Samuel Henshall

Specimens and parts

Containing a history of the county of Kent

Samuel Henshall

Specimens and parts
Containing a history of the county of Kent

ISBN/EAN: 9783337203870

Printed in Europe, USA, Canada, Australia, Japan

Cover: Foto ©ninafisch / pixelio.de

More available books at **www.hansebooks.com**

SPECIMENS AND PARTS;

CONTAINING A

HISTORY OF THE COUNTY OF KENT,

AND A

DISSERTATION ON THE LAWS,

FROM THE REIGN OF

EDWARD THE CONFESSOUR, TO EDWARD THE FIRST;

OF A

TOPOGRAPHICAL, COMMERCIAL, CIVIL, AND NAUTICAL

HISTORY

OF

SOUTH BRITAIN,

WITH ITS

GRADUAL AND COMPARATIVE PROGRESS, IN

TRADE, ARTS, POLITY, POPULATION, AND SHIPPING,

FROM

Authentic Documents.

By SAMUEL HENSHALL, Clerk, M.A.

FELLOW OF BRAZEN-NOSE COLLEGE, OXFORD.

Floreat Historia Britannica. Recordis authenticisque expromatur. Scribatur lentè, maturè, ordinatè, sincerè, dilucidè; sine partium studio, sine pravo consilio, sine omni vili affectu viris literatis indigno.

Disceptatio Epistolaris Thomæ Madox.

Truth requires Sobriety to qualify you for the noble Employment of thinking freely, and thinking justly.

Warburton.

LONDON:

PRINTED FOR THE AUTHOR; R. FAULDER, BOND-STREET; AND F. AND C. RIVINGTON, No 62, ST. PAUL'S CHURCH-YARD.

1798.

PROSPECTUS.

TO collect information, and convey instruction, *to investigate the purest sources* of knowledge, arrange his materials in luminous order, and regular system, and thence render himself clear and accurate; to detail the authority on which each record is framed, and thereby ascertain its credit with precision; and to abhor fiction, and boldly and uniformly deliver truth with simplicity and sincerity, appear the proper object and duty of an historian. To such ends are our views directed, and by such principles shall our Narrative be regulated.

The evidence on which this History will principally depend, for proving its statements at an early period, may properly, perhaps, be termed *internal*. It will be extracted from *authentic documents*, the celebrated Autograph of Domesday, the Fœdera of Rymer, the Anglo-Saxonic and Norman Laws, the National Records, the Rolls of Parliament, Journals, Statutes, &c. &c. —By the liberal and judicious patronage of His Majesty, and both houses of parliament, a great part of this valuable information has been presented to the public, from the press; some lodged in public libraries for the advantage of the student; and the whole is better known and more generally consulted, than at any former æra. When such opportunities are afforded, such advantages presented, it may appear strange that the annals and sentiments of ignorant and bigotted Chroniclers, or [a] Monks,

[a] We place not implicit confidence in ecclesiastical Charters, since we are certain that many Latin ones were forged, to escape the rapacity of the Normans, who could not read the Saxon Records. Vide Hickesii Thesaur. passim.

 should

ſhould have chiefly occupied the attention of Engliſh hiſtorians. It is our deſign to reject every thing that comes in a queſtionable ſhape, our wiſh to tranſmit *facts*, not *opinions*.—But to proceed to our Plan—This Hiſtory, will be comparative and progreſſive, will conſiſt of ſix grand Parts or Diviſions, each containing various Chapters, or Diſſertations, on different ſubjects. The firſt diviſion, or period, will comprehend the preſumed State of the Nation, on the ſubjects we treat upon, in the reigns of Edward the Confeſſor, William, and the ſucceeding monarchs, previous to the firſt parliament ſummoned in 1265, aſſembled probably in 1295.—Here our foundation muſt be eſtabliſhed; and we wiſh to procure every article, that can render it compact, ſolid, and irremoveable.—But though our firſt Æra will occupy two quarto volumes, one comprizing a Topographical Deſcription of South Britain, the other its Civil Hiſtory; no other diſtinctive period will extend beyond half a volume, till we arrive at the eighteenth century, if Providence permits ſo diſtant a continuation. It is preſumed that nine ſimilar numbers will complete our firſt Æra, for in ſubſequent Faſciculos, publiſhed every three months, the Topographical and Hiſtorical Deſcription of two, or occaſionally three or more Counties will be given. It is the wiſh of the Author to continue his Maps on a ſimilar plan with the Specimen exhibited; but, if the Work meets not with encouragement from the Public, he certainly muſt decline the heavy expence of Engraving, abridge his topographical Deſcriptions, and compreſs his arranged matter. To aſcertain this queſtion, he will naturally calculate the number of Copies ſold previous to the continuation of this Work, or the number of Subſcribers who pleaſe to [b] tranſmit their names to Mr. FAULDER,

[b] No Money to be paid previous to the delivery, and the firſt Subſcribers ſhall regularly receive the firſt Impreſſions of the Maps.

BOND-

BOND-STREET, as Patrons of a ſimilar continuation for the Counties of SURREY and SUSSEX, including an Hiſtorical Diſſertation on "Ranks and Services," during the ſame period, or any other of the eight ſubſequent numbers.—Our next diviſion will extend to the æra generally aſcribed to Modern Hiſtory, the concluſion of the reign of the ſeventh Henry. In this, and every ſubſequent diviſion, our diſſertations will particularly ſpecify the *certain* advances in each department, ſince the preceding ſtatement. The ſixteenth and ſeventeenth centuries, terminated nearly with the lives of Elizabeth, and William the third, ſupply us with proper opportunities for other diviſions of our Hiſtory, and a retroſpective and comparative view of our progreſs in Trade, Arts, Polity, Population, and Shipping. The preſent century, furniſhes ſuch extenſive materials in commerce and ſcience, exhibits ſuch aſtoniſhing proofs, even of a quadruple increaſe in our imports and exports, our revenue and ſhipping, our elegant accommodations with the luxurious means of indulgence, and ſuch extent of refinement, and preſumed civilization, as, at leaſt, approximates to a frivolity of manners, that we ſhall pauſe and retrace our ſituation at the cloſe of the reign of George the ſecond, according to our eſtabliſhed arrangement. The ſixth part, or diviſion, will comprehend our farther general progreſs, comparative advance, and unexampled extent of commerce, delicacy, and riches, and will conclude with the eighteenth century, in the important reign of a mild, merciful, and beloved Prince, the [c] patron of arts, navigation, and ſcience, the father of his country.

As

[c] To applaud princes, at the preſent moment, is hazardous and *unpatriotic*; but when any *citizen* ſhall have proved, that George the third encouraged not Navigation, by patronizing a Cooke, a King, a Riou, &c. contributed not to the aſcertainment

As our description of the four first centuries from the Conquest, will very much vary from the representation exhibited by many prior historians, some celebrated antiquaries, and able lawyers; we shall uniformly annex our authority in the original language, lest our veracity might be questioned. By such quotation, the learned may easily determine the propriety and accuracy of our observations, and the truth of our deductions cannot but be admitted. This mode of compiling materials, arranging the subject discussed, and impartially accommodating his sentiment and language to the information presented to him, is certainly an arduous and laborious undertaking for an author; but, by such means, ill-founded prejudices or pre-conceived opinions are more easily dissipated, and misrepresentation avoided; the influence of party warps not so easily the judgment; and candour and equity admit and transcribe the dictates and inferences of reason.

As accuracy and truth are the grand objects of our investigation, we earnestly and anxiously solicit original information, or the perusal of documents that have never been printed. Mr. Faulder, will thankfully receive such records or papers, and guarantee their careful return. With equal gratitude shall we receive intelligence, where such writings are deposited, and the means by which admission to consult them may be obtained. For the present, we particularly request communications for the first p riod of the History, and shall feel ourselves particularly obliged by the loan of any old county map, addressed as above.

ascertainment of a degree of Longitude, by establishing General Roy's base; benefited not Astronomy, by favouring a Herschel; Science, by promoting a Douglas, or a Horsley; History, by the publication of Domesday; or Arts, by discriminating the Grouping of West, or the simple Elegance of Wyatt, we will instantly retract our assertion.

SKETCHES OF OUR ARRANGEMENT, AND *QUERIES* FOR INFORMATION.

ON TRADE AND SHIPPING.

When was the rudder transferred [d] from the ſides of veſſels and placed in the center of the ſtern?—How long was tonnage eſtimated *de tonellis vini?* Was the Navy [e] of Elizabeth, oppoſed to the Armada, calculated from ſuch admeaſurement?—Was 94 feet conſidered the ſtandard previous to the ſeventeenth century?—Were windmills known previous to 1320?—At what period was a pennyweight reduced to 24 grains from 32?—What arts, inventions, or manufactures (and there are certainly many) were introduced into England, or diſcovered at an earlier æra than Anderſon, and others, have aſcribed to them? &c. &c.

ON CUSTOMS, MANNERS, &c.

Is there any proof of coroners previous to 1185?—Is there a ſummons in exiſtence to a county or borough to ſend knights or repreſentatives before Simon Montfort's, 49 Henry IIId.?

[d] Not at the time of the Conqueſt, if the Baieux Tapeſtry is authority.

[e] Mr. Chalmers and hiſtorians in general ſtate it at 31,985 tons, but we can prove, by incontrovertible authority, the Lords Commiſſioners' Enquiry, that it was in fact, one third leſs; and if it was calculated according to the antient ſyſtem, or modern French merchant ſhips, it would not amount to 12,000 preſent Engliſh tons; for in ſeeking information, we began with Modern Hiſtory, in which, at leaſt, we are equally converſant, as in muſty Records, and have courſed the ſtream in oppoſition to its current, ſo long as we are certain of a pure ſource.

ON

ON THE GENERAL STATE OF [f] ENGLAND, ITS CITIES, BOROUGHS, POPULATION, &c.

At what period were the burgeſſes of different cities, &c. liberated from their dependance on patrons, and incorporated? What is the diſtinction between manſio, maſura et domus in Domeſday?—What is the [g] comparative population in the time of the Conqueror and Henry the third?

ON THE ROYAL REVENUE—THE STATE OF LONDON—WEIGHTS AND MEASURES—RANKS AND SERVICES—SCIENCE, ARTS, AGRICULTURE, &c.

The intelligent reader will eaſily collect, indeed, from our title, what information will be ſerviceable to us; though we take leave to premiſe, that war, genealogies, heraldry, or politics, are not the ſubjects ſelected for illuſtration.

[f] This will conſtitute part of the ninth number, and form a general Introduction, with which an appropriate Title-page will be given, for the reſpective Topographical and Hiſtorical volumes.

[g] It is extraordinary, that the number of houſes in ſeveral cities and towns, ſtated by Hume, as extracted from Domeſday, is incorrect in every inſtance.

London, January 10, 1798.

TO

TO THE READER.

AS all our Maps will be conſtructed on a new principle, a few previous directions may be neceſſary to render ourſelves more intelligible.

Geographers have uniformly divided the degrees of latitude and longitude into ſixty parts. But ſince a degree of latitude never varies its proportion, (which is generally eſtimated at 69½ Britiſh ſtatute miles, but more accurately at 69.35 or nearly 69⅓,) and a degree of longitude conſtantly varies in its approximation to the Pole, from the Equinoctial Line, we have attempted to make theſe variations more viſible, and to convey a more adequate idea of diſtance and proportion, to the generality of our nation, by delineating the gradual diminution of the great circles of the globe in the latitude of South Britain. When the variation of a degree of longitude even in Cornwall and Northumberland is * ſix ſtatute miles, ſurely it is an important object to preſent this difference inſtantaneouſly to the eye. This object is certainly accompliſhed by the plan we have adopted, and which we ſhall endeavour regularly to purſue. Farther information may be obtained by a reference to the Map of Kent, which will elucidate our ſyſtem.

* In the fiftieth degree of latitude a degree of longitude is 39,377.15 furlongs or 44.7467 ſtatute miles, in the 55°. 35162.84 furlongs or 38.82 ſtatute miles, and Cornwall is more ſoutherly, Northumberland more northerly.

Explanation of the annexed MAP of KENT.

In delineating the outlines of Kent, and fixing the ſituation of places, we have adopted General Roy's boundaries, aſcertained by longitudinal obſervations. Purſuing his calculations, which are, doubtleſs, ſufficiently accurate for practical purpoſes, when he is certain that he cannot err twenty-ſix yards betwixt Dover and Greenwich obſervatory, we fix a degree of latitude at 61,029 furlongs, ſixty-two parts of a hundred, which is equal to ſixty-nine ſtatute miles thirty-five parts of a hundred, or nearly ſixty-nine miles one third; a degree of longitude, in the latitude of Greenwich, at 38,161 furlongs ninety-ſix parts of a hundred, or forty-three miles thirty-ſix parts, nearly forty-three miles one third. The difference of longitude betwixt Greenwich and Dover is one degree, nineteen minutes, thirty ſeconds, or 51,200 furlongs one-fifth; their difference of latitude is 21,559 furlongs eighty-eight parts; and as theſe lines biſect each other at [a] right angles, the ſquare of the hypotenuſe ſubtending ſuch angle, muſt be equal to the [b] ſquares of thoſe two lines. This is the baſe on which our great triangles are conſtructed; whoſe length is 55,554 fathoms, or ſixty-three ſtatute miles one-tenth. To ſhew how near our calculations approximate to accuracy, we publiſh our double proceſs in the following table.

[a] Vid. Euclid, Book I. prop. 47th.

[b] Square of the longitudinal line 2,621,440,000
Latitudinal 464,833,600

3,086,273,600

Square root 55554,28, or 63.1 √ ſtatute miles, equal to 3,086,273,581.

KENT

Map
of
KENT
from the Autograph of
DOMESDAY
Anno 1086.
SUDTONE
LEST
AILESFORD
LEST DE MILDETO
LEST
SUDRIE
SUDSEXE
Cetcham
Tonebrige
Gravesham
Elesford
Orpinton

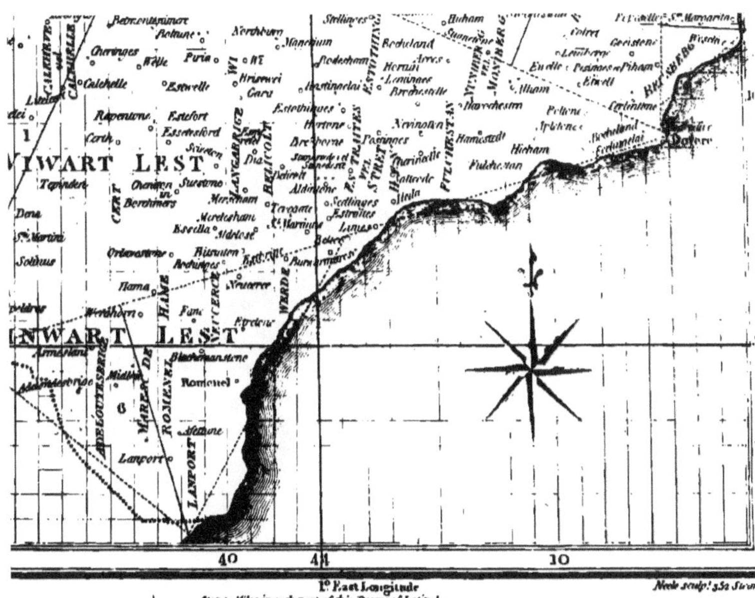

C. Barrington St. Paul's Church Yard, April 10th 1798.

KENT admeasured by Triangles, from a MAP laid down according to its ascertained Latitude and Longitude, on * mathematical Principles.

Dimensions in English Statute Miles and Tenths.

Triangles by Perpendiculars.				Triangles by the three Sides.			
No.	The Base.	The Perpendicular.	Its Area as Half of a Parallelogram.	Dimensions of the first Side.	Second Side.	Third Side.	Its Area by the Square Root.
1	42.	20.7	436.8	42.	32.5	26.7	435.
2	30.5	17.6	268.4	30.5	29.5	18.5	266.
3	24.	13.2	158.4	24.	25.7	13.3	158.3
4	25.7	16.9	217.16	25.7	23.8	19.4	220.
5	18.9	8.2	77.	18.9	13.6	11.5	76.
6	16.8	9.7	81.48	16.8	14.	11.8	81.6
7	21.	10.4	109.2	21.	19.8	11.2	109.2
8	7.2	4.9	17.59	7.2	7.3	5.6	48.5
9	8.	2.4	9.6	8.	5.5	4.	10.
10	5.8	4.6	13.34	5.8	5.5	5.5	13.6
11	7.7	4.	15.4	7.7	6.6	4.7	15.4
12	7.2	.9	3.24	7.2	5.	2.5	3.1
13	3.8	.8	1.52	3.8	2.5	1.8	1.63
14	5.7	2.7	7.7	5.7	5.7	3.	8.25
15	5.9	2.2	6.49	5.9	5.8	2.3	6.6
16	10.2	3.5	17.85	10.2	8.	4.8	17.3
17	9.2	2.7	12.42	9.2	5.4	5.2	12.3
18	12.	3.	18.	12.	11.3	3.5	17.6
19	5.5	1.3	3.67	5.5	3.2	2.9	3.5
20	11.	1.8	9.9	11.	6.5	5.	10.1
21	5.3	2.4	6.36	5.3	4.6	2.6	5.98
22	12.9	5.4	34.29	12.7	10.5	6.6	34.23
23	6.6	1.7	5.5	6.6	5.	2.4	5.5
24	2.	.9	.9	2.2	1.5	1.3	.9
25	8.7	1.8	7.9	8.7	8.7	1.8	7.27
26	5.3	.6	1.59	5.3	4.8	.9	1.6
27	11.6	3.	17.4	11.6	10.	3.8	16.1
28	8.8	2.2	9.68	8.8	8.3	2.4	9.8
29	6.4	3.7	11.84	6.4	5.6	4.2	12.
			1580.62				1577.36
				Medium		—	1578.99
				Total difference			3.26
				or 3¼ statute miles.			
				Acres		—	1,010,561

* A Triangle is half a Parallelogram of the same base and altitude. *Euclid*, book 1. 41. and all Triangles drawn from the same base, and between the same parallels, are equal. *Euclid.* and on another principle, as *demonstrated* in Hawney's Measurer, (p. 81) by adding the three sides together, and taking half their sum; subtracting each side severally from that half; then multiplying the half sum, and the three differences continually, and extracting the square root of the last product, you will obtain the Area of the Triangle.

Explanation of the ſubſequent TABLE.

The difference betwixt the ancient names of places, recorded in Domeſday, and their modern appellation, is ſo great, and the compilers of this autograph have deſignated the ſame place by ſuch various letters, that it would be highly preſumptuous in any man to affect preciſe accuracy from any inveſtigation, or compariſon. That conſiderable attention has been paid to this ſubject, will not, we think, be denied; and though certainty cannot always be obtained, yet, from the frequent ſimilarity in the names of places and their hundreds, which tend mutually to diſtinguiſh each other, there can be little doubt that their general correſpondence is correct. To aſſign every reaſon that influenced us in determining their ſituation, would be tedious in the recital, and of trifling importance.

The titles affixed to the head of each column will convey a general idea of its contents to the reader. But a few obſervations are neceſſary, to prevent miſconception, or convey illuſtration. Where the proprietors under the Confeſſour holding in chief are ſtated, it is neceſſary to remark, that all tenants held not from Edward alone, as from William under the Norman government, but occaſionally alſo from earls Lewin and Godwin, and Alnod and Brixi Cilts, princes or preſidents of the barons. In eſtimating the value, and proportioning it to modern expenditure in articles of neceſſity, at leaſt [a] twenty times the ſum may be calculated. When different ſums are inſerted in the value, under the Conquerour, the higher figures give the aſſeſſed rent, or intermediate eſtimate

[a] See Diſſertation on Weights and Meaſures, and Agriculture.

ſince

ſince Edward's reign, the ſub-figures the actual payment in 1085 or 1086. The gradation of ranks was extraordinary at this period, and there were not only ſub-tenants, but [b] ſub-ſub-tenants to a great extent. To diſcriminate in ſome meaſure on this ſubject, in the column of ploughs, the upper figures ſpecify the ploughs in poſſeſſion of the lord or in his demeſne, the lower figures the ploughs in the hands of villains or ruſtics; though truth commands us to ſtate, that the word ruſtic ony only once occurs in the Survey of Kent, and then it is an alteration of the original record relative to St. Margaret's, near Dover. Borderers and cottagers are ranked in the ſame claſs, for little diſtinction exiſted between them. The clergy here ſtated are conſiderable in number, for we preſume that ſervi means miniſters, whenever immediately following æcclesia, which is generally the caſe, though we are not ignorant that the ſame term was applied to a different [c] order of men. Whenever the ploughs are ſtated in Domeſday, previous to their diviſion into lords and villains [d] ploughs, we calculate four oxen to each, when not ſpecified, the proportion muſt be altered. Of what conſequence hogs were eſteemed, will be fully exemplified in our Hiſtory of Middleſex.

The places to which an aſteriſk (*) is affixed are hundreds; thoſe to which an obeliſk (†) is affixed had a church or churches. When two ſtatements are given in the number of ſowlings, the upper expreſſes the quantity under the Confeſſour, held by the proprietor; the lower, the number held by William's tenants.

Every geographical reader muſt have perceived, that our Map is drawn from Kent, in its preſent ſtate, and that no variation is

[b] See Diſſertation on Ranks and Services.

[c] Inter ſervos & ancillas. Domeſday. Kent.

[d] See Diſſertation on Agriculture, &c.

made in its boundaries, except in fixing the ſcite of a part of Kent in the county of Eſſex. For this alteration we have indiſputable authority, the evidence of the whole [e] ſhire; for it is a moral certainty, that Celca and Hecham, are Chalk and Higham, and the great curvature of the river, with its concave ſhore on the Eſſex coaſt, is favourable to this poſition. We preſume not to infer that ſuch part of Eſſex, lying oppoſite to Woolwich, generally and anciently deſcribed and conſidered as appertaining to Kent, is not to be included in its boundaries, but we are not authorized to make ſuch inſertion by any regiſter in Domeſday. The [f] courſe of the Thames has certainly varied little from this period, or the extent of Kent been conſiderably augmented or diminiſhed, in Romney Marſh or any other quarter, except ſome inconſiderable change in the Iſle of Sheppey, which at this period formed a portion of the three hundreds of [g] Bolton, Feverſham, and Mylton.

[e] Hiſtory of Kent. Scyra teſtificatur, a county court ſanctioned the whole report of the commiſſioners.

[f] See Dugdale's Hiſtory of Embanking.

[g] See Hiſtory of Kent.

A Summary TABLE of LANDS in KENT, with their Situation, Hundred, Value, Proprietors, Occupants, Inhabitants, &c. In the Reigns of EDWARD the Confeffor, and WILLIAM the Conqueror. Compiled from the Autograph of DOMESDAY.

Various Names of Places in Domefday.	Prefumed modern correfponding Names.	In what Hundred or Lath.	Proprietors under the Confeffour, holding in chief.	Value at that Period, in Pounds, Shillings, and Pence. £.	s.	d.	Their Sub-tenants.	Proprietors under the Conqueror.	Value at that Period. £.	s.	d.	Sub-tenants.	Villains.	Borderers or Cottagers.	Sowlings.	Ploughs.	Occurring Obfervations.	Oxen or Cattle.	Agricultural Remarks.	Hogs, or their Pannage.	Folio in Domefday.
*Acheftan	Axtane	Sutton Lath	See Hiftory																		2 b 1
*Adiloutefbrige	Aloes-bridge	Liming Lath	Ditto																		
†Acres	Acryfe	Loningborough	Earl Godwin	2	0	0	TwoBrothers	Earl Bifhop	1 3	10 0	0 0	Anfchil of Rofs.	5	5	1	1½ 1	Separate Halls.	8	1086 1. Manour	10	11 b 2.
Ælvetone	Ebnfton	Prefton	Abbey of St. Auftin's	2	0	0	Demefne Demefne Godeffa	Abbey of St. Auftin's	10 60	0 0	0 0	Ansfrid From Monks Godeffa	3		½	1	From Abbot value 8s. 4d. frank almoig.	3			12 b 2.
†Afettune		Lampert	Earl Godwin	5	0	0	Alfi	Earl Bifhop	4	0	0	Robert Romney	9	3	1	4	2 Retainers	12			10 b 2
Aigleffa [1]	Ayles	Larkfield		3	0	0	Alnod Cilt	Earl Bifhop	4	0	0	Fitz-tyrrel	7	14	½	1 1	1 Minifter.	6	11 Acres	10	7 a 2.
Tunbridge	Moiety								0	9	8										
Alfiholt	Afhholt	See Eiffe																			
Adelofe		Byrcholt	Edward	1	10	0	Godric	Earl Bifhop	2	0	0	Fitz-letard	3		1½	1½		6	Earl's fee		10 b 2
†Aldinton	Aldington	Byrcholt	Archbifhop	62	0	0	Demefne	Archbifhop	101	0	0	Demefne	190	50	21 15	13 70	13 Minifters 3 Mills 3 Fifheries	320	170 Acres Meadow	60	4 a 1
†Alnoitone		Eyhorne	Edward	9	0	0	Seward	Earl Bifhop	10 12	0 0	0 0	Hugh Port	18	6	3	2 6	2 Mills 4 Minifters	24	5 Acres Meadow	40	7 b 2
†Alham	Eleham	Loningborough	Edward	30	0	0	Edric	Earl Bifhop	40 50	0 0	0 0	Demefne	41	8	6	5 18	8 Minifters 2 Mills	92	28 Acres	100	9 b 2
Alteham	Eltham	Grenwich	Edward	5	0	0	Athelwold	Earl Bifhop	5	0	0	Haimo Vifcount	42	12	1	13	9 Retainers	48	22 Acres	50	6 b 2
†Apeldres	Apeldore	Blackburn	Archbifhop	6	0	0		Archbifhop	16	17	0	Demefne	37	41	2	3 11	1 Mill 2 Minifters	50	2 Acres	10	5 a 2
Apletone		Befbrough	Edward	5	0	0	Afered	Earl Bifhop	0 2	10 0	0 0	Ralph Crook-thorn		6	1	2		8			11 a 2
Arclei	Hartley	Shammel	Earl Harold	2	0	0	Hunef	Earl Bifhop	4	0	0	Fitz-tyrrel	6		1	1 ½		6	12 Acres		9 a 1
Afmeflant		Romney Marfh	Archbifhop	2	3	0	Demefne	Archbifhop	2	3	0	Demefne	21		1	3 7	Folet, a fub-tenant	4	25 Sheep		5 a 2
†Audintone		Eyhorne	Edward	4	0	0	Godwin and Alwin	Earl Bifhop	7	0	0	Anfgot	7	5	2	2 1	2 Manours 14 Minifters	10	6 Acres Meadow 1 Mill	10	7 b 2

[1] Aigleffa, probably the Grange, or Abbey, near Aylesford.

Various Names of Places in Domesday.	Presumed modern correſponding Names.	In what Hundred or Lath.	Proprietors under the Conſeſſour, holding in chief.	Value at that Period, in Pounds, Shillings, and Pence.	Their Sub-tenants.	Proprietors under the Conqueror.	Value at that Period.	Sub-tenants.	Villains.	Borderers or Cottagers.	Sowlings.	Ploughs.	Occurring Obſervations.	Oxen or Cattle.	Agricultural Remarks.	Hogs, or their Pannage.	Folio in Domeſday.
				£. s. d.			£. s. d.										
Borowart Borwar	Ward of the Borough St. Auſtin's	See Hiſtory															[illegible]
*Belliſolt	Byrcholt	Borough Lath	See Hiſtory														[illegible]
*Berham	Barham	Eſtrye Lath	Ditto														
*Benſberg	Beſborough	Borough Lath	Ditto														[illegible]
*Blacheborne	Blackburne	Liming Lath	Ditto														
*Boltone	Bolton	Borough Lath	Ditto														[illegible]
*Brige	Bridge	Borough Lath															
*Bronlei	Bromley	Sutton Lath	Biſhop of Rocheſter.	12 10 0	Demeſne	Biſhop of Rocheſter	18 0 0 20 18 0	Demeſne	30	26	6 3	2 11	1 Mill	40	2 Acres Meadow	100	5 b 1
*Brotoham	Wroteham	Aylesford Lath	Archbiſhop	15 0 0 16 0 0	Demeſne	Archbiſhop	24 0 0 35 0 0	In demeſne	76	18	8	$\frac{3}{4}$ 14	3 Mills, at 15 s.	68	9 Acres Meadow	500	3 a 1
Tunbridge	Moiety						15 0 0								[illegible]	[illegible]	[illegible]
Becheham	Beckenham	Bromley	Edward	9 0 0	Anſchil	Earl Biſhop	13 0 0	Anſgot	12	8	2	2 8	1 Mill, 4 Miniſters	32	12 Acres	60	7 a 1
† Badeleſmere	Baſmere [2]	Feverſham	St. Auſtin's	3 0 0		Earl Biſhop	4 0 0	Ansfrid	10		1	1 1$\frac{1}{2}$	2 Miniſters a Fiſhery	10		4	10 a 2
Belice	Bellevieu	Hen	Edward	3 0 0	Turgis	H. Montfort	3 0 0	Demeſne	2	1	1	1		4	3 Acres		13 a 2
†Benindene	Beneden	Rovinden	Edward	2 0 0	Siward	Earl Biſhop	2 10 0	Robert Romney	4	9	$\frac{1}{2}$	$\frac{1}{2}$		10		10 5	11 a 1
Benodeſtede	Nettleſted	Twyford	Alnoid Cilt	1 0 0	Godric	Earl Biſhop	2 0 0	Ethelwold	5		$\frac{1}{4}$	1		4	1 Acre Meadow	6	8 b 1
Berchvelle	Bourſfield	Feverſham	Edward	1 0 0	Wirelm	Earl Biſhop	4 0 0	Wadard	3	3	$\frac{1}{2}$	1	1 Mill	4	10 Acres Alders		10 b 1
Berſreſtone	Barefriſton	Eaſtry		0 10 0		Earl Biſhop		Ralph Crookthorn			$\frac{1}{2}$		A poor Woman 3$\frac{1}{4}$d.			[illegible]	9 b 2
———	———	———	———	———	———	———	———	Ralph Colville			$\frac{1}{2}$		Exempt from Land-Tax				9 b 2
Beretris	Bever.	Eſtret	Archbiſhop	3 0 0		Archbiſhop	7 0 0 11 0 0	William of Eddeſham	9	9	$\frac{1}{4}$	2 1$\frac{1}{2}$		12	18 Acres	20	4 b 2
†Berham	Barham	Barham	Edward	40 0 0	Stigand Archbiſhop	Earl Biſhop	40 0 0 100 0 0	Fulbert	52	20	3 18	3 18	A Mill, a Fiſhery, 3s. 6d. [3] Corve 60s.	80	11 Acres	150	9 b 2

[2] There was a litigation relative to Baſmere, at this period, between the abbey of St. Auguſtine's and the earl Odo. The abbey claimed the manour, as part of its poſſeſſions in the time of the Confeſſor, and ſupported ſuch claim by the teſtimony of the hundred; but the ſon of its late tenant aſſerted that his father was a free man, independant of any Patron, and conſequently holding in chief of the crown or earl. The iſſue of the conteſt is not here ſtated.—Hoc manerium reclamat abbatia Sti. Auguſtini quia habuit tempore regis Edvardi & hundredi atteſtantur ei; ſed filius hominis dicit patrem ſuum ſe poſſe vertere ubi voluerit, et hoc non annuunt monachi. Domeſday, 10 a 2; but folio 11 b 2. the teſtimony of the county declares it in favour of the abbey, and ſtates the tenant to have been its client or dependant. Seyra teſtificatur quod Bedeneſmere fuit Sancti Auguſtini tempore regis Edvardi, & de illo qui eam tenebat habebat abbatia ſacam & ſocam.

[3] De avera id eſt ſervitium 60 ſolid. Domeſday, 9 b 2.

Various Names of Places in Domesday.	Presumed modern corresponding Names.	In what Hundred or Lath.	Proprietors under the Confessor, holding in chief.	Value at that Period, in Pounds, Shillings, and Pence. £. s. d.	Their Sub-tenants.	Proprietors under the Conqueror.	Value at that Period. £. s. d.	Sub-tenants.	Villains.	Borderers or Cottagers.	Sowlings.	Ploughs.	Occurring Observations.	Oxen or Cattle.	Agricultural Remarks.	Hogs, or their Pannage.	Folio in Domesday.
Bermeling	Barming	Maidstone	Edward	4 0 0	Alred	Richard Fitz-gilbert	4 0 0	Demesne	5	8	1	2 5	13 Retainers 1 Mill	16	4 Acres Meadow	10	14 a 2
†Berlinge	Birling	Larkfield	Edward	12 0 0	Sbern	Earl Bishop	6 0 0 12 0 0	Ralph Crookthorn	10	14	6	1 6	1 Mill, a Fishery 400 Eels	28	Pasture 50 Animals	40	7 b 1
Bermelie	Barming	Maidstone		0 15 0		Earl Bishop	2 0 0	Ralph Colville		5		1 2		4		3	8 b 2
Betmontestun	Bampston	Felbrough	Edward	6 0 0	Alric	Earl Bishop	6 0 0	Ralph Crookthorn	13	1	1	3		20	32 Acres Meadow	40	10 b 2
———	———	———	———	6 0 0	———	Hugh Montfort	6 0 0	Demesne					Wood and Pasture				10 b 2
Bichlei	Bickwor	Maidstone	Earl Godwin	0 10 0	Lewin	Earl Bishop	0 15 0	Adam Fitz-hubert	1	2	½	1	1 Mill	4			9 a 1
†Bilsuiton	Blissington	Newchurch	Edward	10 0 0	Alnold Cilt	Earl Bishop	30 0 0 50 0 0 70 0 0	Demesne Robert Romney	47	27	4	5 13	10 Salt-pans 2 Fisheries	60	10 Acres Meadow	50	10 b 2
†Bis	Boxley	Rokesly	Archbishop	12 0 0		Archbishop	20 0 0 30 0 0	Demesne	41	15	3 2	2 10	3 Mills, of 48 s.	40	8 Acres Meadow	100	3 a 1
†Blehem	Blean	Whitestaple	Edward	8 0 0	Norman	Hamo Viscount	6 0 0	Demesne	12		1						
Blacheburne	Blackburn	Blackburn	St. Martin's	0 16 8	Canons	St. Martin's	0 16 8	Sired, Godric and Sewen	9		1	2		8			2 a 2
†Blachemenstone	Blackmanston	Worth	Edward	4 0 0	Blacheman	Hugh Montfort.	3 0 0 6 0 0	Hervey	3	10	½	3	1 Minister	8			13 a 1
Bocheland	Buckland	Besbro'	St. Martin's	5 0 0	Alwi	St. Martin's	4 0 0	Alwy	6	10	1	1½					1 b 1
† ———	———	———	St. Martin's	8 0 0	Godric	St. Martin's	6 0 0	Godric	3	4	1	3					1 b 2
Bocoland	Buckland	Estrye	Archbishop	0 10 0		Archbishop	0 10 0	Godfrey			½		Demesne				4 b 1
Bochelande	Buckland	Stowting		1 0 0		Earl Bishop	2 0 0	Ansfrid	1		½	1					9 b 2
Bochelande	Buckland	Feversham	Edward	4 0 0	Siward	Earl Bishop	3 0 0 3 10 0	Osbern	3	2	½	1½	8 Retainers	6			10 a 2
Bochelande	Buckland	Feversham	Edward	0 12 0	Turgis	Earl Bishop	0 12 0	Turstin	1		½						10 b 1
Betesham	Betshanger	Eastrye	Edward	3 0 0	Godessa	Earl Bishop	2 10 0	Fitz-letard	1	4	½	1		4			11 a 2
Bodesham	Bockham	Stowting	St. Austin's	4 0 0	A Rustic	St. Austin's	4 0 0	Geoffrey		8	1	2		8		15	12 b 2
Boseleu	Boxley	Maidstone	Edward	25 0 0	Alnod Cilt	Earl Bishop	30 0 0 55 0 0	Robert Latin	47	11	7 5	3 16	3 Mills, 16 Retainers	76	20 Acres Meadow	50	8 b 2
———	———	———	———	———	———	Earl Bishop	2 0 0	Helto		1	½	1	A Norman	4	2 Acres	6	8 b 2
†Bogelei	Boxley	Eyhorne	Edward	6 0 0	Turgis	Earl Bishop	7 0 0	Adam Fitz-hubert	2	2	2	2½	4 Ministers 1 Mill	10	6 Acres Meadow	4	8 a 1
†Boltone	Boughton	Eyhorne	Earl Godwin	8 0 0	Lewin	Earl Bishop	6 0 0	Hugh nephw of Herbert	5		1	1		4	2 Acres Meadow	20	8 a 1

Various Names of Places in Domeſday.	Preſumed modern correſponding Names.	In what Hundred or Lath.	Proprietors under the Confeſſour, holding in chief.	Value at that Period, in Pounds, Shillings, and Pence.	Their Sub-tenants.	Proprietors under the Conqueror.	Value at that Period.	Sub-tenants.	Villains.	Borderers or Cottagers.	Sowlings.	Ploughs.	Occurring Obſervations.	Oxen or Cattle.	Agricultural Remarks.	Hogs, or their Pannage.	Folio in Domeſday.
				£. s. d.			£. s. d.										
Boltune	Bolton	Bolton	Archbiſhop	15 16 3¼		Archbiſhop	30 16 3¼	Demeſne	31	31	5½	2 15	A Fiſhery, a Salt-pan	60	4 Acres Meadow	45	3 b 2
†Boltone	Bolton	Eyehorne	Archbiſhop	2 0 0		Archbiſhop	2 0 0	Fitz-tyrrel	3	2	½	3		10	2 Acres Meadow	16	4 a 2
†Boltune	Bolton	Wye		20 0 0	Earl Godwin	Earl Euſtace	30 0 0 40 0 0	Demeſne	67	5	7	3 30	2 Mills, 17 Min. or Retainers	128	26 Acres Meadow	200	14 a 1
†Bonintone	Bonnington	Stret	Edward	4 0 0	Norman	Hugh Montfort	5 0 0	William Fitz-groſs	9	5	1	½	8 Miniſters	10		8	13 b 2
†Borham	Boreham	Larkfield		10 0 0	Earl Lewin	Earl Biſhop	12 0 0	Ralph Crookthorn	15	20	6	2 6	7 Miniſters, 1 Mill	32	10 Acres Meadow	20	7 b 1
Borchtelle	Borden	Rocheſter	Biſhop of Rocheſter	6 0 0	Demeſne	Biſhop of Rocheſter	10 0 0	Demeſne	6		3 1½	2 3	Two Mills See Hiſtory	16	50 Acres Meadow		5 b 2
†Borne	Bourne	Bridge	Edward	18 0 0	Edwin	Earl Biſhop	19 0 0	Fitz-william	44	3	6	3 10	4 Mills, a Fiſhery	40	6 Ac. Paſture ploughed	4	9 a 2
†Burnes	Bourne	Bridge	Edward	12 0 0	Lewin	Earl Biſhop	12 0 0 18 0 0	Demeſne	25	4	2	2 7	6 Miniſters, a Salt-pan, a Fiſhery	24	H.Montfort's Portion, 5s. a Bailiff	6	9 a 2
Borne	Bourne	Bridge	St. Auſtin's	5 0 0	Abbot	St. Auſtin's	5 0 0	Abbot	9	1	1	2	2 Mills	6	3½ Acres Meadow	5	12 a 1
†Burnes	Biſhop's Bourne	Berham	Archbiſhop	20 0 0		Archbiſhop	30 0 0	Demeſne	64	53	6	5 30	2 Mills	145	20 Ac. Mead. Herbage 27d.	15	3 b 2
Breburne	Braborne	Byrcholt	Edward	20 0 0	Godric of Bourne	Hugh Montfort	16 0 0	Demeſne	31	10	7 5½	2 10	8 Min. 2 Mills	48	20 Ac. Mead.	25	13 b 2
†Brieſtede	Braſted	Axtane	Archbiſhop	10 0 0	Alnod Abbot	Archbiſhop	17 0 0	Hamo Viſcount	24	16	1½	2 12	15 Min. 2 Mills	40	Herb. 9s. 6d.	80	4 a 2
Bronlei	Bromley	Bromley	Biſhop of Rocheſter	12 0 0		Biſhop of Rocheſter	18 0 0 20 18 0	Demeſne	30	26	6 3	2 11	1 Mill	52	2 Acres Meadow	100	5 b 1
Brocheſtelle		Beſbrough	Edward	3 0 0	Alnod	Earl Biſhop	2 0 0	H. Montfort			1	1	Herbert, a Sub-tenant	4	Part of his Barony. See Hiſtory		11 a 2
†Brotcham	Wroteham	Wrotcham	Archbiſhop	15 0 0		Archbiſhop	24 0 0	Demeſne	76	18	8	3 14	William Deſpencer Jeffery, and Firman, Sub-tenants	68	9 Ac. Mead. 3 Mills	500	3 a 2
Tunbridge	Moiety		Archbiſhop			Archbiſhop	15 0 0	Fitz-gilbert									
Knight's	Moiety		Archbiſhop			Archbiſhop	11 0 0	3 Knights	14	13	2½	4½	10 Retainers	18			3 a 2
Brunfelle	Bromfield	Eyhorne	Earl Godwin	4 0 0	Alwin												
Burwarmareſc	Burmarſh	Romney Marſh	St. Auſtin's	20 0 0		St. Auſtin's	30 0 0	Abbot	44	5	2½	14		48			12 b 2
*Calehelle	Calehill	Wye Ward Lath	See Hiſtory														
*Canturarie	Canterbury	Borough Lath	Ditto														
*Cert	Chart	Aylesford Lath	Ditto														
*Cetcham	Chatham	Ditto	Ditto														
*Ciſtelet	Chiſlet	Borough Lath	Ditto														
*Corneleſt	Corniloe	Eaſtrye Lath	Ditto														

Various Names of Places in Domeſday.	Preſumed modern correſponding Names.	In what Hundred or Lath.	Proprietors under the Confeſſour, holding in chief.	Value at that Period, in Pounds, Shillings, and Pence.	Their Sub-tenants.	Proprietors under the Conqueror.	Value at that Period.	Sub-tenants.	Villains.	Borderers or Cottagers.	Sowlings.	Ploughs.	Occurring Obſervations.	Oxen or Cattle.	Agricultural Remarks.	Hogs, or their Pannage.	Folio in Domeſday.
				£. s. d.			£. s. d.										
†Cerce	Minſter	Mylton		6 0 0	Siward	Earl Biſhop	6 0 0	Hugh Port		5	2	2	1 Miniſter, a Mill	8			9 a 2
†Celca	Chalk		Edward	7 0 0	Godwin	Earl Biſhop	10 0 0 14 0 0	Adam	13	6	3	2 5	4 Miniſters, a Mill	28	16 Acres Meadow		8 b 2
Celca, in Eſſex	Chalk Manor	Eſſex	Edward		GodwinFitz-Dudeman	R. Peverell		Ral. Peverell					One Hide				9 a 1
Cerlentone	Charlton	Beſbrough	St. Martin's	5 0 0	Lewin, Prebend	St. Martin's	3 10 0	St. Janſon, Prebend	3	4	1	1		4			1 b 1
———	———	———	———	12 0 0	Sired	St. Martins	6 0 0	Fitz-oger	1	7	1	1½	a Norman, 1 plough a monaſtery	6			1 b 1
Cerleſtone	Charlton	Greenwich	Edward	7 0 0	Godwin and Alward	Edward	7 0 0	Fitz-oger	13		1	4	2 Retainers	16	8 Acres Meadow	5	6 b 2
†Certh	Chart Sutton	Eyehorne	Alnod Cilt	12 0 0	Demeſne	Earl Biſhop	12 0 0	Adam Fitz-hubert	20	5	3	1 6	8 Miniſters, 6 Ac. Meadow	22	3 Arp. Vines, Park of Deer	50	8 a 1
Certh	Chart	Chart	Archbiſhop	12 0 0		Archbiſhop	20 0 0 27 0 0	Demeſne	27	11	3	2 22	5 Retainers, 2 Mills, a Salt-pan	48	27 Acres Meadow	100	5 a 1
†Certeham	Chartham	Felbrough	Archbiſhop	12 0 0		Archbiſhop	25 0 0 30 0 0	Demeſne	60	15	4	2 15	1 Miniſter, 5½ Mills	56	30 Acres Meadow	25	5 a 1
†Chenetone	Chillington	Burmarſh, in Longbridge	St. Auſtin's	10 0 0	Villains, or Ruſtics	St. Auſtin's	12 10 0	Abbot	30		4	10	Half a Sowling exempt from land-tax	30		40	12 b 2
Chenoltone	Knowlton	Eaſtrye	Edward	4 0 0	Edward	Earl Biſhop	8 0 0	Turſtin		2	1	2		6			11 a 2
Cherinchelle	Charing-hall	Felbrough	St. Auſtin's	1 0 0		St. Auſtin's	1 10 0	Ansfrid	8		½	3		10			12 b 1
Cheringes	Charing	Calehill	Archbiſhop	24 0 0		Archbiſhop	34 0 0 60 0 0	Demeſne	26	27	8	4 2	12 Retainers, 1 Mill	126	25 Ac. Mead.	26	3 b 2
Cheſtan	Keſton	Rokeſley	Edward	3 0 0	Shern, Com.	Earl Biſhop	2 0 0	G. Maminot	4		½	2		6		5	7 a 1
Cildreſham	Sheldwich	Feverſham		3 0 0		Earl Biſhop	4 0 0	Ansfrid	4	2	1	2	a Knight, Sub-ten.	6	1 Plough		10 a 1
Cilledene	Chillenden	Eaſtrye	Edward	3 0 0	Godwin and 5 Thanes	Earl Biſhop	2 0 0	Fitz-letard	9		1½	2½		8			11 b 1
†Cilleham	Chilham	Felbrough	Edward	40 0 0	Siward	Earl Biſhop	30 0 0 82 10 0	Fulbert	38	12	5	2 12	6 Mills, 2 Fiſheries 13 Houſes in Cant.	56	9 Ac. Mead. Paſt. 18s. 7d.	80	10 a 1
Ciresfel	Chelsfield	Rokeſley	Edward	16 0 0	Tochi	Earl Biſhop	25 0 0 35 0 0	Arnulph of Haſtings	20	4	2	2 6	A Mill	30	10 Acres Meadow	10	6 b 1
†Ciſtelet	Chiſlet	Chiſlet	St. Auſtin's	53 0 0		St. Auſtin's	78 0 0	Abbot	72	68	12	5 39	14 Min. 47 Salt-pans, of 50 Seam	120	3 Arp. Vines 50 Ac. Mead.	130	12 a 2
†Clive	Cliffe	Shammel	Archbiſhop	6 0 0		Archbiſhop	16 0	Demeſne	20	18	3½	1½ 5½	2 Miniſters	24	36 Ac. Mead.		4 b 2
Clive	Cliffe	Shammel	Edward	2 10 0	Alric and Ordric	Earl Biſhop	3 0 0	Arnulph of Haſtings	2			½	100 Sheep	2	10 Ac. Mead.		9 a 1
†Cocleſtane	Cuckſtone	Shammel	Bp. Rocheſter	4 10 0		Bp. Rocheſter	10 10 0	Demeſne	15	9	4½	7	2 Min. 1 Mill	24	20 Ac. Mead.		5 b 2
†Codeham	Cudham	Rokeſley		20 0 0		Earl Biſhop	24 0 0	G. Maminot	15	6	4	10	11 Min. 2 Mills	40		40	7 a 1
Colinge	Colvinge	Shammel	Earl Lewin	2 0 0	Ulwin	Earl Biſhop	4 0 0	Fitz-hubert	5		1½	2½	4 Retainers	10	7 Ac. Mead.	10	9 a 1
Colinges	Colvinge	Shammel	Edward	1 0 0	Godric	Earl Biſhop	1 10 0	Odo		1	½	½		2	4 Ac. Mead.		9 a 1
Colret	Colred	Beſbrough	Edward	8 0 0	Molleve	Earl Biſhop	6 0 0	Crookthorn	6	7	2	3½	2 Retainers	10	4 Ac. Mead.		11 a 1

Various Names of Places in Domeſday.	Preſumed modern correſponding Names.	In what Hundred or Lath.	Proprietors under the Confeſſour, holding in chief.	Value at that Period, in Pounds, Shillings, and Pence. £. s. d.	Their Sub-tenants.	Proprietors under the Conqueror.	Value at that Period. £. s. d.	Sub-tenants.	Villains.	Borderers or Cottagers.	Sowlings.	Ploughs.	Occurring Obſervations.	Oxen or Cattle.	Agricultural Remarks.	Hogs, or their Pannage.	Folio in Domeſday.
†Craie	Cray	Rokeſley	Edward	4 0 0	Leuric	Earl Biſhop	3 0 0	Anſchil	7	6		2	1 Acre Meadow	6	3 Ac. Paſture		6 b ½
Craie-alia	Cray	Rokeſley	Alnold Cilt	4 0 0	Lewin	Earl Biſhop	3 0 0	Anſchil	7	5	½	2	1 Mill, 5 Retainers 2 Manours, T.R.E.	6	1 Man. under the Conquer.	7	6 b 2
Crai	Cray	Rokeſley	Edward	3 0 0	Godwin	Earl Biſhop	4 0 0	Fitz-oger	8	4	½	2½	1 Mill, 1 Retainer	8		6	7 a 1
Crocſtune	Cracking	Rokeſley	Edward	5 0 0	Lewin	Earl Biſhop	6 0 0	Anſchil	3	4	½						7 a 1
Cumbo		Felbrough	Edward	3 0 0	Leuret	Earl Biſhop	4 0 0	Wadard	9	5	1	2	1 military Tenant	6	14 Ac. Mead.	5	10 b 2
*Dunamesfort	Downham-ford	Borough Lath	See Hiſtory														
†Danitone	Denton	Shammel	Bp. Rocheſter	5 0 0		Bp. Rocheſter	7 15 0	Demeſne	6		2½	2	4 Miniſters	6	4 Ac. Mead.	15	5 b 2
†Danetone	Denton	Eaſtrye	Edward	3 0 0	Molleve	Earl Biſhop	3 0 0	Ralph Crookthorn	4	2	½	2	4 Houſes in Canterbury	6			11 b 2
Darenden	Kendington	Wye	St. Auſtin's	1 0 0		St. Auſtin's	1 0 0	Fitz-hubert			½	½	2 Miniſters	2			12 a 1
Dela	Deal	Cornilo	St. Martin's	7 0 0	Stigand Archbiſhop	St. Martin's	8 0 0	Anſchil, Archdeacon	1	6	1	2	100 Ac. belonging to Prebends	8			1 b 2
Addela	Deal	Cornilo	St. Martin's	3 0 0	Athelwold	St. Martin's	3 0 0	Athelwold	3	8		1	The ſame Tenant under Confeſſour	4			1 b 2
Addela	Deal	Cornilo	St. Martin's	2 0 0	Abbot of St. Auſtin's	St. Martin's	1 10 0	Succeeding Abbot	3	8	1	1½		6			1 b 2
Addela	Deal	Cornilo, and Beſbrough	St. Martin's	2 0 0	Derinc	St. Martin's	3 0 0	Fitz-tydald	2	2	½	1		4			1 b 2
Delce	Badelſworth	Rocheſter	Edward	3 0 0	Godric	Earl Biſhop	3 10 0	Fitz-William	5		1½	½		10	12 Ac. Mead.	1	8 b 1
Delce	Badelſworth	Rocheſter	Edward	5 0 6	Siward	Earl Biſhop	5 0 0	Anſgot	1	5	1	2	6 Retainers	8	12 Ac. Mead. 60 Ac. Paſt.		8 b 1
Dene	Shottenden	Felbrough	Edward	2 0 0	Four Thanes	Earl Biſhop	2 0 0	Athelwold		4	1½	1	Seized by the King	4	1 Ac. Mead.	7	10 b 2
Dene	Shottenden	Felbrough	Edward	0 10 0		Earl Biſhop	0 10 0	Crookthorn			½		See Hiſtory for Deans Dingles				10 b 2
†Diſtune	Ditton	Larkfield	Edward	8 0 0	Sbern, Com.	Earl Biſhop	8 0 0	Hamo Viſcount	20	5	1	2 3	6 Miniſters, 1 Mill	16	8 Ac. Mead. 35 Ac. Paſt.	6	7 a 1
†Dodeham	Devington, or Ludingham	Feverſham	Edward	10 0 0	Siward	Earl Biſhop	6 0 0	Fulbert	30		5 2	2 3	6 Miniſters, a Fiſhery of Herrings	16	5 Houſes in Canterbury		19 b 1
Dovere	Dover	Beſbrough	See Hiſtory														
Eſtre-leſt	Eaſtrye lath	See Hiſtory															1 b 1
Elesford-leſt	Aylesfordlath	Ditto															2 b 1
*Eſſame	Shammel	Mylton lath	See Hiſtory														
*Eſtothinges	Stowting	Liming Lath	Ditto														
*Eſtraites	Stret	Liming Lath	Ditto														
*Eſtrei	Eaſtrye	Eſtrye Lath	Ditto														
*Eſturſete	Sturry	Borough Lath	Ditto														
Ece	Aſh	Eaſtrye	Edward	0 12 0	Sbern-bold	Earl Biſhop	0 16 0	Fitz-letard	3		½						11 b 1
†Eddintune	Addington	Larkfield	Edward	8 0 0	Agebred	Earl Biſhop	6 0 0	Fitz-tyrrel	6	9	2	3	2 Mills, 10 Mln.	10	12 Ac. Mead.	10	7 a 1
Edintoge	Addington	Axtane	Edward		Leſlan	Earl Biſhop	4 0 0	Fitz-tyrrel	2	4	½	1	1 Mill	4			6 a 1
Edeſham	Addiſham	Eaſtrye	Archbiſhop	40 0 0	Demeſne	Archbiſhop	46 16 4	Dem. & 2 Kn.	118	19	17	4½	3 Miniſters	100	13 Ac. Mead.		5 a 2

Various Names of Places in Domesday.	Presumed modern corresponding Names.	In what Hundred or Lath.	Proprietors under the Confessour, holding in chief.	Value at that Period, in Pounds, Shillings, and Pence.			Their Sub-tenants.	Proprietors under the Conqueror.	Value at that Period.			Sub-tenants.	Villains.	Borderers or Cottagers.	Sowlings.	Ploughs.	Occurring Observations.	Oxen or Cattle.	Agricultural Remarks.	Hogs, or their Pannage.	Folio in Domesday.
				£.	s.	d.			£.	s.	d.										
Essamellesford	Shamford	Felbrough	Edward	3	0	0	Alred	Earl Bishop	3	0	0	Herfrid	3	1	½	2	E. B.'s Barony	6	8 Ac. Mead.		10 a 2
Essewelle		Eastrye	Edward	10	0	0	Molleve	Earl Bishop	10	0	0	Crook.& Osb.	2	8	4½	5	1 Min. 3 Freemen	16	TimeEdward		11 b 1
Eisse	Ashchurch	Axtane	Edward	7	0	0	Godric	Earl Bishop	7	0	0	Port & Knts.	12	16	3	5	See History	18			6 a 1
†Elentun	Allington	Larkfield	Alnod Cilt	5	0	0	Ulric	Earl Bishop	5	0	0	Anschill	15	2	1	3½	½ Mill, 2 Ministers	11	Shingle wood	8	7 a 1
Elesford	Aylesford	Larkfield	Edward	15	0	0		William	38	17	4	Haimo Visco.	40	5	1	18	1 Mill, See Hist.	42	43 Ac. Mead.	70	2 b 1
††Elesford	Aylesford	Axtane	Archbishop	16	0	0		Archbishop	20	0	0	Fitz-unspac	29	5	6	20	2 Mills, 9 Min.	50	29 Ac. Mead.	20	4 a 2
Elesford	Tonbridge	Moiety						Fitz-gilbert									1 Mill, a Fishery			20	4 a 2
Alteham	Eltham	Greenwich	Edward	16	0	0	Athelwold	Earl Bishop	20	0	0	Haimo Visco.	42	12	1½	13	9 Retainers	30	22 Ac. Mead.	50	6 b 2
Erclei	Hartley	Axtane		3	0	0	a Female	Earl Bishop	5	0	0	Fitz-tyrrel	9	6	1	5	3 Retainers	14		10	6 a 1
†Erhede	Erith	Litelai	Archbishop	12	0	0		Archbishop	21	0	0	Demesne	27	2	4	10	3 Mills, 5 Min.	24	10 Ac. Mead.	40	3 a 1
Ernoltun	Hearne	Feversham	Edward	4	0	0	Burnod	Earl Bishop	5	0	0	Ansfrid	8		1	3	2 Salt-pans	8	10 Acres		10 a 2
†Eslinges	Eastling	Feversham	Edward	10	0	0	Siward	Earl Bishop	8	0	0	Fulbert	30		5	5	1 Mill, 28 Min.	16		30	10 b 2
†Eslinges	Eastling	Feversham	Edward	3	0	0	Unlot	Earl Bishop	2	0	0	Fitz-Anschil		1	1	1	1 Mill	4	2 Acres		10 b 2
†Esledes	Leeds	Eyhorne	Edward	16	0	0	Earl Lewin	Earl Bishop	25	0	0	Athelwold	28	8	3	9	18 Min. 5 Mills	22	2 Arp. Vines	20	7 b 2
Abbot of St.	Austin's, and	Earl of Eu	Value				Earl Lewin		1	10	0	See History			½		for a Park.		and 4 Dingles		7 b 2
Esmetone	Smarden	Marden	Edward	1	10	0	Siward	Earl Bishop	1	10	0	Fitz-letard					a Priest		15 Acres		11 b 1
Esmeresel	Marshamfield	Wye	St. Austin's	2	0	0		St. Austin's	2	0	0	Abbot		5	1	1	Anschil, Sub-ten.	4	6 Acres	10	12 a 2
†Esnoiland	Snodeland	Larkfield	Bp.Rochester	6	0	0	Demesne	Bp.Rochester	9	0	0	Demesne	10	6	6	8	3 Mills, 5 Min.	20	30 Acres	4	5 b 1
Essella	Eastwell	Longbridge	Edward	1	0	0	3 Thanes	H. Montfort	1	0	0	Demesne	4	2	11	2½		8	6 Acres		13 a 2
Esseden	Ashwood	Larkfield	Edward	3	0	0	Earl Lewin	Earl Bishop	3	0	0	Colville	19	3	1	4	3 Retainers	10	8 Acres		7 a 2
†Essetesford	Ashford	Longbridge	Edward	3	10	0	Wirelm	H. Montfort	5	0	0	Manno	2	15	1	7	A Priest & 3 Min.	14	2 Mills		13 a 1
Estefort alia	Ashford	Longbridge	Earl Godwin	1	5	0	Turgis	H. Montfort	1	10	0	Manno	2		1	2	2 Ministers	6	8 Acres		13 a 1
†Estanes	Stone	Axtane	Bp.Rochester	13	0	0	Demesne	Bp.Rochester	24	0	0	Demesne	20	12	6	13	1 Mill, 4 Min.	30	Fishery	60	5 b 1
Tunbridge	Moiety	in Stone	Bp.Rochester				Demesne	Fitz-gilbert	0	15	0	Demesne							a Wood		5 b 1
Estenberge	Stone	Estrye	Archbishop					Archbishop				Folet	12		½	1½	See Flenguessam	3			4 b 1
††Estbrige	Eastchurch	Worth	Earl Godwin	10	0	0	Alsi	H. Montfort	15	0	0	Demesne	2	36	1	7	Salt-pans, Fishery	20		3	13 a 1
Estbrige	Eastchurch	Worth	Edward	1	0	0	Adelelm	H. Montfort				Bertram			7	1		2			13 a 1
Estselve	Eastswale	Bolton	Edward	1	0	0	Godric	Earl Bishop	1	0	0	Fitz-hubert	1	1	½	1	5 Ministers	4	4 Acres	4	8 a 1
Estselve	Essel Street	Eyhorne	Edward	2	0	0	Ulwi	Earl Bishop	2	0	0	H. Fitz-Hub.	1	1	½	1	2 Ministers	4	4 Acres	4	8 a 2
†Estoches	Stoke	Hoo	Earl Godwin	8	1	8	2 Thanes	Bp.Rochester	13	1	8	Demesne	10	5	5	6	4 Ministers	16	4 Acres		5 b 2
†Estothinges	Stowting	Stowting	Archbishop	8	0	0		Archbishop	10	0	0	Earl of Eu	27	13	1	9	1 Mill, 8 Min.	25	20 Acres	10	4 a 1
Estrei	Eastrye	Eastrye	Archbishop	26	10	4½		Archbishop	36	10	4½	Dem.&Monk	78	21	7	29	1 Mill, 3 Salt-pans	61	23 Acres	10	5 a 2
†Esturai	Sturry	Sturry	St. Austin's	2	10	0		St. Austin's	54	0	0	Abbot	39	32	5	14	10 Mills, 7 Fisher.	32	28 Acres	30	12 a 1
†Esturfete	Sturry	Sturry	Archbishop	24	12	6		Archbishop	54	0	0	See History	25	114	7	29	17 Mills, &c.	78	124 Acres	60	3 b 1
Estwelle	Estwell	Wye	Edward	3	10	0	Frederic	H. Montfort	3	10	0	Demesne	5	5	1	3½	See History	11	12 Acres		13 a 1
Eswalt	Wimlingswol	Eastrye	Edward	9	0	0	Alnold Cilt	Earl Bishop	15	0	0	Athelwold	6	2	3	4	2 Retainers	10	Shingle wood		9 b 2
Etretone		Newchurch	St. Martin's	10	0	0	Ulvile Wild	H. Montfort	10	0	0	Demesne		6	5	2	1 Mill	6	See History		13 a 1
Ewelle	Ewell	Besbrough	Edward	12	0	0	Edric	Earl Bishop	12	12	0	Port & Mont.	15	12	3	3	2 Mills. See Hist.	8	4 Acres	4	11 a 1
*Favreshant	Feversham	Wye Lath	See History																		
*Fulchestane	Folkstone	Eastrye Lath	Ditto																		
†Fachesham	Facombe	Axtane	Bp.Rochester	7	0	0		Bp.Rochester	8	0	0	Demesne	15	3	2	5	2 Mills, 3 Min.	12	4 Acres	30	5 b 1
†Fanne	Farnborough	Neuchurch		4	0	0		Earl Bishop	4	0	0	Fitz-hubert	3		½	2	3 Ministers	8	13 Acres	10	10 b 1

Various Names of Places in Domesday.	Presumed modern corresponding Names.	In what Hundred or Lath.	Proprietors under the Confessor, holding in chief.	Value at that Period, in Pounds, Shillings, and Pence.	Their Sub-tenants.	Proprietors under the Conqueror.	Value at that Period.	Sub-tenants.	Villans.	Borderers or Cottagers.	Sowlings.	Ploughs.	Occurring Observations.	Oxen or Cattle.	Agricultural Remarks.	Hogs, or their Pannage.	Folio in Domesday.
				£. s. d.			£. s. d.										
Favreshant	Feversham	Feversham	Edward	59 15 0	Viscount	William	30 0 0	Haimo Vic.	30	40	7	26	A Market, &c.	56	See History	100	2 b 2
Fereburne	Borden	Eyhorne	Edward	1 10 0	Sbern, Com.	Earl Bishop	1 10 0	Crookthorn	2	1	1	1	2 Retainers	4	1½ Acres	6	8 a 2
Fereburne	Borden	Eyhorne	Earl Godwin	4 0 0	Lewin	Earl Bishop	3 0 0	Fitz-hubert	4		1	3½	2 Mills	11			7 b 2
†Ferlaga	Farley	Maidstone	Archbishop	16 0 0		Archbishop	22 0 0	5 Sub-tenan.	42	66	6	59	4 Mills, 6 Fisheries	90	See History	135	4 b 2
Ferlingelai	Capell Fern	Besbrough	St. Martin's	6 0 0	Sired	St. Martin's	4 0 0	Fitz-geoffrey	4		1	2		6			1 b 2
Fletes	Fleet	Wingeham	Archbishop	21 0 0		Archbishop	21 0 0	7 Knights	4	22	6½	10	See History	14			3 b 2
Flengueffam	Finglesome	Eastrye	Archbishop	2 0 0		Archbishop	1 10 0	Folet	6		½	1½		6			4 b 1
*Forevic	Forewic	2 Borough	See History														
Forningeham	Forningeham	Axtane	Archbishop	7 0 0		Archbishop	11 0 0	Ansgot	13	5	1	5	See History	14	6 Ac. Mead.	20	4 a 2
Ferningeham	See History	Axtane		7 15 0	3 Thanes	Earl Bishop	8 15 0	3 Knights	3	6	1	4	2 Mills	16	100 Sheep	15	6 a 2
†Frandesberie	Frindbury	Shammel	Bp.Rochester	8 0 0		Bp.Rochester	25 10 0	Demesne	40	28	10	16	9 Ministers, 1 Mill	42	40 Ac. Mead.	5	5 b 2
†Fredenestede	Frindstead	Eyhorne	Edward	1 0 0	Lewin	Earl Bishop	1 0 0	2 Knights	3		1	3		11	2½ Acres	2	7 b 2
*Grenviz	Greenwich	Sutton Lath	See History														
Gara		Wi	Ditto														
†Gecham	Ickham	Downhamford	Archbishop	22 0 0	Demesne	Archbishop	32 0 0	Demesne	29	60	4	19	4 Mills, 100 s.	48	35 Ac. Mead.	30	5 a 1
Gara	See History	Wye	Feudal Ten.														2 a 1
Gelingeham	Gillingham	Chatham		2 0 0		Earl Bishop	3 0 0	Odo		6	½	2½	1 Mill	10	21 Ac. Mead.		8 a 2
†Gelingeham	Gillingham	Chatham	Archbishop	15 0 0	Demesne	Archbishop	25 19 0	Demesne	42	16	6	15	1 Mill, 3 Fisheries	40	14 Ac. Mead.	20	3 b 1
Geting	See Eastrye	Eastrye	Archbishop			Archbishop		Monks	6		½	2½		10			5 a 2
Gocistone	Guston	Besbrough	St. Martin's	1 0 0	Elric, Preb.	St. Martin's	0 10 0	Ulric	2	6	½	1½	Part in Cornely	6			5 a 2
†Godeselle	Goodneston	Boughton	Edward	4 0 0	Edwin	Earl Bishop	4 0 0	Fitz-hubert	5		1	2½		7			8 a 2
Gollesberge	Woodnesborough	Eastrye	Edward	12 0 0	3 Thanes	Earl Bishop	9 10 0	2 Tenants	26	1	3	2	See History	8			11 a 2
Gomersham	Godmersham	Felbrough	Archbishop	12 0 0	Demesne	Archbishop	30 0 0	Demesne	60	8	8	24	1 Mill	60	12 Ac. Mead.	40	5 a 1
Gravenel	Graveney	Boughton	Archbishop	5 0 0	Demesne	Archbishop	6 0 0	a Knight	8	10	1	3	5 Min. 4 Salt-pans	12	10 Ac. Mead.		4 a 2
†Gravesham	Gravesend	Toltingtrow	Edward	10 0 0	3 Thanes	Earl Bishop	11 0 0	Fitz-ivo	4	8	2½	1½	a Port	6			7 b 1
†Grenvis	Greenwich	Greenwich	Edward	8 0 0	2 Thanes	Earl Bishop	12 0 0	Bp. Lisieux	24	5	2	6	4 Mills	20	62 Ac. Mead.	10	6 b 2
*Haiborne	Eyhorne	Mylton lath	See History														
*Hame	Ham	Liming Lath	Ditto														
*Helmstree	Rokesley	Sutton Lath	Ditto														
*Hen	Hen	Liming Lath	Ditto														
*Hoo	Hoo	Mylton Lath	Earl Godwin	60 0 0	Demesne	Earl Bishop	113 0 0	Demesne	97	61	50	47	6 Church. 12 Min.	188	32 Ac. Mead.	30	8 b 1
Hadone		Shammel	Edward	2 10 0	Siward	Earl Bishop	3 0 0	Arnulph	7	1	½	2		6	6 Ac. Mead.		9 a 1
Hadone		Shammel	Edward	1 0 0	Siward	Earl Bishop	1 0 0	Odo			½			2			9 a 1
Hagelei	Halley	Axtane	Edward			Earl Bishop	15 0 0	Hugh Port	14	3	½	5	A Mill of 20s.	16	12 Ac. Mead.	5	6 a 1
Hagelei	Halley	Axtane	Edward	0 5 0	Ulret, Free.								No Client		20 Acres		6 a 1
†Haintone	Hunton		Edward	1 0 0	Ulf, Priest	H. Montfort	1 0 0	Demesne	1	4	1	1		4	3 Ac. Mead.		13 a 1
Hallinges	Halling	Toltingtrow	Bp.Rochester	7 0 0	Demesne	Bp.Rochester	16 0 0	Demesne	15	9	6	9	2 Ministers	28	30 Ac. Mead.	5	5 b 2
Tonbridge	Moiety	See History					0 7 0	Demesne			2½						
†Hallinges	Halling	Twyford	Edward	30 0 0	Alred	Fitz-gilbert	20 0 0	Demesne	16	12	2	8	15 Min. 2 Mill 4 Fi.	32	5 Ac. Mead.	150	14 a 2
Hama	Ham	Eastrye	Edward	2 10 0	3 Thanes	Earl Bishop	3 0 0	Fitz-letard	1	2		1	2 Followers	4			11 b 1
Hamestede	Hougham	Beusbro'	Edward		2 Freemen	Earl Bishop	0 20 0	R. Valbadon	1				Charter Land				11 b 2

Various Names of Places in Domeſday.	Preſumed modern correſponding Names.	In what Hundred or Lath.	Proprietors under the Confeſſour, holding in chief.	Value at that Period, in Pounds, Shillings, and Pence. £. s. d	Their Sub-tenants.	Proprietors under the Conquerour.	Value at that Period. £. s. d.	Sub-tenants.	Villains.	Borderers or Cottagers.	Sowlings.	Ploughs.	Occurring Obſervations.	Oxen or Cattle.	Agricultural Remarks.	Hogs, or their Pannage.	Folio in Domeſday.
Hamold	Kings-wold	Eaſtrye Lath	Edward		Edward	Earl Biſhop	1 0 0	Adam					Ralph, a Sub-ten.				11 a 1
Hamold	Kings-wold	Eſtrye Lath	Edward		Edward	Earl Biſhop		Fitz-hugh									
Haneheſt	Home Street	Shammel	Earl Godwin	1 0 0	Earl Godwin	Earl Biſhop	2 0 0	Anſgot	2	4	½	1		4			9 a 1
†Hardes	Hardes upper	Bridge	Edward	7 0 0	Edwin	Earl Biſhop	10 0 0	Demeſne	5		2	3	5 Miniſters	8		20	9 a 2
†Hardes alia	Hardesnether	Bridge	Edward	6 0 0	Azor	Earl Biſhop	5 0 0	Colville	5		1	3	8 Miniſters	10	13 Ac. Mead.	4	9 a 2
†Hariardeſham	Harietſham	Eyehorne	Edward	10 0 0	Siward	Earl Biſhop	110 0 0	Fitz herbert	17	4	2	6	11 Min. 2 Mills	24	7 Ac. Mead.	15	7 b 2
†Haſlow	Hadlow	Litefield	Edward	30 0 0	Queen Eddiva	Earl Biſhop	30 0 0	Fitz-gilbert	47	15	6	8	10 Min. 2 Mills 13 Fiſheries	48	12 Ac. Mead.	60	7 b 2
Haſtingelal	Haſtingligh	Byrcholt	Edward	3 0 0	Alnod	Earl Biſhop	3 0 0	Fitz-anſchil	2	6	1	2	3 Retainers	6		1	11 b 2
Haſtingelie	Haſtingligh	Byrcholt	Edward	0 10 0	Alnod	H. Montfort	0 10 0	Demeſne		2							14 a 1
Havocheſten	Hawking	'eſbrough	St. Martin's		Alnod Cilt	Rt. Romney							Canons claim		the Manour		2 a 2
†Hecham	Higham	Hoo	Edward	12 0 0	Godwin, Tol.	Earl Biſhop	6 0 0 15 0 0	Adam	24	12	5	9	Mill, Fiſhery, &c. See Hiſtory	38	200 Sheep, 30 Ac. Mead.		9 a 1
†Hicham-	Higham	Beſbrough	St. Martin's	5 0 0	Edwin	St. Martin's	4 0 0	Baldwin	4	5	1	3		8			1 b 2
Heda	Hythe	Hen	See Hiſtory														
Herbretitou	Harbledown	Whitſtable	Earl Godwin	3 0 0	Alric	Earl Biſhop	7 0 0	Ethelwold	2	1	1	1½	R. Latin farmed it	6	4 Ac. Mead,		8 a 2
Herſte	Hearty	Feverſham	Edward	0 10 0	Siward	Earl Biſhop	1 10 0	Hugh Port	2	2	¾	1		4			10 a 2
Hertang	Hickling	Eaſtrye	Edward	2 0 0	Eddid	Earl Biſhop	3 0 0	Fitz-robert	5	2	1	3		10			11 a 2
†Hoilingeborde	Hoilingborne	Eyhorne	Archbiſhop	20 0 0		Archbiſhop	30 0 0	Demeſne	61	16	6	5	See Hiſtory	96	8 Ac. Mead.	40	4 b 2
Hortun	Monks Horton	Stowting	Edward	2 0 0	2 Freeholders	H. Montfort	1 10 0	Fitz-richard	4		¾	1	1 Mill	4	10 Ac. Mead.	6	13 b 1
Hortune	Horton	Felbrough	Edward	1 10 0	Ordric	Earl Biſhop	3 0 0	Ansfrid	15			1½	1 Min. 2 Mills	4	10 Ac. & wood		10 b 1
†Hortune	Horton	Axtane	Brixi	4 0 0	Godel	Earl Biſhop	6 0 0	Anſchitill		5	1	3	These 3 manrs.		6 Ac. Mead.	3	
Hortune	Horton	Axtane	Edward	2 0 0	Ording	Earl Biſhop	3 0 0	Anſchitill	7	6	½	2	and Sou. Down,		9 do. & a Mill	5	6 b 1
Hortune	Horton	Axtane	Harold	4 0 0	Alward	Earl Biſhop	5 0 0	Anſchitill	7		1	3	1 under William		8 do. & a Mill	15	
Hou	Hall-place	Leſnes or Litelai	Edward	3 0 0	Anſchil	Earl Biſhop	4 0 0	Anſgot	5	2	1	2	1 Mill		12 Ac. Mead.	3	6 b 1
Huham	Wotton	Berham	Edward		Archbiſhop	Earl Biſhop		Fitz-ivo	12			9	See Hiſtory		20 Ac. Mead.		9 b 2
Hulviz	Woolwich	Greenwich	Edward		W. Falconer	Haimo, Viſc.	3 0 0	Demeſne		11					63 Acres		14 a 2
Limenewart-leſt	Ward of Liming	Lath	See Hiſtory														
*Langabrige	Longbridge	Liming Lath	Ditto														
*Lanport	Lamport	Liming Lath	Ditto														
*Liteſelle	Littlefield	Aylesford Lath	Ditto														
*Litelai	Leſnes	Sutton Lath	Ditto														
*Laurocheſel	Larkfield	Aylesford Lath	Ditto														
Langafell	Longfield	Axtane	Archbiſhop	3 10 0		Archbiſhop	5 0 0	Anſchil, Prſt.	9	[illegible]		3		10			5 b 1
Latintone	Nackinton	Canterbury		3 0 0		Earl Biſhop	3 0 0	Haimo, Viſc.		[illegible]	1	1½		6	12 Ac. Pann.		9 b 1
Languelei	Langley		Edward	3 0 0	Turgis	Earl Biſhop	3 0 0	Adam Fitzh.	7	5	1½	5	7 Miniſters	14	3 Ac. Mead.	25	8 a 1
Lanport	Lamport	Lamport	St. Auſtin's	20 0 0		St. Auſtin's	35 0 0	The Abbot	28	63	1½	8	See Hiſtory	32	17 Ac. Mead.		12 a 1
Lanport	Lamport	Lamport	St. Auſtin's	6 0 0		St. Auſtin's	8 0 0	Abbot	9	4	2½	6		12	10 Ac. Mead.	2	12 b 2
Lafela	Leves	Rokeſly	Edward	30 0 0	Brixi Cilt	Earl Biſhop	24 0 0	Geoff. of Roſs	31	14	7	19	10 Retainers	60		75	6 b 2
Tunbridge	Moiety, and					Conquerour	7 2 0										6 b 2

Various Names of Places in Domesday.	Presumed modern corresponding Names.	In what Hundred or Lath.	Proprietors under the Confessour, holding in chief.	Value at that Period, in Pounds, Shillings, and Pence.	Their Sub-tenants.	Proprietors under the Conqueror.	Value at that Period.	Sub-tenants.	Villains.	Borderers or Cottagers.	Sowlings.	Ploughs.	Occurring Observations.	Oxen or Cattle.	Agricultural Remarks.	Hogs, or their Pannage.	Folio in Domesday.
				£. s. d.			£. s. d.										
†Ledesdune	Ludsdown	Toltingtrow		6 0 0	Earl Lewin	Earl Bishop	8 0 0	Fitz-tyrrel	18	4	2½	7	1 Minister	20	3½ Ac. Mead.	20	7 b 1
Lee	Lee	Greenwich	Edward	3 0 0	Lewin	Earl Bishop	5 0 0	Walter, of D.	11	2	½	4	2 Retainers	16	5 Ac. Mead.	10	6 b 2
†Leleborne	Leyborne	Larkfield	Earl Godwin	8 0 0	Turgis	Earl Bishop	8 0 0	Fitz-hubert	17	2	2	10	10 Min. 1 Mill	30	12 Ac. Mead.	50	7 a 1
Tunbridge	Moiety					and Conquer.	1 4 2										
Lertham	Leneham	Eyehorne	St. Austin's	28 0 0		St. Austin's	28 0 0	Abbot	40	7		18	Robert Latin	72	2 Mills, 8 Ac.	40	[illegible] a 1
Lerham	Lenham	Calehill	Archbishop	8 0 0		Archbishop	12 0 0	Geoffrey	15	2		6	3 Retainers	20	1 Mill, 6 Ac.	10	4 b 1
Levelant	Leveland	Feversham	Archbishop	1 10 0		Archbishop	1 0 0	Richard Knt.	2	1		2		6		5	4 a 2
Levesham	Lewisham	Greenwich	Edward	16 0 0	Abbot of Ghent	Abbey of Ghent	30 0 0	Abbot	50	9		19	Toll of Port, 40s. 11 Mills, 8l. 12s.	56	30 Ac. Mead.	50	12 b 2
Leueberge		Besbrough	Edward		Lewin	Earl Bishop	0 5 0	Ansfrid	1	1	¼						11 a 1
Limes	Limpue	Byrcholt	Archbishop	12 0 0	Demesne	Archbishop	27 0 0	Seven Priests	1	18	½	2	Part of Aldington	6			4 a 1
†Leminges	Liming	Loningborough	Archbishop	24 0 0	Demesne	Archbishop	100 0 0	Demesne	101	16	7	9	10 Min. Mill, Fish.	236	30 Ac. Mead.	100	4 a 1
Leminges	Liming	Loningborough	Archbishop			Archbishop	11 0 0	His Knights	20	16		1	1 Minister, a Mill	40	40 Ac. Mead.	11	4 a 1
†Liteborne	Little Bourne	Dunhamsford	St. Austin's	25 0 0		St. Austin's	32 0 0	The Abbot	35	14	7	9	Park, value 60s.	36		4	12 a 1
Litelai	See Loisnes	Litelai															
Litelbroteham	Little Wrotham	Maidstone	Edward	2 0 0	Godwin and Edwin	Earl Bishop	3 4 6	Fitz tyrrel	4	4	1½	3	2 Retainers, 2 Mills	8	2 Ac. Mead.	5	8 b 2
Litelcert,	Little Chart	Calehill	Archbishop	5 0 0	Demesne	Archbishop	8 8 0	Demesne	19	5	5½	9	2 Mills	30	11 Ac. Mead.	15	5 a 1
Litelcert	Little Chart	Calehill	Archbishop				2 0 0	William of Eddesham		4	½	1		4	10 Ac. Mead.	20	5 a 1
Loisnes	Lesnes	Lesnes	Archbishop	20 0 0	Azor	Archbishop	40 0 0	Robert Latin	60	3	14	16	3 Fisheries	60	30 Ac. Mead.	20	6 b 1
Lolingstone	Lullingstone	Axtane	Edward	3 0 0	Brixi Cilt	Earl Bishop	5 0 0	Geoff. of Ross	4	2	1	3	7 Retainers	12	6 Acres	20	6 a 1
Lolingeston	Lullingstone	Axtane	Edward	3 0 0	Bruning	Earl Bishop	3 10 0	Malger	3	6	½	2	William, value 10s.	6	5 Acres		6 a 2
Lolingeston	Lullingstone	Axtane	Edward	3 0 0	Siward, Scot.	Earl Bishop	3 17 0	Osbern Pastforeire	3	1	½	2	William, a Wood, for a Present	6	5 Ac. Mead. 1 Mill	5	6 a 2
Middeltune-lest	Mylton Lath	See History															
*Maresc de Romenel	Romney Marsh	Liming Lath	See History	14 15 0	15 Yeomen	H. Montfort	16 15 0	Demesne	4		2	10	25 Yeomen	20	Tenants		13 a 1
Maresc de Romenel	Romney Marsh	Aloes Bridge	Ditto														
*Meddestan	Maidstone	Mylton Lath	Ditto														
*Moniberg	Loningboro'	Liming Lath	Ditto														
Machelievet		Feversham	Edward	0 4 2	Siward, bold	Earl Bishop	0 5 0	Ansfrid	2		½	½		2			10 a 2
Mapledescam	Maplescomb	Axtane	Edward	4 0 0	Euslan	Earl Bishop	5 10 0	Ansgot	1	4	½	1	4 Retainers	4	1 Ac. Mead.	8	6 a 1
Malpescamp	Maplescomb	Axtane	Earl Harold	3 0 0	Ulstan	Earl Bishop	6 0 0	Wadard	1	4	½	1	5 Retainers	4	1½ Ac. Mead.	8	6 a 2
Marourde	Mereworth	Litefield	Edward	12 0 0	Norman	Haimo, Visc.	19 0 0	Demesne	28	15	2	12	10 Min. 2 Mills, 2 Fisheries	36	20 Ac. Mead.	60	14 a 2
Messeberge	Boroughs Isle	Smarden	Edward		Godwin	Earl Bishop		Turstin	2		½	½		2			11 b 1
Medredive	Near Dover	Besbrough	St. Martin's		Canons	St. Martin's	0 9 4	Canons					Dover Gardens				2 a 2
†Meddestan	Maidstone	Maidstone	Archbishop	14 0 0	Demesne	Archbishop	20 0 0	Demesne	25	21	10	28	10 Min. 5 Mills, 2 Fisheries	112	10 Ac. Mead.	30	3 a 2
Meddestan	Maidstone	Maidstone	Archbishop			Archbishop	13 10 0	3 Knights	32	10	4	9	10 Ret. 1 Mill a Fish.	32	13 Ac. 2 Salt.	23	3 a 2

Various Names of Places in Domeſday.	Preſumed modern correſponding Names.	In what Hundred or Lath.	Proprietors under the Confeſſour, holding in chief.	Value at that Period, in Pounds, Shillings, and Pence.	Their Sub-tenants.	Proprietors under the Conqueror.	Value at that Period.	Sub-tenants.	Villains.	Borderers or Cottagers.	Sowlings.	Ploughs.	Occurring Obſervations.	Oxen or Cattle.	Agricultural Remarks.	Hogs, or their Pannage.	Folio in Domeſday.
				£. s. d.			£. s. d.										
†Meletune	Mylton	Toltingtrow	Earl Lewin	3 0 0		Earl Biſhop	6 0 0	Fitz-tyrrel	21	2	1½	3	1 Mill, a Port, 3 Ret.	10	Tunbridge 5s		7 b 1
Meleſtun'	Mylton	Shammel	Edward	0 10 0	Ulward Wit	Earl Biſhop	1 10 0	Helto		5	½	1		4	1 Ac. Mead.		9 a 1
†Mepeham	Meopham	Toltingtrow	Archbiſhop	15 10 0		Archbiſhop	26 0 0	Demeſne	25	71	17	29	17 Miniſters	116	10 Ac. Mead.	10	4 b 2
Tunbridge	Moiety	Toltingtrow				Fitz-gilbert	0 18 6	Demeſne								20	4 b 2
†Mellingetes	Malling	Larkfield	Bp. Rocheſter	2 0 0		Bp. Rocheſter	4 0 0	Demeſne	5	6	4½	½	1 Retainer	12	2 Ac. Mead.	10	5 b 1
†Merſeham	Marſham	Longbridge	Archbiſhop	10 0 0		Archbiſhop	20 0 0	Demeſne	39	9	7	19	2 Mills, 2 Salt-pans	48	13 Ac. Mead.	30	3 b 2
Mereleſham	Merſham	Longbridge	St. Martin's		Alnod Cilt	R. Romney		Demeſne					See Hiſtory				2 a 2
†Midelea	Medley	Lamport	Earl Biſhop	3 0 0	Godric	Earl Biſhop	3 0 0	Alred	5	9	½	2		6	10 Ac. Mead.	10	11 b 1
Mideltune.	Mylton	Mylton	See Hiſtory	200 0 0	Siward, Viſc.	William	200 0 0	Haimo, Viſc.	10	74	84	167	6 Mills, Toll 40s.	500	Guards, corvè	220	12 b 2
††Monoeſtune	Monkſtown	Thanet	Archbiſhop	20 0 0		Archbiſhop	40 0 0	Demeſne	89	21	38	25	1 Mill, Fiſh. Salt-p.	100		10	5 b 2
†Mundingeham	Mongeham	Cornilo	St. Auſtin's	22 0 0		St. Auſtin's	26 0 0	Demeſne			2½	5	See Hiſtory	20			12 b 1
Mundingeham	Mongeham	Cornilo	St. Auſtin's	10 0 0		St. Auſtin's	10 0 0	Wadard	8	2		¼	Monks, a Mill, &c.		Gavel Ten.		12 b 1
*Neucerce	Newchurch	Liming Lath	See Hiſtory														
†Neteſtede	Nettleſtead	Twyford	Edward	8 0 0	Norman	Earl Biſhop	8 5 0	Haimo, Viſc.	14		3	6	14 Min. 2 Mills Fiſh.	24	7 Ac. Mead.	35	8 b 1
†Neventone	Newington	Beuſbrough	Edward	12 0 0	Edric	H. Montfort	12 0 0	Demeſne		21	3	5	3 Mills	12	See Hiſtory		13 b 2
Nevingtone	Newington	Beuſbrough		3 0 0		Earl Biſhop	3 0 0	H. Montfort		1							11 b 1
Newedene	Newendene	Selbrittenden	Archbiſhop	5 0 0	Demeſne	Archbiſhop	18 0 0	Demeſne	25	4	1	5	See Hiſtory	15		40	14 a 1
Newetone	Queenboro'	Mylton	Queen Eddiva	40 0 0	Siward	Albert, Chan.	34 0 0	Several	10	48	7½	5	Ditto	20	12 Ac. Mead.	30	14 b 1
Neucerce	Newchurch	Blackburn	Edward	3 0 0	6 Yeomen	H. Montfort	4 15 0	Harold		31	½	5	1 Retainer	14	See Hiſtory		14 a 1
Neucerce	Newchurch	Newchurch	Edward	8 0 0	Azor	H. Montfort	9 0 0		8	3	1	5	No Hall	15			13 a 2
Nordeude	Norwood	Canterbury	St. Martin's		Canons	St. Martin's		Canons	3	9		1½	See Hiſtory	6			2 a 2
Nordeude	Norwood	Canterbury	Archbiſhop	17 0 0		Archbiſhop	17 0 0	Demeſne	7	26	1	3½	3 Mills. See Canter.	12	24 Ac. Mead.	30	
†Norfluet	Northfleet	Toltingtrow	Archbiſhop	10 0 0	Demeſne	Archbiſhop	39 0 0	Demeſne	36		11	12	7 Min. a Fiſhery	48	20 Ac. Mead.	20	5 a 1
Norborne	Norbourne	Cornilo	St. Auſtin's	80 0 0		St. Auſtin's	76 0 0	Demeſne	79	49	30	42	See Hiſtory	216	40 Ac. Mead.	10	3 a 2
Nordeſlinge	Nor-eaſeling	Feverſham	Edward	1 0 0	Turgod	Earl Biſhop	1 10 0	Her. Fitz-ivo		2		1		4			12 b 1
†Nortone	Norton	Rocheſter	Archbiſhop	24 5 0	Demeſne	Archbiſhop	50 13 2	Demeſne	92	40	13	61		104	10 Ac. Mead.	50	3 b 1
†Norton	Norton	Rocheſter	Archbiſhop				14 6 6	Vital		29	3½	5	7 Salt-pans	20	12 Ac. &c.		3 b 1
Nortone	Norton	Feverſham	Edward	8 0 0	Siward	Earl Biſhop	12 0 0	Hugh Port	18	6	4	8	3 Mills, 2 Fiſheries	22		40	10 a 1
*Oiſtreham	Weſterham	Sutton Lath	Edward	30 0 0	Earl Godwin	Earl Euſtace	40 0 0	Demeſne	42	7	4	32	10 Retain. a Mill	120	16 Ac. Mead.	100	14 a 1
*Oxenai	Oxney	Liming Lath	See Hiſtory														
Obtrepole	Orgarſwick	Stret	Edward	2 10 0	Alred bold	H. Montfort	4 0 0	Hervey	11		1	½	1 Retainer	12	10 Ac. Mead.	Pan.	14 a 1
Oſeham	Offham	Larkfield	Edward	2 0 0	Godric	Earl Biſhop	1 10 0	Hugh Port	6	1	1	2	1 Mill, 4 Retainers	6	4 Ac. Mead.	10	7 a 2
Oſeham	Offham	Larkfield	Alnod Cilt	5 0 0	Ulric	Earl Biſhop	5 0 0	Anſchil	6	2	1	2	1 Mill, 4 Retain.	16	7 Ac. Mead.	10	7 b 1
Oiſtreham	Weſterham	Weſterham	Edward	30 0 0	Earl Godwin	Earl Euſtace	40 0 0	Demeſne	42	7	4	32	10 Retain. 1 Mill	68	16 Ac. Mead.	100	14 a 1
†Oldeham	Woldham	Larkfield	Bp. Rocheſter	8 0 0		Bp. Rocheſter	12 0 0	Demeſne	13	16	9	8	6 Min. a Fiſhery	20	60 Ac. Mead.	20	5 b 1
†Olecumbe	Combe	Axtane	Archbiſhop	10 0 0	Alſer	Archbiſhop	11 0 0	Earl of Eu	23	8	2	9	1 Mill	36	8 Ac. Mead.	80	4 a 2
†Ore	Ore	Feverſham	Edward	4 0 0	Turgis	Earl Biſhop	5 0 0	Fitz-hubert	10	10	2	½	Mill, 2 Fiſh. Salt-p.	10		6	10 a 1
†Ore	Ore	Feverſham	Edward	1 0 0	Lewin bold	Earl Biſhop	1 0 0	Fitz-hubert	2		½	1	2 Villains farm it	4		5	10 a 2
†Orpintun	Orpington	Rokeſley	Archbiſhop	15 0 0		Archbiſhop	28 0 0	Demeſne	46	25	3	25	2 Mills. See Hiſt.	80	10 Ac. Mead.	50	4 b 2
††Orlaveſtone	Orlaſton	Ham	Edward	3 0 0	11 Freemen	H. Montfort	5 0 0	William	15	9	½	5½		12	20 Ac. Mead.	6	13 b 1
†Oſpringes	Oſpringe	Feverſham	Edward	20 0 0		Earl Biſhop	20 0 0	Fitz-herbert	36	17	9	14	1 Mill, a Fiſhery		13 Ac. Mead.	80	10 a 1
†Oteham	Otham	Eyehorne	Edward	3 0 0		Earl Biſhop	4 0 0	Geoff. of Roſs	9	3	1½	2	2 Min. 1 Mill	6	3 Ac. Mead.	8	8 a 2

Various Names of Places in Domesday.	Presumed modern corresponding Names.	In what Hundred or Lath.	Proprietors under the Confessour, holding in chief.	Value at that Period, in Pounds, Shillings, and Pence. £. s. d.	Their Sub-tenants.	Proprietors under the Conquerour.	Value at that Period. £. s. d.	Sub-tenants.	Villains.	Borderers or Cottagers.	Sowlings.	Ploughs.	Occurring Observations.	Oxen or Cattle.	Agricultural Remarks.	Hogs, or their Pannage.	Folio in Domesday.
Otefort	Otfort	Axtane	Archbishop		Demesne	Archbishop	60 0 0	Demesne	101	18	8	51	8 Retain. 6 Mills	168	50 Ac. Mead.	150	3 a 1
Otefort	Otfort	Axtane	Archbishop			Archbishop	22 0 0	3 Thanes and Fitz-gilbert	16	11	1½	7	2 Mills, 5 Retain.	24	28 Ac. Mead.	30	3 a 1
Otrinberge	Wateringbury	Twyford	Edward	4 0 0	Godil	Earl Bishop	5 0 0	H. Braibow	5	4	2	3	3 Retain. 1 Mill	12	3 Ac. Mead.	2	8 b 2
†Ottringberge	Wateringbury	Twyford	Edward	2 0 0	Leveva	Earl Bishop	6 0 0	Fitz-tyrrel	6	8	3	5	2 Mills, a Fishery	16	2 Ac. Mead.	2	8 b 2
Otringdene	Otterden	Eyehorne	Edward	0 10 0	Alward	Earl Bishop	1 10 0	Fitz hurbert	2	4	½	1¾	2 Retainers	6	1 Ac. Mead.	5	3 a 1
*Piteham	Petham	Borough Lath	See History														
*Prestetune	Preston	Borough Lath	Ditto														
†Palestrei	Paster Court	Oxney	Edward	2 0 0	Edwy, Priest	Earl Bishop	3 0 0	Osbern		9	½	2	2 Min. 5 Fisheries	6	10 Ac. Mead.	10	10 b 2
†Pecheham	Peckham	Litefield	Archbishop	12 0 0		Archbishop	8 0 0	Demesne	16	14	6	6½	10 Min. 1 Mill	26	6 Ac. Mead.	10	4 b 2
Pecheham	Peckham	Litefield						Ar. Bp's Knt.			½		Free Land				4 b 2
Tunbridge	Moiety						4 0 0	Fitz-gilbert	27		2½	7		20		10	4 b 2
Pecheham	Peckham	Litefield	Edward	12 0 0	Earl Lewin	Earl Bishop	12 0 0	Corbin	12	8	2	6	5 Retainers, Conquerour 4 Villains	20	3 Ac. Mead.	10	7 b 1
Pesinges et Piham }	Pincham	Besbrough	Edward	5 0 0	6 Thanes	Earl Bishop	6 0 0	Hugh Port	6	14	2	3½					10 b 2
†Pivestone	Pevington	Calehill	Edward	8 0 0	Sbern	Earl Bishop	6 0 0	Earl Bishop	7	7	1	4	9 Min. 1 Mill, held of the Barony	10 16	Montfo. sub-ten. 20 Ac.	60	10 b 2
†Pelleforde	Badlesworth	Larkfield	Edward	1 0 0	Godric	Earl Bishop	2 0 0	Hugh Port	1	4	½	1¾	2 Ministers	7	5 Ac. Mead. 1 Ac. Pasture		7 a 2
Pinpa	Pembury	Twyford	Edward	0 6 0	Godric	Earl Bishop	0 15 0	Fitz-hubert		2	½	¼	Half a Fishery	2	4 Ac. Mead.	6	8 b 1
Pinnedene	Pinnenden		Edward	0 16 0	Alred	Earl Bishop	0 16 0	Malger	6		½	1		7	6 Ac. Mead.		6 a 2
Perie	Perry Street	Feversham	Edward	0 16 0	Ulwi	Earl Bishop	0 16 0	Ansfrid		1	½						10 a 1
Perie	Perry Street	Feversham	Edward	1 4 0	Ulweva	Earl Bishop	1 4 0	Ansfrid		3		1	A House in Canter.	4			10 a 1
††Piteham	Petham	Petham	Archbishop	17 6 3		Archbishop	20 0 0	Demesne	32	21	7	22	2 Ministers	80	13 Ac. Mead.	20	9 b 1
Piteham	Petham	Petham	Archbishop			Archbishop	9 0 0	Godf. & Nigel	4	8	1½	7	Monk's Portion 8s.	22			9 b 1
Platenout		Besbrough	St. Austin's	1 0 0		St. Austin's	2 0 0	Abt. & Crook.	4	3	1	1½		6	25 Ac. Mead.		12 b 1
Pluchlei	Pluckley	Calehill	Archbishop	12 0 0		Archbishop	20 0 0		16	7	1	13	8 Retainers	44	12½ Ac. Mea.	140	3 b 2
Plumestede	Plumstead	Litelai	Edward	10 0 0	Brixi Cilt	Earl Bishop	12 0 0	Abbot	17	3	2½	5		20		5	6 b 1
Plumstede	Plumstead	Litelai	St. Austin's	10 0 0		St. Austin's	14 8 3	Abbot	17	6	2¼	7		24		5	12 a 1
Poltone	Polton	Besbrough	Edward	2 0 0	Lewin	H. Montfort	1 10 0	Herfrid	3		1	2					13 b 2
††Postinges	Posting	Hen	Edward	10 0 0	Sbern	H. Montfort	14 0 0	Roger	17	11	1	10	3 Mills	40	45 Ac. Mead.	40	13 a 2
Popeselle	Popeshall	Eastrye Lath	Edward	3 0 0	2 Freemen	Earl Bishop	5 0 0	Osbern	1	4	1	2½	A Knight	8			9 b 2
†Prestetone	Preston	Feversham	Archbishop	10 0 0		Archbishop	15 0 0	Demesne	13	14	1	5	1 Min. 1 Mill, a Fishery of Eels	24	2 Ac. Mead.	5	5 a 1
Prestetune	Preston	Preston	St. Austin's	10 0 0		St. Austin's	19 0 0	Abbot	25	34	5	13	Vital, a Sub-tenant	40			12 b 1
*Rovecestre	Rochester	Aylesford Lath	See History														
*Rovindene	Rovinden	Liming Lath	Ditto														
Rapentone	Ripton	Calehill	St. Austin's	3 0 0	Abbot	St. Austin's	4 0 0	The Abbot	2	12	¼	1	Ansfred, Sub-ten. Part of a Mill	4	11 Ac. Mead.	10	12 a 2
Redlege	Ridley	Axtane	Edward	3 0 0	Siward	Earl Bishop	4 10 0	Fitz-hubert	6	5	1	4	5 Retainers	10	A Dingle to Tunbr. Moi.		6 a 1

Various Names of Places in Domeſday.	Preſumed modern correſponding Names.	In what Hundred or Lath.	Proprietors under the Confeſſour, holding in chief.	Value at that Period, in Pounds, Shillings, and Pence.			Their Sub-tenants.	Proprietors under the Conqueror.	Value at that Period.			Sub-tenants.	Villains.	Borderers or Cottagers.	Sowlings.	Ploughs.	Occurring Obſervations.	Oxen or Cattle.	Agricultural Remarks.	Hogs, or their Pannage.	Folio in Domeſday.
				£.	s.	d.			£.	s.	d.										
†Rieſc	Ryarſh	Larkfield	Edward	8	0	0	Alric	Earl Biſhop	6	0	0	Hugh Port	10	2	2½	5	10 Miniſt. 1 Mill	16	9 Ac. Mead.	5	7 a 2
Ripa & Brandet	Ripple	Beſbrough	St. Martin's	1	0	6	Frank-almo.	St. Martin's	1	0	6	Frank-almo.									2 a 2
Ringeſtone	Rowling	Eaſtrye	Edward	6	0	0	Edward	Earl Biſhop	13	0	0	Herbert	4	7		4	Of the Barony 1 Mill	12			11 a 1
Rochelei	Rokeſley	Helmſtrei, now Rokeſley	Edward	4	0	0	Edward	Earl Biſhop	4	0	0	Malger	10	10	1	1½ 2	1 Mill	12		3	6 b 1
Rotinge	Roching	Calehill	St. Auſtin's					St. Auſtin's	0	15	0	Abbot			½	1		4			12 a 2
†Roculf	Rocheſter	Rocheſter	Archbiſhop	14	0	0		Archbiſhop	35	0	0	Demeſne	90	25	8	3 27	1 Mill, additional Rent 7l. 7s.		1 Fiſh. 5 Salt-pans, 33 Ac.	20	3 b 1
Roveceſtre	Rocheſter	See Hiſtory																			
Romenel	Romney	Lanport	See Hiſtory																		
Rongoſtone	Rodmerſham	Feverſham	Edward	2	0	0	Ulwi	Earl Biſhop	2	0	0	Richard	2		1	1		4			10 b 1
Sudtone-leſt	Sutton Lath	See Hiſtory																			
*Sm. Marden	Marden	Liming Lath	See Hiſtory																		
*Sanwice	Sandwich	Eſtrye Lath	Ditto																		
*Salebriſt	Selbrittenden	Liming Lath	Ditto																		
*Stretes	Stret	Liming Lath	Ditto																		
†Salteode	Saltwood	Hen	Archbiſhop	16	0	0		Archbiſhop	29	6	4	H. Montfort	33	12	7 3	2 9	2 Miniſters, 9 Mills 225 Burg. in Hythe	44	33 Ac. Mead.	80	4 b 1
Sancta Margaretta	St Margaret's	Beſbrough	St. Martin's	21	10	0	7 Prebends	St. Martin's	24	9	2	7 Prebends	12	31	6	5	See Hiſtory A Ruſtic Sl.	36	100 Acres		1 b 1 2 a 2
Sanctus Martinus	St. Martin's	Byrcholt	Archbiſhop	11	0	0	Demeſne	Archbiſhop	11	0	0	Demeſne	3	39	1½	6	5 Mills, 7 Burgeſſes Ralph, a Sub-ten.	16	See Hiſtory		4 a 1
Sanwice	Sandwich	Sandwich	See Hiſtory																		
Scape		Therham	Archbiſhop	1	10	0		Archbiſhop	5	0	0	Geoff. Purve.		2	½	1	4 Retainers	4			4 b 1
Schildriceham	ſee Cildreſham																				
Seleſburne	Sittingbourn	Eyhorne	Earl Godwin	1	0	0	Lewin	Earl Biſhop	1	0	0	Fitz-herbert		1	¼	½	5 Ret. & Land free	2	1½ Acres		7 b 2
Sedlinges	Selling	Stret	Edward	8	0	0	Siward	H. Montfort	7	0	0	Hervey	8	25	1	½	1 Mill	20	36 Ac. Mead.	6	13 b 2
Selinges	Selling	Eaſtrye	Edward	4	0	0	Ulwin	Earl Biſhop	5	0	0	Coiville	4	3	1	1½		6			11 b 2
Selinge	Selling	Eaſtrye	Edward	3	0	0	Lewin	Earl Biſhop	2	0	0	Fitz-letard	1		1						9 b 2
Siborne		Stret	Edward	3	0	0	Siward	H. Montfort	4	0	0	Demeſne	1	4	1	2	1 Retainer	6			13 b 1
†Setlinges	Stelling	Bolton	St. Auſtin's	15	0	0		St. Auſtin's	13	0	0	Abbot	30		6	10	No Hall	30			12 a 1
†Sentlinges	Chevening	Rokeſley	Archbiſhop	8	0	0	Bonde	Archbiſhop	8	0	0	Fitz-herbert	20		1½	4	9 Miniſters	12	6 Ac. Mead.	8	7 a 1
†Scivetone	Sevington	Longbridge	Edward	1	10	0	Brixi the bold	H. Montfort	1	10	0	Maigno	1	6	½	1	A Prieſt, a Mill	4	8 Ac. Mead.		13 a 1
Sueſton	Sevington	Longbridge	Edward	0	2	6	A Yeoman	H. Montfort	0	3	0			1							14 a 1
†Seſaltre	Seaſaltre	Canterbury	See Hiſtory																		
†Sibertſwalt	Shebbertwold	Beſbrough	St. Auſtin's	8	0	0		St. Auſtin's	8	0	0	Abbot	11	6	2	4		12			12 b 1
Sibertefwalt	Shebbertwold	Beſbrough	St. Martin's	10	5	0	5 Prebends	St. Martin's	6	15	0	Prebends	8	13	2	3	See Hiſtory	14			1 b 2
Sifletone		Larkfield		2	0	0	Lewin & Ulwin, as Peers	Earl Biſhop	5	0	0	Vital	6	1		1½	6 Retain. 1 Mill	6	10 Ac. Mead. 30 Ac. Paſt.		7 a 1
Soaneclive	Swale Cliff	Witenſtaple	Edward	1	1	0	Edw. Snoch	Earl Biſhop	1	10	0	Vital		8	½	1½		6		20	10 a 1
Soaneclive	Swale Cliff	Witenſtaple	Edward	0	10	0	Ulfi	Earl Biſhop	1	0	0	Vital		4	¼	½		2		10	10 a 1

Various Names of Places in Domeſday.	Preſumed modern correſponding Names.	In what Hundred or Lath.	Proprietors under the Confeſſour, holding in chief.	Value at that Period, in Pounds, Shillings, and Pence.	Their Sub-tenants.	Proprietors under the Conqueror.	Value at that Period.	Sub-tenants.	Villains.	Borderers or Cottagers.	Sowlings.	Ploughs.	Occurring Obſervations.	Oxen or Cattle.	Agricultural Remarks.	Hogs, or their Pannage.	Folio in Domeſday.
				£. s. d.			£. s. d.										
Soltone	Sheldon	Beſbrough		15 0 0		Earl Biſhop	1 10 0	Hugh Port	3	1	1	1	20 Ac. allodial land	4	held by Godric		11 a 1
Soles	Sole Ropers	Eaſtrye	Edward	5 0 0	Elmer	Earl Biſhop	6 0 0	Anſfrid	8		2	2½		10			11 a 2
†Sondreſſe	Sundriſh	Axtane	Archbiſhop	12 0 0		Archbiſhop	18 0 0 23 0 0	Demeſne	27	9	1½	11	8 Min. 3 Mills, 1 Knight's Service	28	8 Ac. Mead.	60	3 a 1
†Stanceſelle	Stalisfield	Feverſham	Earl Godwin	3 0 0	Turgis	Earl Biſhop	5 0 0	Fitz-hubert	10		2	3	6 Miniſters	10	6 Ac. Mead.	60	10 a 1
Stanetdeſte	Stanford	Stret	St. Martin's	0 16 8	The Abbey	St. Martin's	0 16 8	The Abbey	7	7	1	2	See Hiſtory for	8			2 a 2
Stanceſtede	Stanford	Byrcholt	St. Martin's	0 8 9	The Abbey	St. Martin's	0 8 9	The Abbey	7	7	1	4	6 Vill. 9 Borderers	12	5 Dingles		2 a 2
†Stochingeberge	Stockbury	Eyhorne	Edward	4 0 0	Elveva	Earl Biſhop	6 0 0	Anſgot	5	9	2	3	2 Miniſters, 1 Mill	10		15	8 a 1
Stoches	Stoke	Hoo	Edward	5 0 0	Anſchil	Earl Biſhop	5 10 0	Anſgot		7	2	2	A Fiſhery	8			8 b 1
†Stellinges	Stelling	Bridge	Edward	3 0 0	Alred	Earl Biſhop	2 0 0	Demeſne		1	⅛	1½		6		2	9 a 2
Sudcrai	South Cray	Rokeſley	Edward	6 0 0	Toli	Earl Biſhop	10 0 0	Fitz-hubert	13	1	1	3	6 Retainers	10	10 Ac. Mead.	10	6 b 2
†Sudfleta	Southfleet	Axtane	Bp. Rocheſter	11 0 0		Bp. Rocheſter	45 0 0	Demeſne	25	9	11	13	7 Miniſters	52	20 Ac. Mead.	10	5 b 1
Tunbridge	Moiety	in Southfleet	See Hiſtory			Fitz-gilbert	1 0 0	Demeſne					Wood and Paſture				5 b 1
†Sudtone	Chart Sutton	Eyhorne	Edward	10 0 0	Levenot	Earl Biſhop	30 0 0	Fitz-hubert	15	9	1½	5	10 Miniſters	14	8 Ac. Mead.	50	8 a 1
†Sudtone	Sutton	Eyhorne	Earl Lewin	12 0 0	Demeſne	Earl Biſhop	32 0 0	Fitz-hubert	18	5	4	6	1 Mill	16	4 Ac. Mead.	50	8 a 1
Suineſcamp	Swanſcombe	Axtane		20 0 0		Earl Biſhop	32 0 0	Helto	33	2	10	16	A Knight, 10 Ret. 1 Port & 5 Fiſher.	56	40 Ac. Mead.	3	6 a 1
Tunbridge	Moiety						0 4 0						A Wood				6 a 1
Suanetone	Swingfield	Beſbrough	Edward	10 0 0	Coloen	Earl Biſhop	4 0 0	Crookthorn	3	3	2	1½	Two Sub-tenants	6			11 a 2
Stepedone		Mylton	Edward	1 10 0	Siward	Earl Biſhop	1 10 0	Hugh Port	1	5	1	2		8			9 a 2
*Tanet	Thanet	Borough Lath	See Hiſtory														
*Therham	Therham	Sutton Lath	Ditto														
*Tuiſerde	Twyford	Aylesford Lath	Ditto														
*Tonebridge Leuga	Lowy of Tonbridge	Aylesford Lath	Ditto														
†Tangas	Tong	Mylton	Edward	7 0 0	Siward	Earl Biſhop	10 10 0	Hugh Port	5		2	3	4 Min. 1 Mill	10		4	9 a 2
†Tanet	Thanet	Thanet	St. Auſtin's	80 0 0	Abbot	St. Auſtin's	100 0 0	Abbot	150	50	48	65	A Prieſt, Salt-pa. 1 Mill	260	A Fiſhery, 3 Knights		12 a 2
Tarent	Darent	Axtane	Archbiſhop	14 0 0		Archbiſhop	18 0 0	Demeſne	22	7	2	8	6 Reta. 2 Mills, 5 Burg. in Rocheſter	18	8 Ac. Mead.	20	3 a 2
Tarent	Darent	Axtane	Edward	5 0 0	Alric	Earl Biſhop	5 0 0	Anſc. of Roſs	4	4	½	2	2 Mills	6	3 Acres	3	6 a 2
Tarent	Darent	Axtane	Edward	3 0 0	Siward	Earl Biſhop	3 10 0	Anſchill	5	5	½	1	1 Mill	4	3 Acres		6 a 2
†Tarenteſort	Dartford	Axtane	Edward	60 0 0	Siward, Viſc.	William	102 13 2	Haimo Viſco.	141	10	1½	55	3 Min. 1 Mill, two Quays	160	See Hiſtory		2 b 1
Tepindene	Tipenden	Blackburn	Edward	0 8 4	Norman	H. Montfort	0 8 4	Demeſne	2		½	½		2			13 b 2
Teſtan	Teſton	Twyford	Edward	5 0 0	Edward	Earl Biſhop	5 0 0	Athelwold	7	3	1	3	1 Mill, 12 Retain.	10	8 Acres	20	8 b 2
Tevegate	Smethe	Longbridge	Edward	1 0 0	Earl Godwin	H. Montfort	1 0 0	Demeſne	1		½	1		4	8 Acres		14 a 1
Ticheteſte	Icovehurſt	Smarden	Edward	4 0 0	Edric	Earl Biſhop	5 0 0	Turſtin		4	1½	1		4	a ſmall Wood		11 b 1
Tilemanſtone	Tilneſtone	Eſtrye	Archbiſhop	1 0 0		Archbiſhop	1 10 0	Will. Folet		5	1	2		4			4 b 1
†Tintentone	Tenterden	Blackburn	Edward	12 0 0	Alnold Cilt	H. Montfort	7 0 0	Demeſne	21	6	1	9	9 Min. 3 Fiſheries	20	38 Ac. Mead.	40	13 a 2
Titentone	Tantariden	Aloes Bridge		0 15 0		Earl Biſhop	0 15 0	Rt. Romney	1	3		½	2 Fiſheries	2			11 a 1
Titentone	Tenterden	Newchurch				H. Montfort	0 12 0	Demeſne		2			Lords Ploughs				13 a 1

Various Names of Places in Domeſday.	Preſumed modern correſponding Names.	In what Hundred or Lath.	Proprietors under the Confeſſour, holding in chief.	Value at that Period, in Pounds, Shillings, and Pence.	Their Sub-tenants.	Proprietors under the Conqueror.	Value at that Period.	Sub tenants.	Villains.	Borderers or Cottagers.	Sowlings.	Ploughs.	Occurring Obſervations.	Oxen or Cattle.	Agricultural Remarks.	Hogs, or their Pannage.	Folio in Domeſday.
				£. s. d.			£. s. d.										
†Tivedell	Tudely	Watliſton	Edward	0 15 0	Eddeva	Earl Biſhop	0 15 0	Fitz-gilbert			¼	1		4		2	7 b 2
Totentune	Ditton	Larkfield	Edward	1 10 0	Alnod Cilt	Earl Biſhop	2 0 0	Robert Latin	3	9	½	1½	Preſented to Wm. from Earl Biſhop	6	4 Retainers, 5 Ac. Mead.	2	7 a 2
Totentune	Ditton	Larkfield	Edward	0 10 0	Earl Godwin	William	0 10 0								2 Ac. Mead.		7 a 2
†Toteſclive	Treteſcliff	Larkfield	Bp. Rocheſter	3 0 0		Bp. Rocheſter	7 0 0	Demeſne	10		4	½	1 Miniſter	10	2 Ac. Mead.	10	5 b 1
†Trevelai	Throwley	Feverſham	Edward	7 0 0	Alnod Cilt	Earl Biſhop	8 0 0	Herfrid	24	5	3	7	5 Min. 3 Houſes in Canterbury	28		20	10 a 2
Tuneſtelle	Tunſtall	Mylton	Edward	7 0 0	Siward	Earl Biſhop	8 0 0	Hugh Port	9		3	3	9 Retainers	10	Salt-pan	10	9 a 2
*Wiwart-leſt	Wye-ward Lath	See Hiſtory															
*Wachelſtan	Watliſton	Aylesford Lath	See Hiſtory														
*Werde	Worth	Liming Lath	Ditto														
*Wi, a †manour	in Wye	Wye Lath	Ditto	10 0 0		Haimo, Viſc	14 0 0	Demeſne	16	15	2	10	7 Min. 1 Mill	32	20 Ac. Mead.	30	14 a 2
*Wingeham	Wingham	Baſtrye Lath	Ditto														
*Witeneſtaple	Whitſtable	Eorough Lath	Ditto														
Walwaleſere	Walderſhare	Eaſtrye	Edward	7 10 0	Ulward	Earl Biſhop	7 0 0	Crockthorn	13		2	4		12			13 b 1
Warwintone	Wanderton	Downhamfort	Sbern	4 0 0	Edric	St. Auſtin's	4 0 0	Abbot		3	½	1		4			12 a 1
Waneſberge	Glaſenbury	Smarden	Edward	0 7 6	Tochi	Earl Biſhop	0 10 0	Turſtin		2							11 b 1
Welle	Well	Calehill	Archbiſhop	17 11 4		Archbiſhop	24 0 4 40 0 0	Demeſne	51	5	12	16	1 Mill, 8 Retainers	48	20 Ac. Mead.	80	5 a 2
Werahorne	Warehorne	Hame	Archbiſhop	1 0 0		Archbiſhop	3 0 0	Demeſne	6	3	1	2		6	12 Ac. Mead.	6	5 a 2
Weſtſelve	Weſtſwale	Mylton	Edward	4 0 0	Queen Eddiva	Earl Biſhop	4 0 0	Fitz-robert	10	1	1	3	1 Mill, 5 Retain.	10	1 Ac. Mead.	15	8 a 1
Weſclive	Weſtcliffe	Beuſbrough	Edward	8 0 0	Edric	Earl Biſhop	8 0 0	Hugh Port	17		2	3	2 Mills, belonging to H. Muntfort	10			11 a 1
†Wi	Wye	Wye	Battle Abbey	85 6 8		Battle Abbey	125 0 0	Abbot	114	22	7	26	7 Min. 4 Mills	104	133 Ac. Mea.	300	11 b 2
†Wirentone	Warden	Feverſham		2 0 0		St. Auſtin's	4 0 0	Abbot	9		1	2		6	2 Ac. Mead.	5	12 a 2
†Wichebam	Wickham	Rokeſley	Edward	8 0 0	Godr. Fitz-c	Earl Biſhop	13 0 0	Fitz-hubert	24		1	6	1 Mill, 13 Min.	16		10	6 b 1
†Wicheham	Wickham	Downhamfort	Edward	25 0 0	Alred	Earl Biſhop	30 0 0	Demeſne	36	32	2	11	A Prieſt, paying 40s. per an. a Park, 2 Mills, a Salt-pan	44	½ Sow. free-l. 300 ſheep, 31 Horſes, 32 Ac.	80	9 a 2
Wingeham	Wingeham	Wingeham	Archbiſhop	77 0 0		Archbiſhop	100 0 0	Demeſne	55	20	40 35	65	8 Retain. 2 Mills, D'arcey, 6 Knights holding 6 ſowlings,	140	Ploughs, Vil. Ruſtics, &c. See Hiſtory	5	3 b 2
Winchelſmere	Winmill-Creek	Feverſham	Edward	5 0 0	Ulwi	Earl Biſhop	2 0 0	Fitz-herbert		3		1	3 Houſes in Canterbury, 3 Ret.	4		5	8 a 2
Witenemers		Greenwich	Edward	5 0 0	Anſchil	Earl Biſhop	5 0 0	Fitz-tyrald	11	2	1	4		12	4 Ac. Mead.	15	6 b 2
Places omitted.																	
Aia	a Hall	Stret	Edward	1 0 0	a Sockman	H. Montfort	1 5 0	Nigel, Phyſi.		6	1	½	2 Retainers	2	5 Ac. Mead.		13 b 2
Beveaſel	Beawfield	Cornilo	St. Auſtin's			St. Auſtin's	6 0 0	Oidelard		10	½	2	Norborne Manour	4			12 b 1
†Eſtraites	Stret	Stret	Edward	12 0 0	Ulnod	Earl Biſhop	35 0 0	Robert Latin	33	4	16	13	15 Retain. 6 Fiſh.	32	20 Ac. Mead.		8 b 1
Ceteham	Chatham	Chatham	Edward	0 10 0	Godwin	H. Montfort	8 0 0	Mandeville	12	27	2½	9	1 Mill, 2 Sub-ten.	24	30 Ac. Mead.		13 b 1

It cannot be ſuppoſed that Tables on ſuch conſtruction can give the exact population of the county of Kent, ſince many perſons are mentioned in the Autograph of Domeſday, though their appropriate reſidence is not ſpecified. For preciſe accuracy on this ſubject, we muſt refer the reader to the Tables of Hundreds, inſerted in the body of our Hiſtory, where the inhabitants are computed with the greateſt certainty.

THE

HISTORY OF SOUTH BRITAIN;

FROM

Authentic Documents.

CHAP. I.

The Topographical, Civil, and Political History of the County of Chenth, Chent, or Kent, from the Æra of Edward the Confeſſor, 1065, *to the Reign of Edward the Firſt,* 1272, *a Period of* 207 *Years.*

IN the kingdom of Great-Britain there are two grand diviſions, South and North Britain; a ſecond ſeparation into the nations of England, Scotland, and Wales; and a diſtinctive ſubdiviſion of each into particular diſtricts, or counties. To aſcertain the preciſe period, when this arrangement was adopted, is foreign to our purpoſe; but we have certain proofs, that little alteration has taken place in the demarcation of their boundaries [a], from the reign of Edward the Confeſſor to the

CHAP. I. 1065—1272.

[a] To avoid cavil, we juſt note that Rutland was partly included in Nottinghamſhire (Hæc duo Wapentac adjacent Vicecomitatui Snotingeham ad Geltum Regis. Domeſday. 293. b. 1.) and Lancaſhire, betwixt the Ribble and Mercy, (inter Ripam & Merſam) ſeparated from the other part of the county, &c.

CHAP. I. 1065—1272.

present day. In each particular county there were ftill fubordinate fections, as laths, rapes, wapentakes, baronies, ridings, hundreds, or manors; but the diftinction of parifhes, or the regular payment of [b] tithes to a particular church, was certainly not generally eftablifhed, when the autograph of Domefday was compiled.

That portion of the ifle, which engages our immediate attention, is fituated in its fouth-eaftern extremity. It extends from fifty degrees fifty-three minutes, northern latitude, to fifty-one thirty minutes; comprehends the [c] focus from whence the Englifh meridian is calculated, and extends one degree nineteen minutes and a half eafternly, three minutes wefternly from fuch centre; or, to fpeak in more intelligible language to an Englifh reader, is fixty-five miles in length from its caftern to weftern extremities, and forty in breadth, from the ifle of Grain to Romney.

The gently-fwelling tide of the Thames bounds it on the north, the Downs and the Straits of Dover on the eaft, the extremity of the Englifh Channel and Suffex on the fouth, and the counties of Suffex and Surrey border on its weftern line. The form of Kent is irregular, but it approximates neareft to a trapezium, or four-fided figure, whofe eaftern bafe is forty-one miles; whofe northern fhore fixty-three miles; whofe interfecting fide with Surrey, twenty-five miles; and whofe length, from Bafeing to the extremity of Romney Marfh, is forty-three miles.

[b] De ftori anteceffore Walterii de Aincurt dicunt (teftes duarum fcirarum,) quod fine alicujus licentia potuit facere fibi æcclefiam in fua terra & in fua foca & fuam decimam mittere quo vellet. Snotinghfcire. Domef. 280. a. 2.

Tempore regis Edvardi erant præbendæ communes, modo funt divifæ per fingulos per epifcopum baiocenfem. Domef. p. 1. b. 1.

[c] Royal Obfervatory, at Greenwich.

This

This county constitutes nearly one fortieth part of South Britain, contains more than one thousand five hundred and seventy-eight square-miles of English [d] statute measure, and one million ten thousand five hundred and sixty-one acres, exclusive of such augmentation as must arise from inequality of surface. For farther particulars we refer the reader to an annexed map, with copious explanations; and shall proceed with the more immediate object of our pursuit, the existing state of Kent, as reported by the commissioners to the Norman prince, from the collected evidence of counties and hundreds.

CHAP. I. 1065—1272.

To avoid the confusion that would arise from pursuing the unconnected entries in Domesday, or that inaccurate perspective of objects or manners, which the perambulation of a county presents; we must necessarily adopt some systematical arrangement, if we would comprehensively convey our presumed information, or beneficially transmit the documents of antiquity. For such strong reasons, we shall endeavour to collect and concentrate each scattered ray, that may possibly illumine an obscured medium, or enable the judicious and well directed eye to receive with accuracy and precision such image, as a mirror of considerable diameter may reflect from distant objects. On such principles, we shall survey the eastern hemisphere, its general horizon, primary planet, constellations, and stars of various magnitude; or in simple language, East Kent, with its prevailing laws, customs, and manners, its conspicuous city, boroughs, towns, villages, and hamlets. We shall afterwards contemplate on the western district, pursuing the same plan.

The county of Kent constituted a part of that division of England, which was controuled by the [e] West-Saxon laws.

[d] Of 1760 yards, or 880 fathoms, equal to 937½ French Toises.

[e] Surrey, Sussex, Hants, Dorset, Berks, Somerset, Gloucester, and Devon, were wholly, or partially, regulated by such laws.

 William

CHAP. I. 1065—1272. William had certainly ratified the [f] laws of the Confeſſor, before the Roll of Winton was compiled; and in the record of ſuch ratification, the laws are divided into three grand claſſes, which prevailed in different parts of the realm, the Saxon, Mercian, and Daniſh Laws. As this county was undoubtedly regulated by the principles and cuſtoms eſtabliſhed under the Saxon government, the beſt authority that can be reſorted to, for the elucidation of diſputable points, will be found in the records of thoſe counties, governed by ſimilar laws. To theſe then we may occaſionally refer for information or illuſtration.

When the royal commiſſioners ſurveyed the eaſtern diſtrict of Kent, juries from each [g] lath, or diviſion, were aſſembled, that the prevailing laws might be aſcertained by their concurring teſtimony. The Norman nobles, that ſucceeded the Saxon princes, or barons, held their lands by the tenure of their predeceſſors, and were preſumed to guarantee, to their tenants, the privileges and cuſtoms they had enjoyed, in the reign of the Confeſſor. On this account the [h] feudal lands of Alnod, and his peers, are particularly ſpecified, the [i] obſervation of ancient uſages frequently remarked, or a [k] deviation from them pointed out.

[f] Vide Wilkins Leges Saxonicas, p. 202. ſub titulo legum Edwardi per Willielmum confimatarum.

[g] Laths, from ȝelaðian, to aſſemble together.

Lambardes Perambulation of Kent, p. 26. 4to. 1596.

Has infra ſcriptas leges regis concordant homines de quatuor leſtis hoc eſt, *Borwar* leſt, et *Eſtre* leſt & *Linwar* leſt & Wiwar leſt. Domeſ. 1 a 2. Lathes of the Borough ward, (Canterbury) Eaſtrye ward, Liming ward, & Wi ward.

[h] De terris ſupra nominatis Alnodi (Cild) & ſimilium ejus habet rex cuſtodiam. Domeſday, 1 a 2.

[i] Omnes hæ Conſuetudines erant ibi, (Dovere) quando Willielmus rex in Angliam veniebat. Ibid. 1 a 1.

[k] Nec domus fuit ibi tempore regis Edvardi. Ibid. 1 a 1.

In

In conformity to the fame affumed principle, Odo earl of Kent, exercifed princely authority, and divided the revenue of his boroughs, with the fovereign of the realm. He was not only the patron of powerful barons, the Montforts and Romneys, but the liberal [l] donor of ample poffeffions to them. [m] Earls were his retainers, and bifhops his dependants. With fuch [n] powers were Lewin and Godwin invefted under the Saxon conftitution, and inheriting their poffeffions, he exercifed their prerogative.

The peers of Alnod (independant of three ecclefiaftical [o] abbots) confifted only of feven nobles. An affembly of fuch [p] warlike chiefs poffeffed more than baronial jurifdiction, or the court of an hundred; were invefted with the cognizance of all caufes in the eaftern divifion of Kent; and, when affembled on the heath of Pinneden, tumultuoufly decided the controverfies of their fubordinate chieftains. To fuch county meetings thefe powerful lords were [q] fummoned, by their feudal chief, with their knightly train, and their non-attendance was punifhed by a heavy [r] fine.

[l] De his (Domibus in Dovere) habet Robertus de Romenel duas, Radulfus de Curbefpine tres, Willielmus filius Goisfridi tres, in quibus erat *Gihalla* Burgenfium, Hugo de Montfort unam cum multis aliis.

Domefday, 1 a 1.

[m] Earl of Ow (or Eu) and Bifhop of Lificux ; both in Normandy.

[n] All the lands in Kent are recorded to have been held from Edward the Confeffor, Lewin and Godwin, earls, and Brixi and Alnod, Cilts, or, perhaps, prefidents of the barons, *and from them alone.*

[o] Of the Holy Trinity, St. Auguftines, and St. Martins.

Domefday, 1 a 2.

[p] Invenerunt Cuftodiam Regis—were his feudal vaffals.

Domefday, 1 a 1.

[q] Si fuerint præmoniti ut eveniant ad Sciram, ibunt ufque ad Pinnedennam, non longiùs. Domefday, 1 a 2.

[r] Si non venerint, de hâc foris-facturâ & de aliis omnibus rex 100 folidos habebit. Ibid.

Such

CHAP. I. 1065—1272. Such an assembly was convened, when the commissioners of William visited this district, to ascertain the laws that prevailed, examine the title of the respective proprietors of land, enregister the value and quality of their possessions, assert the rights of the crown, and augment its revenue. At this period, the privileges, tenures, and services of different descriptions of men, were examined; and the claims of individuals admitted, proved, or controverted, by the impanelled evidence of the four [a] laths.

Throughout the whole eastern division of Kent, there were only eight persons, independant of ecclesiastics, whose lands paid not relief to the crown, on the demise of their occupiers. The [b] eight excempted persons, whose names are recorded, we decidly state (in opposition to the authority of every English antiquary) to have been feudal tenants of the Confessor.

[a] Concordant Homines de quatuor Lestis. Vid. supra.

[b] Nomina eorum de quatuor Lestis, Borwar, Eestre, Linwart, et Wiwart non relevantium terram, similium Alnodo Cilt.

First occurring Name.	Words, probably designating the same Person.
Alnod, Cilt	Ulnod Unlot Alsi
Ciret de Cilleham	Siret, Osiert, Seward, Sewart * *Sot* Sired, Oswart, Siward, Sewold, i. e. Sewart the Bold.
Esbern Biga	Sbern Biga Bernolt—Sbern the Bold.
Norman	
Godric de Burnes	Ordric
Godric Carlesone	
Turgis	
Azor	

* Seward, the celebrated earl of Northumberland, then included in Scotland, and one of the sheriffs of the county in the reign of Edward.

These

Thefe men were Saxons, not Normans. They ceafed to exift, or, at leaft, to occupy fuch eftates; but the cuftoms, that had obtained, were continued to their fucceffors. By fuch military tenants was the king guarded fix days at Canterbury, or Sandwich. They were [u] fupplied with provifions at the expence of the monarch, or, in defect of maintenance for themfelves, and their retainers, were exempted from [x] perfonal contributions, or the payment of [y] fuch penalties as had devolved to the crown, within the liberties of their jurifdiction. A circumftance ftill more remarkable, and contrary to the general opinion, is here alfo recorded, that the powers and [x] freedom of the occupants had been lately augmented; that at the æra this ftatement was compiled, fines only affected their perfons, not property, and the inheritance was fecured to the pofterity of fuch nobles, without burthenfome mulcts. Many authorities will be hereafter quoted, to prove that the fyftem of military array had been eftablifhed previous to the Norman monarchs, and the payments of different diftricts had been long [z] adjufted, if their proprietors were not fummoned to difcharge

[u] Ibi habent de rege Cibum et Potum; fi non habuerint, fine foris-facturâ recedunt. Domefday, 1 a 2.

[x] Super iftos habet rex foris-facturam de *Capitibus eorum* tantum *modò*. Ibid. 1 a 2.

[y] Pro Handfocam, Gribrige, Foriftellum. Ibid. 1 a 2.

[z] In terrâ Sophis habet rex 12 denarios pro uno Inewardo, et de uno Jugo de Northburg 12 den. aut unum Inewardum, et de Dena 18 den. & de Gara unum Ineward. Hæ terræ jacent in Wi & homines de his terris * *cuftodiebant* regem apud Cantuariam & apud Sanwice tres Dies, fi rex illuc veniffet. Domefday, 1 a 2.

De terris eorum habet relevamen, qui habent fuam Sacam & Socam. Ibid.

* This word is ftated at full length, and, doubtlefs, refers to the days of the Confeffor: it is frequently difficult to meet with an habet, or habebat; for *ht* is generally found, even when fpeaking of Saxon cuftoms, probably left the writer might expofe himfelf.

the

CHAP. I. 1065—1272. the perfonal attendance, they owed their fovereign as his body-guards, if he vifited their county.

Independent of thefe eight exalted peers, the Saxon princes received reliefs from every other occupant in the divifion; from the [a] refpective lord of each manour, and the [b] poffeffor of privileged land by royal charter, or hereditary fucceffion. The fubordinate claffes are not noticed in this furvey, becaufe they appertained not to the monarch, but were the [a] property of the lord of the foil; and every fervice that the fovereign required from his tenants or vaffals, was exacted from the [b] villains, by their refpective owners, with accumulated oppreffion.

If the high fpirit of the bold yeomanry of Kent fhould indignantly read this defcription, or contemptuoufly reject our pofitions, without examination; we can only lament, that the ignorance, or mifreprefentation of former writers, fhould have reduced the advocate of hiftoric truth, to the neceffity of [c] contradicting their affertions, or difproving their conclufions. But if they will judge by comparifon, by a view that will hereafter be prefented, they will find their fuperiority in population, in privileges, in wealth, and power, as fully eftablifhed, as their fondeft wifhes can defire.

Before we attempt to defcribe the city or inhabitants of Canterbury, we muft previoufly confider the nature of different

[a] Erga Dominum cujus homo fuerit. Domefday, 1 a 2. et Uluret non pertinens ad illud Manerum.—Not more than twelve of this defcription, exclufive of burgeffes, fpecified in the whole county of Kent. This fubject will be difcuffed in an appropriate differtation on " Ranks and Services."

[b] Quando moritur alodiarius rex inde habet relevationem terræ. Ibid.

[a] Vide Magnam Chartam, &c.

[c] Lambarde, in his Perambulation, ftates, that there never was a villain in Kent, (p. 14, no bondmen, or villains, in Kent) when there are 309 in a manour, Mylton, and we believe not one manour without them.

kinds

kinds of tenure; for we find the burgeſſes clearly diſtinguiſhed in the ſecond line of its [d] repreſentation. The laborious diſquiſitions that have been written on Gavelkind tenure, are ſo numerous and voluminous, that we ſhall not preſume to ſtate every opinion, or diſcuſs each argument; but briefly deliver the ſentiments we entertain on the ſubject, and the foundation on which they are grounded. CHAP. I. 1065—1272.

The word [e] Gablum, or Gable, approximates ſo nearly in ſound to the word Gavle (the word [f] Landgable alſo is interpreted by *Domeſday* itſelf as a payment of rent in lieu of ſervices) is uſed in the deſcription accurately to diſcriminate betwixt the orders and privileges of citizens: 58 [g] ſhillings are farther ſtated to have been paid to the manour of Newton, (our modern Queenborough) for the rent of nine ſowlings; and burgeſſes paying rent, are peculiarly ſtiled [h] allodial tenants: that from all theſe concurring circumſtances, we certainly entertain little doubt that this tenure originated from a compromiſed payment in money, for thoſe ſupplies of proviſions, which dependants were formerly obliged to furniſh to the

[d] In civitate Cantuaria habuit rex Edwardus 51 burgenſes reddentes *Gablum* & alios 212, ſuper quos habebat ſacam & ſocam. Domeſday, 21 a.

[e] Gabellum. Vectigal. Voſſius.

This may, originally, have been derived from the Saxon ᵹaꝼol, but the etymology from 'give all kynd' can ſcarcely be admitted.

[f] Landgable, i. e. unus denarius de unaquàque domo. Great Domeſday, 336.

[f] In Mideltune 309 villani et 74 bordarii. Domeſday, 2 b 1.

[g] De novem * Solins de Middeltone pertinent in Neutone 58 ſol. de Gablo. Domeſday, 14 b.

[h] 80 acras terræ, quas tenebant burgenſes in † alodia de rege, 2 a 1.

* Vid. Diſſertation on Weights and Meaſures. Solin, 160 acres of the Cheſhire meaſure, eight yards to the rood, as will there be proved.

† Tenentes in liberum Socagium per Redditum. Littleton.

 hall

CHAP. I. 1065—1272.

[i] hall of their lord. We state provisional supplies, because this tenure did not exonerate all tenants from other [k] slavish services at this period. But, to hold some [l] species of land by this title, was certainly considered as an honourable tenure, since [m] Odo, bishop of Baieux, earl of Kent, and half-brother to the Conqueror, held eighty acres in Hoilingeborde on such conditions.

Canterbury.

In the days of the Confessor, the city of Canterbury was a royal borough, and governed by a [n] mayor, or superintendant of the monarch. It was divided into several districts, and its inhabitants possessed privileges, or were subjected to exactions, according to the power or description of their patron. The ecclesiastical possessions of the [o] Holy Trinity, and St. Augustine, the clients of queen Eddiva, Alnod the prince, Sbern the commissary, and Siward of Chilham, were exempt from the suit, services and fines, demanded from the tenants or dependants of others. The archbishop of Canterbury, abbot of

[i] Ibi una Piscaria serviens Hallæ—in Newton, ibid.—& Manerio Neutone pertinent 28 pensæ Caseorum. Ibid.

[k] Et de his 9 solid. reddebat Sigar (tenens de reginâ Eddid sive Eddiva) apud M[illegible]tone * *Averam.* Ibid.

De avera, i. e. servitium 60 solidi. Domesday, 9 b 2.

[l] Vid. Dissertation on Ranks and Services.

[m] Hunc dimidium Solinum, qui nunquam reddidit Scotum tenet episcopus Baiocensis de Archiepiscopo ad Gablum. Domesday, 4 b 2.

[n] Quidam præpositus Brumanno nomine. Domesday, 2 a 1.

[o] Per totam civitatem Cantuariæ † habebat rex sacam & socam, excepta terra ecclesiæ Stæ. Trinitatis & Sancti Augustini, & Eddevæ reginæ & Alnod Cild, & Esber Biga, & Siret de Cilleham. Domesday, 2 a 1.

* Synonimous with the late French Corvè; work done for the lord of the soil, without remuneration.

† It is written *H*. but it must necessarily be habebat, not habet, since specifying the possessors in the time of the Confessor.

St. Auftins, thofe princes and nobles had knights in their train of followers, who held their poffeffions by the fame military fervices, their patrons paid to the crown, and were truly feudal tenants, of a higher rank than the moft free, allodial or foccage tenant. CHAP. I. 1065—1272.

Edward had [p] fifty-one burgeffes of a fuperior defcription, the defcendants probably of [q] freeholders, who appertained not to any manour, but rented their poffeffions or dwellings. It is evident that it was the habitations of thefe men, not their perfons, that were the property of the lord, fince eleven were deftroyed in the foffe of the city, feven transferred to the archbifhop, and fourteen exchanged with the abbot of St. Auftins, for the caftle he furrendered; fo that nineteen only remained to the Conqueror, when Domefday was compiled. 1086.
To this [r] fraternity of burgeffes, forty-five houfes in the fuburbs belonged, thirty-two acres were annexed to their guild, and they held eighty acres from the king by tranfmitted inheritance, or a perpetual leafe. But they had no manorial [s] rights, power, or privileges; for thefe were attached, in their diftrict,

[p] Modo burgenfes gablum reddentes funt 19. De triginta duobus aliis qui fuerant, funt vaftati undecim in foffato Civitatis, et archiepifcopus habet ex eis feptem, et Abbas Sti. Auguftini alios quatuordecim pro excambio Caftelli.

Domefday, 2 a 1.

[q] On a farther perufal, the reader will entertain little doubt, that the inferior burgeffes were villains, that had emigrated from his manours, whofe property and perfon were the lords.

[r] Burgenfes habuerunt quadraginta quinque Manfuras extra Civitatem, de quibus ipfi habebant gablum & confuetudinem, rex autem habebat facam et focam. Ipfi quoque burgenfes habebant de rege triginta duas acras terræ in *Gildam fuam*.—Octoginta acræ terræ quas tenebant burgenfes in *Alodia* de rege.

Domefday, 2 a 1.

Co-liberti, qui tenent in liberum Socagium per Redditum. Littleton.

[s] Rex autem habebat facam et focam. Domefday, 2 a 1.

CHAP. I. 1065—1272. to the monarchy. Of all these houses, lands, and tenures, were they despoiled at the conquest, by [t] Ralph de Colville, a creature of the [u] Earl Bishop, who guaranteed them to him.

Of the inferior order of burgesses, Edward the Confessor possessed [x] two hundred and twelve, and such number continued annexed to the monarchy twenty years subsequent. But with this class, we may rank another description of citizens, those men who still appertained to the lords of different manours, though resident in Canterbury, and honoured with the appellation of burgesses. To place this matter beyond all [y] controversy, and to calculate more accurately its population, we shall enlarge considerably on this subject, and specify the manours, and the proprietors, prior to the destruction of the Saxon government. We shall begin with ecclesiastics, whose manours were always the most populous, whose clients were the most favoured, who were the greatest [z] merchants and promoters of trade, and most highly encouraged the industry of their vassals. From such men did the liberty of boroughs originate, for warlike chieftains oppressed all but military retainers.

[t] Has domus et hanc terram tenet Rannulfus de Columbels; habet etiam quatuor viginti acras super hæc, &c. de his omnibus revocat isdem Rannulfus ad Protectorem, Episcopum Baiocensem. Domesday, 2 a 1.

[u] Odo, bishop of Baieux, and earl of Kent.

[x] Et alios (burgenses) 212, super quos habebat sacam & socam, &c. et adhuc sunt 212 burgenses super quos habet sacam & socam.

Domesday, 2 a 1.

[y] To silence the Towers's and Oldfields, (admirers of the forgeries of Pettyt) babblers continually yelping after Saxon liberty, and the Saxon constitution.

[z] Scarce a ship is mentioned in Domesday that belonged not to an ecclesiastic. Vid. Dissertation on Trade, Commerce, and Shipping.

To

To [a] Norwood, a manour of the archbiſhop's monks, ſituated CHAP. I.
in the vicinity of Canterbury, ninety-ſeven burgeſſes apper- 1065—1272.
tained, who yielded a yearly revenue of [b] eight pounds four ſhillings. To [c] Sturry fifty-two manſions belonged in the time of the Saxon prince, but twenty-ſeven had been deſtroyed for the ſcite of the archbiſhop's palace. The abbot of St. Auſtins had [d] ſeventy burgeſſes, part of his manour of Lamport, the church of St. Martins ſeven; the proprietor of Chilham [e] thirteen; and the ſucceſſor of Sbern eleven. On the whole, there were burgeſſes belonging to ſeventeen different proprietors or manors, that had their abode in the city of Canterbury, though they belonged to a different ſoil, and conſtituted part of its value. [f] The manours are ſpecified to ſilence gainſayers, and ſatisfy the inquiſitive or incredulous.

The

[a] Manerio * Nordeude pertinent in civitate Cantuariâ 100 burgenſes, tres minus, reddentes 8l. 4s. Domeſday, 5 a 1.

[b] Equal to 168l. of our preſent money, in providing neceſſaries at the different period, including the variation of weight.

Vid. Diſſertation on Weights and Meaſures.

[c] Ad manerium Eſturſete pertinuerunt tempore regis Edvardi in civitate 52 maſuræ, & modò non ſunt niſi 25, quia aliæ ſunt deſtructæ in novâ hoſpitatione archiepiſcopi. Domeſday, 3 b 1.

[d] 70 burgenſes erant in Cantuaria civitate manerio Lanport pertinentes. Domeſday, 12 a 1.

Ad terram Sancti Martini pertinent 7 burgenſes in Cantuaria. Ibid. 4 a 1.

[e] In Cantuaria civitate 13 maſuræ pertinent huic manerio. Ibid. 10 a 1.

Iſdem Radulſus tenet alias 11 maſuras de epiſcopo Baiocenſi in ipſa civitate, quæ fuerunt Sbern Bigæ. Ibid. 2 a 1.

[f] Vid. ſupra, et 4 manſuræ in civitate quas tenuit quædam Concubina Heraldi. Manerio Otringberie pertinent 2 manſuræ terræ in Cantuaria, 8 a 1. Manerio Weſtſelve pertinebat tempore regis Edvardi una domus reddens 25 denarios

* Situated between Seſaltre and Canterbury, including North Blean and Clowes Wood.

CHAP. I. 1065—1272. The learned reader muſt have obſerved in the cited paſſages, that ſometimes the burgeſſes are named, ſometimes their manſions, and ſometimes their houſes [g]. But we have already proved [h] that the regiſter, whether of citizens or their habitations, is intended to convey the ſame idea, and it is doubtleſs evident to every clear-ſighted eye, from ſuch concentrated repreſentation, that whatever poſſeſſions ſuch burgeſs acquired, appertained to his lord; and if a dwelling belonged to a manour, its inhabitant (if not a military vaſſal of ſome potent noble,) was equal in condition to the villains reſident in his juriſdiction.

Canterbury contained five hundred and thirty-one burgeſſes, including every deſcription, in the days of the Confeſſor. The corporation were proprietors of forty-five houſes in the ſuburbs. The knights of the archbiſhop, abbots, and privileged nobles, with their attendants, and the monks of Trinity and St. Auguſtines, who had each a public mart, frequented by [i] merchants, muſt, upon the moſt moderate computation, be equally numerous, and far more powerful.—However other perſons

narios, 8 a 1.—Mancrio Winchelſmere T. R. E. pertinebant 3. Domus 8 a 2.—Mancrio Wiccham pertinent 3 maſuræ reddentes 6 ſolidos 9 a 2.—In hundret et in civitate Cantuarienſi habet Adam fil. Huberti de epiſcopo 3 Domus, & duas foris Civitatem 9 b 1.—Mancrio Oſpringes pertinet una manſura in Cantuaria 10 a 1. Perie una Maſura in Civitate 10 a 2.—4. Maſuræ Danetone pertinentes 11 b 2.

[g] That the reader may not ſuppoſe this tautology, we take leave to ſtate, that in Nottingham there were three manſions, in which eleven houſes were ſituated at this period. Rogerus de Buſli habet in Snotingham tres manſiones, in quibus ſedent undecim domus. Domeſ. 280 a 1.

[h] Vid. p. 11.

[i] According to modern ideas, pedlars, for they carried a pack; mercator truſſellum deferens. Domeſday. Cheſter. p. 263 a 1.

were

were oppreſſed by the Norman Conqueror, [k] eccleſiaſtics certainly recovered ſome privileges in his reign, of which they had been deprived under the Saxon government. This aſſertion is amply corroborated by the following fact. [l] Bruman, the ſuperintendant and receiver of the royal income of Edward, in Canterbury, had demanded and received the [m] cuſtomary payments from the traders not reſident in the diſtrict, for the liberty of opening [n] their packs or vending their wares, within the clerical juriſdiction of the Trinity and St. Auguſtines. This right was conteſted under the Conqueror, and the cauſe was tried before Lanfranc, the archbiſhop, and Odo, the earl of Kent. It appeared in evidence, that the collector had tolled them unjuſtly, for in the early part of the Confeſſor's reign, ſuch church-lands were exempted from ſimilar contributions, and a verdict was therefore given in favour of ſuch right, and

CHAP. I. 1065—1272.

[k] Land held in frank almoigne (in elemoſina) in the time of the Confeſſor, in Colcheſter, paid the regal cuſtoms, but was exempted in William's days; & tempore regis Edvardi reddebant conſuetudinem & modo non reddunt. Little Domeſ. 107.

The burgeſſes of Colcheſter alſo enjoyed greater privileges, which we ſhall exhibit fully in Eſſex.

[l] Quidam præpoſitus Brumanno nomine tempore R. E. cepit Conſuetudines de extraneis mercatoribus in terrâ Stæ. Trinitatis & Sti. Auguſtini: qui poſtea tempore regis Willelmi ante archiepiſcopum Lanfrancum & epiſcopum Baiocenſem recognovit ſe injuſte accepiſſe & ſacramento facto juravit, quod ipſæ æccleſiæ ſuas Conſuetudines quietas habuerunt regis Edvardi tempore: et exinde utræque eccleſiæ in ſua terra habuerunt Conſuetudines ſuas judicio baronum regis qui placitum tenuerunt. Domeſ. 2 a 1.

[m] Scavagium, modern ſcavage, Scheuage.—Shewage. Si abſque licentia miniſtri epiſcopi *diſſoluerit* truſſellum mercator, &c. Ibid. 263 a 1.

[n] It is aſtoniſhing that writers, of ſuch high authority as Blackſtone, ſhould ſtate, that there were no cuſtoms paid previous to the Conqueror, when Conſuetudo is found in almoſt every county of Domeſday, and Theloneum in moſt Saxon laws.

ror

CHAP. I. 1065—1272. for the future the archbishop and abbot received such customary payment from the non-resident inhabitants.

Independant of the ecclesiastical districts, (which were extensive and populous, and in which there was a fraternity of clerical [o] merchants,) the city of Canterbury produced a [p] revenue to Edward of fifty-one pounds. Such was its value when delivered to Haimo, the sheriff of William, and in the year 1086, it was estimated at fifty pounds; yet it produced thirty pounds of pure silver and good weight, twenty-four pounds in tale; and 110 shillings, to the viscount, or sheriff. So little variation, indeed, took place in the rental of all the cities and boroughs throughout the kingdom, under the Saxon and Norman monarchs, that it is impossible for William to have been that devastating plunderer or spoiler, which monkish historians have represented him; for, however his followers may have ravaged the English possessions, such character is not found applicable to the natural son of duke Robert, when we accurately examine these authentic records.

To avoid chronological confusion, we shall discontinue our observations on Canterbury, for the present, and proceed in our detail of other districts in East Kent, under the Saxon Edward, and his Norman successor. Agreeable to our system, we shall visit boroughs or towns successively, in proportion to their consequence, occasionally, to the similarity of their customs or privileges, that our illustration may be more concise, comprehensive, and regular. Adopting such arrangement, the Dover. borough and port of Dover are immediately presented to our

[o] Clerici in Gildham suam Domesday, 3 a 1.

[p] Inter totum tempore regis Edvardi valuit 51 libras & tantundem quando Haimo Vicecomes recepit & modo 50 libr. appreciatur; tamen qui tenet, nunc reddit 30 libr. arsas & pensatas, et 24 libr. ad numerum, super hæc omnia habet Vicecomes 110 sol. Domesday, 2 a 1.

view,

view, and demand our obfervation. This important harbour, that is only feparated from the continent of Europe by [q] twenty-two ftatute-miles, was of confiderable magnitude in the days of the Confeffor, and was honoured with extraordinary privileges. In lieu of military array, it equipped for the ufe of the monarch twenty [r] veffels, manned with 420 mariners, that were at the command and fervice of the king fifteen days each year, and tranfported the horfes of the meffengers of the monarch for a [s] trifling confideration. For this fpecies of feudal duty, its inhabitants were exempted from all fuit, fervice, and ordinary fines to their lord's court; and a refident [t] burgefs was exonerated from tolls and cuftoms throughout the realm of England. [u] The rental of Dover was eighteen pounds, of which fum Edward had twelve, and earl Godwin fix. In addition to this, the [x] toll of the borough yielded eight pounds to the abbey of St. Martin's. Such cuftoms [y] exifted when William invaded England. In a fhort time fubfequent to his [z] arrival, the town was confumed by

CHAP. I. 1065—1272.

[q] 21.97 by the French triangles, or 49,800 French toifes. Vide Philofophical Tranfactions, for 1787, Part I. 151.

[r] Burgenfes dederunt viginti naves regi una vice in anno ad quindecim dies, et in unaquâque navi erant homines viginti et unus. Hoc faciebant pro eo qood eis perdonaverat faccam et foccam. Domef. 1 a 1.

[s] Dabant (Miffatici) pro caballo tranfducendo 3 denarios in Hieme & 2 in Æftate. Ibid.

[t] Quicunque manens in villa affiduus reddebat regi confuetudinem, quietus erat de theloneo per totam Angliam. Ibid.

[u] Dovere tempore regis Edvardi reddebat 18 libras, de quibus denariis habebat rex Edvardus duas partes et comes Godwin tertiam. Domef. 1 a 1.

[x] Theloneum de doure tempore reg. Edv. valebat 8 libras. Ibid. 2 a 2.

[y] Omnes hæ confuetudines erant ibi quando Willielmus rex in Angliam venit [ebat.] Domef. 1 a 1.

[z] In ipfo primo adventu ejus in Angliam fuit ipfa villa combufta, et ideo pretium ejus non potuit computari quantum valebat, quando epifcopus Baiocenfis eam recepit. Ibid. 1 a 1.

CHAP. I. 1065—1272. fire [a], so that its value could not be estimated, when delivered to the custody of the earl of Kent. But in the year [b] 1086, it was valued at forty pounds, yet produced fifty-four; of which the sovereign had twenty-four standard pounds, Odo thirty pounds, whose purity or weight were not particularly examined.

The abbey of St. Martin's, in Dover, had been despoiled of some property in the reign of the Confessor, but its wealth and power were astonishingly reduced by the military retainers of the bishop of Baieux. [c] Alnod, the superior baron of the district, with the tyrannical concurrence of Harold, had dispossessed its canons of the manours of Mersham and Hawking. But the land and income of the abbey were still immense. The tenants occupied [d] eight thousand and fifty acres in different lathes and hundreds, the three canons [e] seven hundred; its demesne consisted of four hundred, and several [f] manours held in frank-almoigne, or found [g] cloathing for its ecclesiastics.

[a] From the frequent fires, by which whole towns were consumed, at this æra, we may rationally presume, that the curfeu originated not (if then originating, which we much doubt) so much from the tyranny, as the precaution of William; for eight o'clock, at this period, was a very late hour for retiring to rest; and there were customs, in some counties, by which a neighbour could recover damages from the person in whose premises the fire began.

[b] Modò appreciatur 40 libr. et tamen præpositus inde reddit 54 lib. regi quidem 24 libr. de denariis qui sunt viginti in ora, comiti vero 30 lib. ad numerum. Domes. 1 a 1.

[c] Alnod Cilt per violentiam Heraldi abstulit Sancto Martino Mereleham et Havochesten, pro quibus dedit canonicis iniquam commutationem. Ibid. 2 a 2.

[d] 24 Solini hæc omnia adquietant. Domesday. 1 b 1. et 2 a 2.

[e] Habent simul tres canonici quatuor solinos et quinque denas et 16 acras. Ibid. 2 a 2.

[f] Terra Nordewode et terra Ripe et terra Brandet reddunt viginti solidos et sex denarios ad Sanctum Martinum in elemosina. Ibid. 2 a 2.

[g] Lx solidi ad calciamenta canonicorum. Ibid.

The

The demesne of the abbey, the possessions of the canons, and the land held by elemosynary title, were exempt from all contributions [h] to the government; for the possessions of [i] prebendaries and colonists, with their respective villains, complete the twenty-four sowlings that were assessed to the [k] land-tax. The annual income of the canons would have amounted to sixty pounds, even subsequent to the Conquest, if their rights had not been infringed upon by insolent fraud, and shameless rapine. The half-brother of William was indeed a bishop in Normandy, but this dignitary of the church was an earl in England, and supporting such character, we must contemplate him, as mounted on his [l] charger, as justifying and encouraging the rapacity of his military retainers, and violently seizing the possessions of the abbey. The [m] Colvilles, the Romneys, and

[h] Hæc terra nunquam reddit aliquid consuetudinis vel scoti, quia 24 solini hæc omnia adquietant. Ibid.

[i] Ulric de *Oxneford*, Spirites tenent in præbenda. 1 b 2. Rusticus reddens 8 lib. 2 a 2.

[k] A sowling paid one pound to the king in the days of the Confessor, two pounds in the time of William, for Monocstune tempore regis Edvardi pro xx libras, et modo * xl libras 4 b 2. et 5 a 1.

[l] In a seal appendant to a deed in the possession of Mr. Astle, he is represented, on one side, as an earl mounted on his war-horse, in armour, and a sword in his hand; on the reverse, as a bishop, pontifically arrayed, pronouncing the benediction. Archæologia, Vol. I. p. 337.

[m] Rannulfus de Columbels aufert eis unum pratum. Robertus de Romenel aufert eis singulis annis 20 denarios et unam salinam et unam piscariam. Herbertus filius Jvonis dedit episcopo Baiorensi Marcam Auri pro uno Molino eorum nolentibus illis. Lambartus Molinum unum. Wadard unum Molinum. Raduldus de Curbespine unum. Domes. 2 a 2.

* If a solin is equal to one quarter of our modern statute square mile, (which we believe we shall prove in our dissertation on weights and measures,) and each paid two pounds; estimating South Britain at 65,000 statute miles, and deducting 15,000 for Wales and the Northumbrian kingdom, 10,000 for waste and exempted land, there will be 40,000, yielding 320,000l. equal in expenditure to 6,400,000 l. at the present day, from this source alone; but this subject we shall more fully discuss, in our chapter on the royal revenue.

the

CHAP. I. 1065—1272. the Herberts, his martial followers, ſeized the mills, the fiſheries, the meadows and ſalt-houſes, of this religious foundation, and deprived it of more than [n] one-fifth of its revenue, under the auſpices, or by the connivance of Odo. The [o] three churches of Dover ſtill, however, appertained to the abbey, though, of the ten mills, [p] four were certainly taken away from it.

To avoid confuſion in our repreſentation, we deem it neceſſary to ſtate thoſe nobles of Kent, who were immediate tenants of the crown, and the true peers of the realm. The members of the royal council [q] conſiſted only of eleven perſons, ſeven of whom were eccleſiaſtics; the archbiſhop of Canterbury, the biſhops of Rocheſter and Baieux, the abbots of Battle, (in Suſſex,) St. Auguſtines, and Ghent, Albert, the chaplain (or chancellor,) of William, Hugh Montford, Earl Euſtace, Richard of Tonebridge, (or Fitzgilbert) and Haimo

[n] Modo non habent niſi, 47 l. 6 s. 4 d.

[o] Tres æcclefiæ apud doueram reddunt, 36 s. 6 d.

[p] Vid. ſupra.

[q] HIC ANNOTANTUR TENENTES TERRAS IN CHENT.

Rex Willielmus,	5. Abbatia St. Auguſtine,
1. Archiepiſcopus Cantuarenſis,	6. Abbatia de Gand,
{ * Terra Militum ejus,	7. Hugo de Montford,
{ Monachi & homines ejus,	8. Comes Euſtachius,
2. Epiſcopus Roſeceſtrenſis,	9. Richard de Tonebrige,
3. Epiſcopus Baiocenſis,	10. Haimo Vicecomes,
4. Abbatia de Batailge,	11. Albertus Capellanus.

*. Though in the original record, recording the liſt of tenants in capite, at one view, the monks of the archbiſhop are inſerted, yet we entertain not the leaſt doubt, that it is a miſtake of the ſcribe who arranged the materials, for in the body of the Survey, the knights of the archbiſhop have precedence of them (4 a 2.) and there is not even *one* acre recorded to have been held by *any* monk from the monarch in this county.—Haſted and others, inattentive to this diſcrimination, have ſtated twelve peers.

the

the viſcount. Eccleſiaſtics poſſeſſed their property at this period, by baronial tenure, were the immediate vaſſals of the crown, members of the high national aſſembly, and equally reſponſible to their feudal chieftain, as a military retainer. At this time, we are certain, that not only biſhops, but abbots, had votes in the houſe of lords. Even ſo late as the reign of Henry the third, when the clergy were ſuperior to civil juriſdiction, and above the controul of laical courts, the monarch could effectually diſtrain the refragatory eccleſiaſtics, by ſeizing the *feudal* poſſeſſions of the [r] biſhop; who could eaſily ſummon and puniſh his inferior clergy, to indemnify himſelf.

We will not deciſively ſtate, that ſuch nobles were the only freemen in the kingdom of England, though we are warranted in this ſuppoſition, by a curious obſervation in Domeſday, relative to the future noble family of [s] Bruce, from whence monarchs and nobles are deſcended, that their anceſtor, Robert Bruce, was inveſted with poſſeſſions in Yorkſhire, after he had been acknowledged, or admitted, a freeman in a national aſſembly at Wincheſter. This order certainly ſolely conſtituted the high council, but their feudal dependants, knights, or minor barons, were admitted into the great aſſembly of the nation.

In the recorded Survey, the diſtinction of Eaſt and Weſt Kent is ſtill obſerved, when the cuſtoms are delineated; but

[r] Epiſcopo Exonienſi. Rex eidem. Quia Johannes Wak non habet laicum feodum per quod poſſit diſtringi: Vobis mandamus, ſicut *pluries*, quod diſtringatis ipſum per eccleſiaſticum beneficium, ad reddendum nobis prædictum debitum;—Alioquin ſciatis quod præceperimus Vicecomiti Devoniæ, quod illud capiat de Baroniâ veſtrâ. Ex Memor. 28. Hen. 3. Rot. 7 a.
Madox. Vol. II. 248.

[s] Hic eſt feudum Roberti de Bruis, quod fuit datum, poſtquam liber de Wintonia ſcriptus fuit. Domeſday. 332. b. a.

these

CHAP. I. 1065—1272. these potent nobles had lands in both divisions, and consequently were peers of the whole county; but their military retainers were still particularized, and observed those Saxon usages in forming a separate shiremote at Pinneden, which are still retained in the two grand juries of the present day. We now proceed according to our proposed plan.

Sandwich. [t] Sandwich was situated in its own hundred, was under the protection of the archbishop, though it appertained, in a certain degree, to the monks of the Holy Trinity, by a donation of Edward the Confessor, to provide them with apparel. Its burgesses performed similar services with the men of Dover, and most probably enjoyed equal privileges on account of those services. Under the Saxon government there were three hundred and seven houses inhabited, and yielding a revenue, but the population of the borough had since increased considerably; for when Domesday was compiled, three hundred and eighty-three are recorded. If its inhabitants might be believed, (but we give not much credit to such interested evidence,) its rental, previovs to Edward's benefaction to the abbey, was only fifteen pounds. At the Confessor's death there was no assessed rent. When Lanfranc first rented it from William, he paid forty pounds, and supplied the monks with forty thousand herrings; but in the year 1086, the rental was augmented ten pounds, and the supply of herrings still continued to the abbey. In

[t] Sandwice jacet in suo proprio hundret. Hoc burgum tenet archiepiscopus, et est de vestitu monachorum, et reddit simile servitium regi sicut Dovere et hoc testificantur homines de isto burgo, quod antequam rex Edwardus dedisset illud Sanctæ Trinitati reddebat regi xv. libr. tempore mortis regis Edvardi non erat ad firmam. Quando recepit archiepiscopus reddebat 40 l. de firma et 40 millia de allecibus ad victum monachorum. In anno quo facta est hæc descriptio, reddit Sanwic 50 l. de firma et alleces sicut prius. Tempore regis Edvardi erant ibi 307 mansuræ hospitatæ modo sunt plus 76, id est, simul 384. Domesday. 3 a 1.

this

this borough there were inhabitants of an inferior deſcription, the ſons of villains, for [u] thirty-two manſions belonged to the manour of our modern Woodneſbury, and paid their rental in that diſtrict to the archbiſhop. CHAP. I. 1065—1272.

Of the liberties, and ſervices, attached to the borough of Hythe, the record of Domeſday tranſmits no particular accounts. With what ſuperior privileges the inhabitants of [x] boroughs were inveſted, that market-towns and villages poſſeſſed not, is a bold ſubject to diſcuſs, after the laborious inveſtigation, and learned diſquiſitions of Brady. However, we briefly ſtate, that we believe burgeſſes, under the Saxon government, to have conſtituted ſuch a corporate body, as mutually guaranteed the good conduct of its members, conjointly paid [y] aſſeſſed [z] tribute to its proprietor, was reſponſible for the defalcation of its [a] individuals, poſſeſſed the power of [b] trafficking or negociating with merchants or pedlars, (conſequently the Hythe.

[u] In Sandwice habet archiepiſcopus 32 maſuras ad manerium (* Golleſberge) pertinentes et reddentes 42s. 8d. Domſday. 11 a 2.

[x] Boꞃh, a pledge, or buꞃꞃ, a houſe of aſſembly; though in general we rely not much on etymological certainty or preciſion; for what unclaſſical reader would believe that the Engliſh *journal* comes from the Latin *dies*, not one letter the ſame; yet no etymology is more probable; dies, diurnus; Italian, giorno; French, jour; Engliſh, journal.

[y] As their opulence increaſed, their talliage increaſed.

[z] Guildhall. Gelti Halla, the court where their aſſeſſments were rated.

[a] To their reſpective lords, or different owners.

Honor Comitis de Arundel, et de Petewurda, Comitis, Conſtabulariæ, et Coronæ. Great Roll. paſſim.

[b] Habebat Thol, quod nos dicimus Theloneum, ſcilicet quod habeat libertatem vendendi & emendi in terrâ ſuâ.

Leges Edv. per Will. confirm Will. p. 202.

True villains could neither buy or ſell, for their perſons and their property were the chattels (catalla) of their lord.

* Recorded. alſo Waneſberge, but muſt be the modern Woodneſborough, ſince ſituated in Eaſtrye hundred.

inhabitants

CHAP. I. 1065—1272. inhabitants of a borough possessed some property of their own,) and had a house of assembly, for regulating its internal polity, where the reeve of the lord presided, distinct from the court-leet or baron of the feudal chieftain, though still dependant on his controul, and considered as part of the value of his manour, or the honour of a major baron, a bishop, an earl, or monarch.

Hythe, or the Haven.

In conformity to this delineation, we find two hundred and twenty-five burgesses resident in [c] Hythe, that had emigrated from the manour of Saltwood, the property of the [d] archbishop of Canterbury, though Hugh Montford had the custody of it as his [e] martial retainer, not as a [f] peer of the realm, or a tenant of the crown. In addition to these the archbishop retained six [g] burgesses in his own possession, which were not farmed out to either knight or ecclesiastic, as part of his manour of Liming in his own demesne, or peculiar administration. The value of this borough is not distinctly specified. But the six burgesses, under the immediate jurisdiction of the archbishop, were probably opulent [h] ecclesiastics, that traded to foreign ports; for their value, with the manour of Liming,

[c] Salteode. Ad hoc manerium pertinent 225 burgenses in burgo Hedæ. Domesday. 4 b 1.

[d] Cinque ports not established at this period, for Sandwich, Romney, and Hythe belonged to the archbishop wholly or partially.

[e] In Domesday, under the title Terra Militum Archiepiscopi, p. 4 a 2. et Hugo de Montfort tenet de Archiepisco Salteode. Domes. 4 b 1.

[f] Hugh Montfort was a *great* baron, or peer, in Kent, Essex, Norfolk, and Suffolk.

[g] Leminges pertinent 6 burgenses in Hede, ipse archiepiscopus tenet in dominio. Domesday. 4 a 1.

[h] We are certain of a clerical guild in Canterbury. Vide supra.

4 Ibi pertinent 6 burgenses in Hede. Tempore regis Edvardi valebat 24 l. et postea 40 l. et modò similitèr reddit. Ibid. 4 a. 1.

was

was eſtimated at twenty-four pounds, in the early part of the reign of the Confeſſor, their property, in this ſhort period, was ſo much augmented, that they were aſſeſſed at forty pounds at the time of his deceaſe; ſuch was their eſtimated rental, twenty years ſubſequent, yet they annually paid ſixty pounds. The two hundred and twenty-five burgeſſes of Montfort were of an inferior deſcription. Though the extent of the manours of Saltwood and Liming were equal, for each was aſſeſſed as ſeven [i] ſowlings, yet the rental of [k] the two hundred and twenty-five burgeſſes, and the value of the manour, only produced ſixteen pounds under the Saxon government; when Hugh Montfort obtained poſſeſſion of it, only eight pounds; but in the year 1086, produced twenty-nine pounds ſix ſhillings and four-pence. Theſe men, conſequently, muſt conſiſt of the inferior order of mechanics, or of ſuch tradeſmen, who can be ranked little higher than pedlars, or petty dealers.

Romney.

In the borough of Romney, were burgeſſes of three deſcriptions. Earl [l] Godwin was its proprietor in the days of Edward, and Alſi the prince, his tenant. Odo ſucceeded him, and occupied all his poſſeſſions by ſimilar tenure. The military retainer of the uterine brother of the Conqueror that was inveſted with the occupancy of the borough, was ſurnamed from the place, Robert of Romney. To him [m] appertained fifty burgeſſes of a ſuperior order, for they were under the immediate protection

[i] Leminges pro 7 ſolingis ſe defendebat. Domeſday. 4 a 1.
Saltcode pro 7 ſolingis ſe defendebat tempore regis Edvardi. Ibid. 4 b. 1.

[k] Inter burgum et manerium valebat tempore regis Edvardi 16 libr. quando recepit (Hugo de Montfort) 8 libr. modò inter totum 29 libr. 6 ſol. et 4 den. Ibid. 4 b. 1.

[l] Alſi tenuit de comite Godwino.

[m] Robertus de Romenel habet 50 burgenſes in burgo de Romenel. 10 b. 2.

CHAP. I. 1065—1272. of the [n] monarch, who exempted them from every service and payment, as a compensation for the fleet and mariners they furnished to the royal navy, except the customary fines, for the violation of the king's peace, public robbery, or infringement on the forests or national roads, of which the established forfeitures belonged to the crown. There were [o] twenty-one burgesses that enjoyed similar privileges, for similar services, who, in a corporate capacity, received their own ordinary fines and forfeitures; but the archbishop of Canterbury, as lord paramount of the manour of Lanport, received such fines from them as the monarch received from the preceding fifty, though they were guarded by the protection of the royal peace. In addition to these there were [p] eighty-five other burgesses that belonged to Lanfranc, as part of his manour of Aldinton, which were in his own immediate custody, and produced him only an annual income of six pounds. These were certainly of an inferior order, for the twenty-one Lanport burgesses yielded [q] ten pounds to their lord, in the days of Edward, and sixteen in the reign of William. The fifty burgesses that partly

[n] De eis habet rex omne servitium & sint quieti pro servitio maris ab omni consuetudine præter tribus, Latrocinio, pace infracta et * Forstel.

Domesday. 10 b. 2.

[o] Ad hoc manerium (Lamport) pertinent 21 burgenses qui sunt in Romenel, de quibus habet archiepiscopus tres foris-factas. Latrocinium, pacem fractam foristellum. Rex vero habet omne servitium ab eis & ipsi habent omnes consuetudines & alias foris-facturas pro servitio maris & sunt in manu regis.

Domes. 4 b. 1.

[p] In Romenel sunt 85 burgenses qui pertinent ad Aldinton manerium archiepiscopi & valuerunt & modo valent domino 6 libras. Domes. 4 a. 1.

[q] Tempore regis Edvardi et post valuit 10 libras & modo 16 libras. 4 b. 1.

* Many antiquaries interpret this word as synonimous to viæ obstructio, itineris interceptio; but as we meet with Foresta, Foristarius, &c. in Domesday, it may perhaps apply to the Forest Laws, which are universally known to have been severe at this period. Lambardes *Forestelling* is certainly wrong.

appertained

appertained to Robert Romney, were not productive to their proprietor, for they were only estimated at [r] forty shillings, in the year 1064, but had increased in value ten shillings in twenty years. CHAP. I. 1065—1272.

[s] Sesaltre was a *borough* of a still inferior description, that properly belonged to the kitchen of the archbishop, and whose eight fisheries were held by gavelkind tenure at a rent of twenty-five shillings, by a sub-tenant of the name of Blize, from the monks of St. Austin's. There were forty-eight rustics annexed to this borough, which was situated in Canterbury lath, possessed two ploughs, one of which appertained to the demesne, had a church, and pannage for ten hogs. Sesaltre.

[t] Forewic is the remaining borough situated in East-Kent, at this period. Before the Confessour's reign two-thirds of this district was annexed to the crown. Edward had presented his portion to the abbey of St. Augustine's. When Odo succeeded to Earl Godwin's third share, he obtained permission from Forewic.

[r] Tempore regis Edvardi et post valuit 40 solid. modo 50 sol. Domes. 11 a 1.

[s] In eodem Borowart Lest, jacet parvum burgum nomine Sesaltre, quod proprie pertinet Coquinæ Archiepiscopi. Quidam nomine Blize tenet de Monachis. In dominio est una Caruca et 48 bordarii cum una Carucâ. Ibi æcclesia et 8 piscariæ cum *gablo* de 25 solidis. Silva 10 porcorum. Tempore regis Edvardi et post valuit 25s. Domes. 5 a 1.

[t] Ipse abbas (Sancti Augustini) tenet unum parvum burgum, quod vocatur Forewic. Hujus burgi duas partes dedit Edwardus Sancto Augustino. Tertiam verò partem, quæ fuerat Godwini Comitis, Episcopus Baiocensis concessit eidem Sancto annuente rege * Willielmo. Ibi fuerunt 100 masuræ terræ, 4 minus, reddentes 13 s. modo sunt 73 masuræ tantundem reddentes. Domes. 12 a 2.

* This passage corroborates Alfred's will, where the West-Saxon Nobles are represented holding their liberties and property at the pleasure of their lord, which they could not enjoy, or transfer, without his consent. But more on this subject hereafter. See Alfred's Will, edited Oxon. 1788, from a MS. of Mr. Astle.

 William

CHAP. I. 1065—1272. William [u] to transfer the remaining part to this ecclesiastical foundation. Here were situated ninety-six houses, or [x] burgesses, for these were synonimous in boroughs, under the Saxon prince, but were reduced to seventy-three, under the Norman monarch; the general state of the place had, notwithstanding, been so much improved by its clerical possessors, that its value had increased from five pounds to eleven pounds two shillings. In addition to these inhabitants, there were six burgesses appertaining to the abbey, that held in gavelkind tenure twenty-four acres, at a rent of twenty-two shillings. These were still retained, because possessions attached to this religious house from time immemorial; but seven mansions in the borough, which were only possessed by St. Austin's in the Confessour's reign, were exempted from services to his ecclesiastics by Lanfranc, archbishop, but [y] certainly not for the benefit of the occupants, but his own emolument.

Having surveyed the situation of the city and boroughs in East Kent, we shall now pervade the four laths, with their respective hundreds. We shall commence with the neighbourhood of Canterbury, and the reader will easily be enabled to accompany us in our progress, by consulting the annexed map. To mark the precise boundaries either of laths or hundreds, at this period, is impossible, since several hundreds are situated in more than one lath, and many manours extend to different hundreds. Hence we attempt not to *delineate* their extent or figure, but shall endeavour to particularize them with such

[u] Ibidem sunt 24 acræ terræ, quas *semper* habuit Sanctus Augustinus, ubi fuerunt & sunt 6 burgenses reddentes 22 solidos. In isto burgo tenet archiepiscopus Lanfrancus septem masuras terræ, quæ tempore regis Edvardi serviebant Sancto Augustino, modo archiepiscopus aufert ei [eo] Servitium. Dom. 12 a 2.

[x] Vide supra, p. 11.

[y] Aufert.

fidelity

fidelity and accuracy, as the tranſmitted documents enable us. To avoid that tedious detail and tireſome repetition which muſt neceſſarily reſult from a tranſcript of the entries in Domeſday, we have arranged, with conſiderable labour and expence, a ſummary Table of the Lands in Kent, their ſituation, hundred, value, proprietors, occupants, and inhabitants, in the reſpective reigns of Edward the Confeſſour and William the Conqueror. That table and this hiſtory will mutually illuſtrate each other, and their authority reſts on the ſame baſe.

Borough-ward Lath.

In the ward, or lath, of the borough of Canterbury, diſtinguiſhed in modern days by the title of St. Auguſtine's lath, eleven hundreds were ſituated. Since Bolton occupies its north-weſtern diſtrict, we ſhall there commence our deſcription, and ſucceſſively viſit, in a ſouth-eaſternly direction, the reſpective hundreds.

Bolton.

Bolton was not remarkable either for its extent, population, or riches. It comprized probably ſix manours, or hamlets, and appertained to the Saxon monarch Edward, Stigand Archbiſhop, Earl Godwin, and the Abbey of Saint Auſtin's. It comprehended [z] Selling, Bolton, Goodneſton, Graveney, Eaſt-Swale, and part of the iſle of Sheppey, near Muſcle Creek. Hence it is reaſonable to imagine that a ſhoal extended from the main land to this iſle, which the name, Eaſt-Swale, perhaps imports. The whole hundred was eſtimated at more than [a] fifteen ſowlings to the general land-tax, equal in extent

[z] Sedlinges, 12 a 2—Boltun, 3 b 2—Godeſelle, 8 a 1—Gravenel, 4 a 2 *—Eſtſelve, 8 a 2—Winchelcſmere, 8 a 2. Domeſday.

[a] 15½ ſowlings, each equal to 160 computed, or Cheſhire acres, give 2480, or 5243.7 ſtatute acres of land, proper for cultivation.

* We preſume that Eſtſelve and Weſtſelve, are Eaſtſwale and Weſtſwale, or the Eaſtern Shelve or Shoal, and Weſtern Shelve or Shoal; but we are leſs certain relative to the eighth ſolio in Domeſday, eſpecially its firſt page, denoted by a, than any other part of Kent, ſince *not one hundred* is ſpecified in either column diſtinguiſhed by the figures 1 and 2.

to

CHAP. I. 1065—1272. to more than five thousand statute acres, or eight square miles. Its rental, under the Confessour and Conquerour, with other particulars, will be found in a general subsequent table of the hundreds, to which the reader is referred for information. The land of the [b] ecclesiastics in this district constituted four-fifths of the whole hundred, they possessed thirty ploughs, sixty-nine yeomen or villains, thirty-one borderers or rustics, fisheries, and salt-works, which were uninterruptedly transmitted to their successors; whilst the feudal property of the royal Edward, and Earl Godwin, with their sub-tenants, Lewin, Edwin, and Ulwi, were transferred to the uterine brother of William, who portioned it to his military retainers, Hugh, the nephew of Hubert, and Richard, his knight.

Whitestable. Whitestable hundred was composed of [c] Blean, Swalecliff, and Harbledown. The soil was solely occupied by feudal chieftains, and the value or cultivation was comparatively inconsiderable, when we view the regularly transmitted possessions of ecclesiastical foundations; its inhabitants and oxen were few, its assessed taxes to the government, or support of the realm, trifling. Edward and Earl Godwin were demesne lords, under the Saxon monarchy, and committed their possessions to the custody of [d] four warlike nobles, with manorial privileges. The Conqueror transferred them to the opulent and powerful Odo, and Haimo the Viscount of the county, who parcelled them to their respective dependants, and Norman followers.

Canterbury. The city of Canterbury, at this period, gave denomination to a hundred. This district, independant of Sesaltre, which

[b] Archbishop of Canterbury and abbey of St. Austin's. See general alphabetical Table of Places.

[c] Blchem, 14 a 2—Soaneclive, 10 a 1—Herbretitou, 8 a 2.

[d] See subsequent Hundred Table.

has

has been deſcribed, comprehended [e] Norwood and Nackington. CHAP. I. 1065—1272.
The burgeſſes annexed to the manour of Norwood have already been [f] ſpecified. The archbiſhops were its proprietors, and the major part of their vaſſals had relinquiſhed their agricultural occupations, to live as tradeſmen, under the immediate auſpices of their patron at Canterbury. But though they had abandoned the place of their nativity, their ſervile ſtate ſtill attached to them, or perhaps they were fortunate, at this period, in receiving the protection of an eccleſiaſtical patron. The number of yeomen, or villains, ruſtics, borderers, cottagers, or inhabitants of the ſkirts of the manour, will be found in a ſummary table of the hundreds of each lath. Nackington, another hamlet, included in this diviſion, had been held by the [g] burgeſſes of Canterbury, under the Saxon government; but the tyrannical Earl biſhop had wreſted it from their hands, and transferred it to Haimo, the Norman viſcount. As this land had been occupied by perſons incapable of exerciſing manorial powers, we could little expect to find either mills, fiſheries, ſalt-works, or a church in the diſtrict.

Sturry.

Sturry was wholly occupied by eccleſiaſtics, or their dependants, previous and ſubſequent to the conqueſt. The archbiſhop of Canterbury had one moiety in demeſne, which, in proportion to its extent, was excellently cultivated, abounded with [h] mills and paſture, and whoſe inhabitants had built fifty-two houſes in the city, where many of the ruſtics reſided, with the appellation of burgeſſes. The major part of theſe were deſtroyed, when the palace was erected by Lanfranc. In this

[e] Nordeude, 2 a 2. & 5 a 1—Latintone, 9 b 1.

[f] See Hiſtory Canterbury.

[g] Has terras tempore regis Edvardi tenuerunt burgenſes Cantuariæ, et uſque ad epiſcopum baiocenſem, qui ab eis cepit. Domeſday, 9 b 1.

[h] Duodecim molini et 100 acræ paſturæ. Domeſday, 3 b 1.

manour

CHAP. I. 1065—1272. manour [i] five knights of the archbiſhop, and Haimo, ſheriff, or viſcount, had poſſeſſions, with ſubordinate retainers, cottagers, mills, and paſture. The abbey of St. Auſtin's had the other portion. This diſtrict alſo was chiefly arable, and was well furniſhed with [k] mills and fiſheries, for the benefit of this eccleſiaſtical foundation. The abbot retained this manour under his immediate ſuperintendance, which, like all other clerical poſſeſſions, was highly rated to the land-tax at this period, for this ſmall hundred paid for twelve ſowlings, and though eſtimated ſo high as [l] fifty pounds, yielded a revenue of fifty-four pounds annually, when the Autograph was compiled.

Forewic. Forewic hundred has been generally deſcribed, when we treated on boroughs. In addition to our former obſervations, we curſorily ſtate that [m] eighty acres adjoining to Canterbury, ſituated in this diſtrict, poſſeſſed by the abbot of St. Auſtin's, were exempt from all land-tax, and cultivated by fifteen borderers. Here likewiſe four nuns reſided, under the patronage of this eccleſiaſtical eſtabliſhment, and held four acres in frank-almoigne, at the rent of two ſhillings and one ſeam of wheat.

Chiſlet. Chiſlet appertained likewiſe to St. Auſtin's, and was under the immediate controul of the abbot. Its general ſtate and value will eaſily be known, from the table of hundreds comprized in each lath, ſince it only conſiſted of one manour. Vines were conſiderably cultivated at this æra, for three [n] arpents,

[i] See ſummary Table of Places.

[k] 10 molini de 8 libris, et 7 piſcariæ, 12 a 1.

[l] This portion of the abbot is ſtated, in Domeſday, to have been valued at 50 ſhillings, but moſt probably is an error of the ſcribe, writing fifty ſol. for 50 lib.

[m] Juxta civitatem Cantuarienſem habet Sanctus Auguſtinus dimidium ſolinum, quod ſemper fuit quietum, & 4 moniales in elemoſinâ de abbate, et reddunt 2 ſol. et unam ſummam farinæ. Domeſday, 12 a 2.

[n] Tres arpenni vineæ, 12 a 2.

or

or French acres, belonged to this foundation, and to many other clerical poſſeſſors, not only in Kent, but in Middleſex, Eſſex, and moſt of the midland, ſouthern, and weſtern counties. At this period alſo, when moſt animal food was preſerved by ſeaſoning, and herrings conſtituted a great portion of eccleſiaſtical proviſion, the acquiſition of a ſufficient quantity of ſalt, as an article of the firſt neceſſity, was a great deſideratum for ſupplying the monks with muttons, bacons, beeves, and fiſh. Hence they received their rent in kind, and [o] ſtipulated with their tenants for fifty ſeam of ſalt, and one hundred and thirty hogs, for annual ſuſtenance. In this ſmall hundred four [p] Norman knights reſided, as military vaſſals of the church, and occupied premiſes of twelve pounds yearly value.

Downham-ford.

The hundred of [q] Downhamford was compoſed of four manours; Wickham, Ickham, Littlebourne, and Wanderton. The particular value of each ſeparately may eaſily be found in the ſummary table of places prefixed to this hiſtory, and of the whole conjointly, at the completion of each lath. But there are many occurrences that cannot be remarked on ſuch a confined plan, and we muſt neceſſarily enter into detail upon ſome occaſions. Wickham, in the days of the Confeſſour, was occupied by [r] Alred, the commiſſary of the monarch, or general proveditor for the royal retinue, whenever he viſited that part of the county. In this manour, one hundred and

[o] 47 ſalinæ de 50 ſummis ſalis. De paſnagio 130 porci.
Domeſ. 12 a 2.

[p] De iſto manerio tenent quatuor francigenæ milites, quod valet per annum 12 l.
Domeſ. 12 a 2.

[q] DUNAMESFORT—Wicheham, 9 a 2—Gecham, 5 a 1—Liteburne, 12 a 1—Warwintone, 12 a 1.

[r] Hoc manerium tenuit Alured biga de rege Edvardo. Domeſ. 9 a 2.

CHAP. I. 1065—1272. ſixty-ſeven acres of [s] free or chartered land were ſituated, which Siward occupied under the Saxon government, and which were tranſferred to Maltravers, with ſimilar privileges, by the Earl of Kent. This diſtrict was in the immediate poſſeſſion of Odo Earl and Biſhop, under the Norman dynaſty, and was amply ſupplied with the neceſſary requiſites for the caſtle of a feudal chieftain. There was a [t] park for him to ſport in; an exalted prieſt to attend his devotional hours; mills, and ſalt-works, to prepare ſuch proviſions as ſixty-eight agricultural ruſtics, a paſture of [u] three hundred ſheep, fiſheries, and a wood yielding pannage for eighty bacons, could furniſh for the round table of the knightly hall. What is more remarkable, there were thirty-one [x] chargers, to accommodate his military train, and three [y] manſions in Canterbury, appendages to the manour, to receive his followers, when they attended him in the city.—Ickham had a greater quantity of arable land, and more numerous labourers, had four extremely productive [z] mills, and was more [a] valuable to the archbiſhop, its poſſeſſor, who retained it in demeſne. In this manour,

[s] *Adhuc* jacet ad hunc manerium dimidius * ſolinus liberæ terræ, quam Sired tenuit de Alured Biga, et modo tenet Goisfrid filius malæ terræ de epiſcopo Baiocenſi et valet et ſemper valuit 60 s. Domeſ. 9 a 2.

[t] Ibi unus parcus, æccleſia et preſbytor qui dat 40 s. per annum.

[u] There are not 300 ſheep, or paſture for them, to be found in five places of Domeſday, the part of Higham manour, in Eſſex, fed 200, whilſt in ſome counties many manours fed 2000 hogs. See Diſſertation on Agriculture, &c.

[x] 31 animalia, 9 a 2; a very uncommon entry.

[y] Maſuræ, not domus, not houſes ſimply, but manſion-houſes. Vid. ſupra.

[z] Quatuor molendini de 100 ſolidis. We find mills varying in value, from 30 ſhillings to 30 pence. Vid. Domeſday, 177 b 2, and 5 a 1.

[a] For the value we ſhall generally refer to the prefixed table of places arranged alphabetically.

* 80 Cheſhire acres, equal to 167 ſtatute. See Diſſerta. on Weights and Meaſures.

William,

William [b], a knight of Lanfranc's, resided, possessing landed property of seven pounds annual income.—The abbot of St. Austin's was proprietor of one moiety of Littlebourne, and the whole of Wanderton, in the reign of the Conquerour. Under the Saxon prince, Wanderton appertained to Sbern, the commissary, was farmed by Edric, and probably included in Preston hundred. But when Odo succeeded to his possessions, and was desirous of extending his [c] park of Wickham, he exchanged, for an adjoining portion of Littlebourne, his manour of Wanderton, with the abbey, though Ralph [d] Crookthorn was continued its Sub-tenant under the mitred abbot.

Petham.

In Petham hundred there is little deserving our attention, that may not easily be collected from the edited tables. It consisted of one manour, was occupied in demesne by the primate, though [e] Godfrey, his purveyor, and Nigell, an ecclesiastic and physician, held extensive premises in the district, with the accustomed appendages of yeomen or villains, rustics or borderers, to the amount of nine pounds. A small portion appertained to the monks of Canterbury, independant of the archbishop.

Bridge.

[f] Bridge hundred comprehended the three Bournes, Hardes, and Stelling. One Bourne belonged to the abbey of St. Austin's, was in the hands of the abbot, and thence probably had the addition of Bishop's Bourne; for though Odo, the

[b] De terra hujus manerii tenet Willielmus *homo* suus tantum quod valet 7 l. Domesf. 5 a 1.

[c] De isto manerio (Liteburne) habet episcopus Baiocensis in suo parco tantum quod valet 60 s. Domesf. 12 a 1.

[d] Hoc manerium tenuit Edricus de Sbern Biga, et modò tenet Radulphus. (i. e. de Curvâ spinâ.) Domesf. 12 a 1.

[e] Godfrid Dapifer, 4 b 1, et Nigellus medicus tenuit in præbenda, 1 b 2.

[f] BRIGE.—Borne, 9 a 2—Hardes, 9 a 2—Stellinges, 9 a 2—Burnes, 9 a 1—Borne, 12 a 1. Domesf.

CHAP. I. 1065—1272. proprietor of the others, was a biſhop in Normandy, we muſt ever conſider him as an earl in Kent. Its value was inconſiderable, its [g] mills ill conſtructed, or with ſmall power of ſtream, or fall of water. A ſecond Bourne was farmed from the uterine brother of the Conqueror, by Richard [h] Fitz-William. This manour was more productive, but there is little remarkable which cannot be collected from the tables. One circumſtance indeed may give us ſome idea of the ſtate of ſociety and agriculture at this period, that [i] ſix acres of paſture could be converted into arable land by ſtrangers, or, in other words, that men could plough the ground, ſow the ſeed, and reap an harveſt, yet continue unknown to the proprietor of the diſtrict. Of the other three manours Odo was lord paramount, but [k] Ralph Crookthorn was his ſub-tenant, though Hugh Montfort had a ſmall moiety in the remaining Bourne. As half a fiſhery is here firſt ſpecified, we take an opportunity of obſerving, that fiſheries conſiſted of dams or wears erected on a ſtream, where, when two * wheels were fixed in the water-courſe, the lords of the adjoining bank had each their own. Mills were divided on a ſimilar principle, each proprietor poſſeſſing one courſe of water, or occaſionally, one pair of mill-ſtones. In this hundred were four churches, but their number can always be ſo eaſily aſcertained from one table, and their ſituation from the other, that we ſhall deſiſt from noticing them.

Berham. [l] Berham hundred was under the ſole dominion of Stigand, under the Saxon government. In the Norman monarchy it

[g] Value 9s 6d. 12 a 1.

[h] Willielmus Tahun. 8 b 1.

[i] Paſtura unde araverunt *extranei* homines ſex acras terræ. 9 a 1.

[k] Hæc tria maneria epiſcopi Baiocenſis tenet Rannulfus ad firmam. Quod Hugo de Montfort tenet valet 5s. 9 a 1.

* An inſtrument of wicker-work, placed in the water-courſe, at floods, for eels and other fiſh.

[l] BERHAM, 9 b 2—Huham, 9 b 2—Burnes, 3 b 2.

was divided. Odo became the proprietor of [m] Berham, for the archbifhop poffeffed it not, as a portion of his ecclefiaftical domain, but as a baronial fief, but Bourne continued in the hands of the primate. In Berham manour an unequivocal proof of flavery, or the French [n] corvè, is tranfmitted. If the yeomen or villains were not called upon to erect [o] buildings for their lord, to grant him the ufe of their ploughs, to place fhingles round his court, or perform fuch fervices to which their tenure fubjected them, fuch immunity was purchafed at the high fum of fixty fhillings, in this diftrict. Of this [p] manour Herbert Fitz-ivo poffeffed Huham, and Ofbern, the verdurer, another hamlet, by the donation of Odo, earl of Kent, and jufticiary of England, with the accuftomed fuit of dependants. Lanfranc regularly fucceeded to Bourne, the poffeffion of his predeceffor, a populous manour, well cultivated, and productive to its proprietor.

CHAP. I. 1065—1272.

Thanet.

Thanet hundred, or ifle, appertained to the abbey of St. Auftin's, and archbifhop of Canterbury. This diftrict was eftimated at fixty-fix fowlings, which, according to our [q] pre-

[m] Hoc manerium tenuit Stigandus archiepifcopus, fed non erat de archiepifcopatu, fed fuit de dominicâ firmâ regis Edvardi. 9 b 2.

[n] De averâ id eft fervitium 60s. 9 a 2.

[o] Faciebant domos regis ficut villani. Thanes of Lancafter. Hence the *gable* end of buildings, in lieu of rent gablum.

[p] De ifto manerio dedit epifcopus unam Berewicham Herberto filio juonis, quæ vocatur Huham. De eodem quoque manerio dedit epifcopus Ofberno Pais-forere unum folinum. 9 b 2.

[q] 48 fowlings belonging to the abbey, of 160 computed, or Chefhire, acres each, equal to 331 ftatute acres, give 15,888 acres, equal to 24½ miles; and this part of the ifle approximates as nearly as poffible to this admeafurement; if to this we add the 18 fowlings of the archbifhop, adjoining to Monks-Town, equal to 5,958 acres, or 9½ miles, we have good reafon to prefume that little alteration has taken place in its boundaries to the prefent day. See Differtation on Weights and Meafures, and Map of Kent.

fumed

CHAP. I. 1065—1272. sumed proportion, corresponds with its present extent. [r] St. Mildred's was the distinguishing title of the abbey's manour. Here one hundred and fifty [s] yeomen and fifty rustics resided, though the former must have been daily labourers, since two hundred cultivated the ground with [t] sixty-five ploughs, and superintended salt-works, fisheries, and a mill. In the days of William, three knights had succeeded to a considerable portion of land, formerly possessed by the sub-tenants, which was of nine pounds value, when their isle was not [u] harrassed by invaders, or plunderers.—In [x] Monks-Town no particular circumstances are recorded deserving our attention, that cannot easily be known from the tables. A *new* [y] fishery indeed had been established, and the manour much increased in value, since the days of the Confessour.

At the conclusion of our review of each lath, it is intended to publish a summary Table, similar to the annexed; and, before we conclude this portion of the History, we shall give a general Table of the Laths, Cities, and Boroughs, and thereby form an accurate estimate of the population of the county, the proportion of different classes of the community, and general state of society and agriculture, in the reigns of the Saxon and Norman princes, Edward, and William, in the years 1064, and 1086.

[r] Sancta Mildreda. 12 a 1.

[s] We shall generally render villanos yeomen, and bordarios rustics; the former certainly, according to its modern acceptation, is too honourable a title, but originally signifying ȝemen, common.

[t] See Dissertation on Agriculture, &c.

[u] Quandò pax erat in terrâ. Domesday, 12 a 2.

[x] Monocstune. 4 b 2.

[y] Nova piscaria. 4 b 2.

A Summary

A SUMMARY TABLE OF THE HUNDREDS,

SITUATED IN THE

LATH OF THE BOROUGH OF CANTERBURY,

IN THE

REIGNS OF EDWARD THE CONFESSOUR, AND WILLIAM THE CONQUEROUR;

THEIR VALUE, POPULATION, &c. &c.

Hundreds.	Value under the Confessour.	Value under the Conqueror.	Number of Villains.	Borderers.	Lords Ploughs.	Villains Ploughs.	Oxen.	Churches.	Ministers, or Retainers.	Fisheries.	Salt-pans.	Acres of Meadow.	Thanes, or Knights, under the Confessour.	Knights, or Military Tenants, under the Conquerour.	N° Manours.
	£. s. d.	£. s. d.													
Bolton	54 16 3½	64 1 3½	80	47	6	30	84	4	8	3 of 4s. 10d.	5	22	Lewin, Edwin, Alwi.	Hu. Fitz-herbert, Rich. Knight.	6
Whitstable	12 11 0	12 16 0	14	13	3½	2½	20	1					Norman, Edward, Alfi, Alred.	Vital, Athelwold, Robert Latin.	3
Canterbury	25 0 0	29 0 0	6	39	4	5½	30					28	Burgesses of Canterbury.	Haimo, Viscount.	2
Sturry	69 12 6	108 0 0	64	146	13½	30	114	2	1	7 of 5s.		162	Abbot of St. Austin's.	Haimo, 5 Knights.	2
Forewic	10 2 0	16 4 0	96	15	1		4		4 Nuns			35	Abbot of St. Austin's.	Abbot of St. Austin's.	2
Chiflet	52 0 0	78 0 0	72	68	5	39	98	1	14		47	50	Abbot of St. Austin's.	Abbot, 4 Norman Knights.	1
Downhamford	76 0 0	98 0 0	100	109	9	33	102	3		3 of 4s.	2	89	Edric, Sbern, Alred, Siward.	William, Kt. Colville, Maltravers.	4
Petham	17 16 3	29 0 0	36	29	6	19	62	2	2			13	Stigand, Archbishop	Lanfranc, Nigell, Godfrey.	1
Bridge	46 0 0	54 0 0	87	9	8½	21	76	5	20	1½ 10d.	1	19	Edwin, Alred, Lewin, Azor.	R. Fitz-william, Montfort, Colville	5
Berham	61 0 0	148 0 0	132	73	10	58½	157	2		25 34s. 8d.		61	Stigand, Archbishop.	Fulbert, Herbert, Osbern.	3
Thanet	100 0 0	149 0 0	239	71	9	90	216	3		1	1		Stigand, and Abbot of St. Austin's.	Lanfranc, Abbot, 3 Knights.	2
BOROUGH LATH	524 18 0½	776 15 3½	926	618	76	328	963	23	45	40½ 2l. 9s. 4d.	56	479	See future general Recapitulation.	See future general Recapitulation.	31

CHAP. I. 1065—1272. Eaſtrye-lath conſiſted of ſix hundreds; Preſton, Wingham, Sandwich, Eaſtrye, Corniloe, and Beſborough. We ſhall continue our route, in the ſame direction we purſued, when writing the hiſtory of the Borough Lath.

So long as we continue in the neighbourhood of Canterbury, eccleſiaſtics will be found to poſſeſs the major part of all property. Preſton. Preſton hundred appertained to the abbey of St. Auſtin's, and included the manour ſo called and the modern hamlet of Elinton [a]. In each diſtrict was a ſub-tenant in the days of the Conquerour, and a female, by name [b] Godeſſa, held by all odial tenure, which is here repreſented as ſimilar to frankalmoigne, and paid to St. Auſtin's a ſmall annual rent.

Wingeham. Wingeham conſiſted only of one manour, but had a hamlet dependant upon it of the name of Fleet. This diſtrict had been eſtimated at forty [c] ſowlings, under the Confeſſour, but having been over-rated, in the days of William it only paid for thirty-five, including the poſſeſſions of [d] William D'arcey, who had a ſubordinate military tenant, and five knights of the archbiſhop, with the accuſtomed train of numerous yeomen, ruſtics, and attendants; the neceſſary and general appendages of mills, fiſhery, and ſalt-work; and two [e] woods, for forming the wattled courts of the lord, or ſupplying ſhingles for his palaces or edifices.

[a] Ælveton, Alwis Town. 12 b 2.

[b] Godeſſa tenuit in alodium & dedit inde Sancto Auguſtino 25d. in elemoſinâ unoquoque anno. Domeſday, 12 b 2.

Godeſſa held Bedeſham, in Eaſtrye lath, from Edward the Confeſſour. We believe this lady to have been Godiva Comitiſſa, by corrupt abbreviation Godeſſa. Godiva Counteſs widow of Godwin.

[c] Pro 40 ſolinis ſe defendebat tempore regis Edvardi, modò pro 35. 3 b 2.

[d] De hoc manerio tenet Willielmus de Arcis unum ſolinum in Fletes et habet in dominio unam carucam, 4 villanos, et unum militem. 3 b 2.

[e] Duæ ſilvulæ ad clauſuram. Ibid.

Sandwich

[f] Sandwich hundred cannot with propriety be omitted in our perambulatory defcription, though we have already defcribed it, when we reviewed the boroughs of Eaft Kent. CHAP. I. 1065—1272.

The hundred of Eaft-rye is fo peculiarly connected with thofe of Befbrough and Corniloe, is fo irregular in its form, and comprehends fuch a variety of places within its diftrict, that it is particularly difficult to infert them with precifion, in a map of fuch fmall dimenfions, or accurately afcertain the number of manours or hamlets contained in it, with its various proprietors, in three lines of a table. This hundred certainly comprized at leaft twenty-four [g] places, with diftinct names, or different occupiers. As the tables cannot poffibly convey fome interefting intelligence, we muft occafionally enter into detail. Eaftrye.

This diftrict was occupied by numerous tenants and fub-tenants, equally, under the [h] Saxon and [i] Norman monarchy. The communication betwixt England and the Continent was confiderable under Edward; and the fituation was peculiarly de-fireable to poffeffors of property in Normandy, that occafionally

[f] Sandwice jacet in fuo proprio hundredo. 3 a 1. See page 22.

[g] Hama, 11 b 1—Hertange, 11 a 2—Hamolde, 11 a 1—Ece, 11 b 1—Eftenberge, 4 b 2—Flengueffam, 4 b 2—Eftrei, 5 a 2—Geting, 5 a 2—Cille-dene, 11 b 1—Gollefberge, 11 a 2—Chenoltone, 11 a 2—Edefham, 5 a 2—Ringeton, 11 a 1—Berfreftone, 9 b 2—Efwalt, 9 b 2—Walwalefere, 11 b 1—Danetone, 11 b 2—Brocheftelle, 11 b 2—Effewelle, 11 b 2—Selinges, 11 b 2—Selinge, 9 b 2—Popefelle, 9 b 2—Soles, 11 a 2—Bedefham, 11 a 2.

[h] Queen Eddiva, Earl Godwin, Sbern, Alnod, Edward, Wluard or Ulwi, Alwin * or Lewin, Elmer, Molleve, and Godeffa.

[i] Sub-tenants. Ansfrid, Adam Fitz-herbert, Athelwold, Crookthorn, Colville, Ernold, Folet, Fitz-letard, Fitz-robert, Turftin, and various knights.

* In afcertaining fynonimous terms, indicative of the fame perfon, confonants muft principally affift our judgment; this idea is ftrongly corroborated by the Hebrew language, and the various vocabularies of South-fea voyagers.

 vifited

CHAP. I. 1065—1272. visited both countries. Hence the politic Odo obliged his military retainers with small portions of land, for their particular accommodation in this neighbourhood; for this wise and powerful Earl Bishop, and the metropolitan, were alone tenants in chief of this hundred. Some feudal [k] knights possessed only sufficient ground to maintain themselves and followers, though Colville, Crookthorn, and Fitz-letard possessed extensive tracts in various parts. The [l] names of the same place were varied in such a manner, as easily to distinguish their limits and scite, their peculiar situation, and quality. Even the subordinate tenants appear to have possessed, at this period, a species of legislative power, for [m] Osbern Fitz-letard, who was invested with Hame and Chillenden, by the earl of Kent, under seperate jurisdiction in the reign of the Confessour, formed them into one manour, under the immediate controul of his own hall, or court.—The two manours, of Adesham and Eastrye, that nearly equalled in [n] value the other twenty-two portions, were occupied by the archbishop. These, and other particular circumstances, will easily be observed and distinguished by an intelligent examiner of the tables. Indeed if we include the fine [o] for favour and protection paid to the primate, these manours were more productive than the whole hundred.

Besbrough. [p] Besbrough hundred comprized the manours of Norbourne, Mundingeham, and Deal, with a small portion of St. Mar-

[k] Adam, Herbert, 1 jugum, equal to 20 Cheshire acres.

[l] Hama, Hamold—Ece, Eisse, Estenberge—Eswalt, Walwalesere.

[m] Osbernus misit terras eorum (Hama et Cilledene) inunum manerium. 11 b 1.

[n] Estric, 36l. 10s. 4½d.—Edesham, 59l. 16s. 4d. Equal to 96l. 6s. 8½d. Total of the Hundred, 192l. 14s. 4½d.

[o] De Gersumne, 100s.

[p] BEUSBERG, Dela, 1 b 2—Norborne, 12 b 1—Mundingeham, 12 b 1—Sancta Margaritta, 1 b 2—Ripa, 2 a 2—Bevessel, 12 a 1. Domesday.

garet's,

garet's, and the hamlets of Ripple and Beawfield.—Norbourne was a manour of great extent, value, and population. It was under the immediate jurifdiction of the abbot of St. Auftin's, but eight Norman knights poffeffed extenfive diftricts there, fome of whom held of him by [q] gavel-kind tenure, and were exonerated from thofe flavifh fervices, which the [r] villains that formerly refided there, were accuftomed to perform under the Saxon government. Some of thefe military [s] vaffals poffeffed diftricts of from five hundred to a thoufand acres in extent; and could we by any means find a correfpondence in their titles, we might have prefumed that they were the eight feudal chieftains, that Lambarde [t] reports to have been appointed by William, for the cuftody of Dover caftle.—[u] Mongeham was occupied by the monks of St. Auftin's, and Wadard, a military retainer. The portion of the ecclefiaftics had been exempted, from time immemorial, from every national contribution; but the laical poffeffors paid to the land-tax, equally under the Saxon and Norman monarchs, though the two divifions conftituted one manour. This [x] knight held by gavelkind tenure of the abbey, at a rent of thirty fhillings per

[q] Ipfe vero nullum fervitium reddit abbati nifi 30 s. quos perfolvit in anno. Domef 12 b 1.

[r] De terrâ villanorum tenent, 12 b 1.

[s] Wadard tenet 3 folins—Oidelard tenet de terrâ villanorum 1 folin, et de hoc manerio unum folinum & vocatur Bevesfel. Domefday, 12 a 1.

[t] William of Albrance, Fulbert of Dover, William Arficke, Galfride Peverell, William Maynemouth, Robert Porthe, Hugh Crevequer, and Adam Fitz-williams. Lambardes Perambulation, 4to. 1596. p. 153.

Oidelard, Gilbertus, Wadard, Odelin, Marcherius, Ofbern Fitz-letard, Ranulfus de Columbellis, Ranulfus de Valbadon. Domef. 12 b 1.

[u] In hoc manerio, terra, quam tenent monachi, nunquam geldavit, et Wadard tenet ibi terram, quæ tempore regis Edvardi femper geldavit, & illo tempore erat manerium infimul. Domef. 12 b 1.

[x] Nullum fervitium inde reddit nifi 30s. per annum abbati. 12 b 1.

annum.

CHAP. I. 1065—1272. annum.—Deal, and a portion of St. Margaret's, were solely occupied by clerical possessors. The abbot of [y] St. Austin's held one moiety, as prebendary of St. Martin's, Dover: Anschil [z], arch-deacon, held one portion of Stigand's and others, as prebendary; [a] Edwin, and [b] Athelwold inducted under the Saxon government, continued to hold their prebends; though the bishop of Baieux, when dividing them, appropriated a share of Edwin's to Alan, his secretary, to which Ulric of Oxford succeeded; and Robert Black and Fitz-tydald occupied other districts, which Goldstan and Derinc had enjoyed, as prebendaries, under the Confessour.

Besbrough. Besbrough hundred comprehended at least twenty-four distinct [c] hamlets, or parts of manours, for we cannot presume that there were so many distinct jurisdictions in so small a district. Indeed it appears highly probable that the whole hundred, independant of the possessions of St. Martin's, and the borough of Dover, was under the baronial government of Hugh Montfort. He possessed sixteen mills, distinguishing

[y] In Addelam tenet abbas Sti. Augustini, &c. Antecessor ejus tenuit in præbenda similiter. Domes. 1 b 2.

[z] Anschil, archdiaconus tenet, &c. hanc terram tenuit Stigand archiepiscopus. Hæ 100 acræ erant de præbendis. 1 b 2.

[a] Edwin tenet, &c. ipsemet tenuit tempore regis Edvardi de hac præbendâ sumpsit episcopus baiocensis 8 acras, et dedit Alan Clerico suo, modò habet Ulric de Oxeneford. 1 b 2.

[b] In Addelam tenet Adelold, &c. Ilsemet tenuit tempore regis Edvardi. Domes. 1 b 2.

[c] BEUSBERGE—Apletone, 11 a 2.—Bocheland, 1 b 2.—Cerlentone, 1 b 1—Brochestelle, 11 a 2.—Leuiberge, 11 a 1. & 11 a 2.—Ewelle, 11 a 1—Etwelle, 13 b 1.—Colret, 11 a 1.—Hamestede, 11 b 2.—Hicham, 1 b 2.—Havochesten, 2 b 2.—Medredive, 2 a 2.—Neventone, 13 b 1. & 11 b 1.—Oxenai, 10 b 2.—Poltone, 13 b 2.—Ferlingelai, 1 b 2.—Pesinges—et Piham, 10 b 2.—Gocistone, 1 b 1.—Pars Stæ. Margarettæ, 1 b 1.—Sibertefwalt, 1 b 2.—Soltones, 11 a 1.—Wesclive, 11 a 1.—Suanetone, 11 a 2.

appendages

appendages of manorial right, at this æra; of the two others situated in this division, one in Dover, occupied by Hugh Port, is particularly specified not to be annexed to any manour; the other at [d] Charlton, was attached to a monastery in Dover, and its prior Fitz-oger; of which St. Martin's canons had been unjustly deprived by Odo; but the distantly-situated mills of Ewell, Eastwell, Westcliff, and Newington, were all solely occupied by the lord paramount of the district, who held from the sovereign by [e] Saxon peerage, and governed the district as [f] baron of the realm. The villages of Sibertswold, Gurson, Charlton, Buckland, and Farthingloe, were the property of the canons of St. Martin's, as a corporate society, in the reign of the Confessour, and principally occupied by their [g] prebendaries; the bishop of Baieux divided their [h] seven thousand acres in Corniloe and Besbrough, and appropriated particular portions to each canon and prebendary, and thereby had a convenient opportunity of providing for some of his ecclesiastical dependants. In general the sons of the prior possessors

CHAP. I. 1065—1272.

[d] In Dovere unum Molendinum de 48 ferlingis frumenti non pertinens ulli manerio. 11 a 1.

In eadem villa (Cerlentone) Willielmus filius Ogeri tenet unum Molendinum & unum Monasterium in Dovere de episcopo. Canonici calumniantur. 1 b 1.

[e] Tenuerunt in *paragio*. Domesday passim.

[f] Hugo de Montfort habet *caput* manerii (* Ewelle) et ibi 5½ Molini de 61. Domes. 11 a 2.

[g] Baldwin, Alwi, Alric, Alred, Esmelt, (chaplain of the Confessour) Lewin, Edwin, Spirites, and Ulric.

[h] 21 Solin. in hundred de Cornely & Beusberge. 1 b 1.

* Ewell and Westcliffe were estimated at 2600 acres, were occupied by Crookthorn and Hugh Port, powerful and opulent knights, as sub-tenants of Odo, yet the mills were transferred to Montfort, tenant in chief of the crown, and controuling lord of these manours of the Earl Bishop, with baronial jurisdiction.

succeeded

CHAP. I. 1065—1272. succeeded to the inheritance of their [i] fathers, though the abbey was despoiled of numerous [k] mills, manours, fisheries, and salt-works, to accommodate the Norman dependants of the Earl, with a convenient and well-supplied mansion, in their general intercourse with their continental possessions. The laical proprietors of Pincham, and other districts in this neighbourhood, possessed uncommon privileges under the Saxon monarchy. Six Thanes had a [l] right of choosing their patron under Edward, and in the days of William, a [m] freeholder continued to retain his possessions in Newington, but the [n] chartered land which two Thanes possessed in [o] Hamstead, under the Confessour, were seized by Odo, and transferred to a [p] Norman knight.

For farther particular information, relative to this lath, we refer the reader to our general Tables of Places and Hundreds, but as we find it possible to render this table of Eastrye-lath, more complete than the edited Borough-lath, we take an opportunity of stating, that Bolton, or Boughton hundred was estimated at 15½ sowlings, and contained 1 mill; Whitstable, at 2½; Canterbury, at 2, with 8 mills; Sturry, at 14, with 27 mills; Chislet, at 12; Downhamford, at 16, with 5 mills; Piteham, at 7; Bridge, at 11, with 4 mills; Berham, at 13, with 5 mills; and Thanet at 48, with 3 mills; and that the whole Lath of the Borough was estimated at 161 sowlings, and contained 23 mills.

[i] Ulstan, to his father Ulwin; Sired, to his father's prebend; Alred, to his father's, &c. Domes. 1 b 2.

[k] Vide Domesday, 2 a 2.

[l] Poterant ire quolibet cum terris suis Lesstan, et Lewin, et Eluret, et Sired, et duo alii, tempore regis Edvardi. 10 b 2.

[m] Sochemannus tenens 16 acras terræ, et ipse idem tenuit de rege Edvardo. Domes. 13 b 2.

[n] Quod tenuerunt duo liberi homines de rege Edvardo in *Bechelande*. 11 b 2.

[o] Hougham court.

[p] Ranulfus de Valbadon.

A SUMMARY

A SUMMARY TABLE OF THE HUNDREDS,

SITUATED IN

EASTRYE LATH,

IN THE

REIGNS OF EDWARD THE CONFESSOUR, AND WILLIAM THE CONQUEROUR;

THEIR VALUE, POPULATION, &c. &c.

Hundreds.	Value under the Confessour. £. s. d.	Value under the Conqueror. £. s. d.	Sowlings.	Number of Villains.	Borderers.	Lords Ploughs.	Villains Ploughs.	Oxen.	Churches.	Ministers, or Retainers.	Fisheries.	Mills.	Salt pans.	Acres of Meadow.	Hogs.	Thanes, or Knights, under the Confessour.	Knights, or Military Tenants, under the Conquerour.	N° Manours.
Preston	12 0 0	22 0 0	5½	26	34	5	10	42								Godessa.	Abbot, Vital, Ansfrid.	2
Wingeham	77 0 0	123 0 0	40	89	42	9	58	146		16	1	2	1		5	Archbishop.	Archbishop, 6 Knights, D'arcey.	2
Sandwich																See History, p. 22.		1
Eastrye	166 2 4½	192 14 4½	50½	289	87	39	81	282	2	6	1	2½	3	36	10	Eddiva, Sbern, Godwin, Edward, Alnod, Wluard, Molleve, Ulwi, Alwin, Elmer, Godessa.	Adam, Ansfrid, Athelwold, Crookthorn, Colville, Ernold, Osbern, Fitz-robert, Folet, Turstin, Wlbert, Herbert and 3 Knights.	23
Cornilloe	124 0 0	156 11 4	42½	109	109	17	46	147	1	2		1		15	14	Stigand, Athelwold, Abbot of St. Austin's, Derinc, Edwin, Goldstan.	Abbot St. Austin's, and 8 Knights. See History.	6
Besbrough	101 0 0	133 3 6	38½	79	164	24	28½	124	4	9		18		34	4	9 Preb. and Canons. Alnod, Godric, Edric, Molleve, Coloen & Freemen.	10 Prebends, H. Montfort, and 13 Knights.	14
EASTRYE Lath	480 2 4½	627 9 2¼	136½	592	436	94	223½	741	7	33	2	23½	4	85	33	See future general Recapitulation.	See future general Recapitulation.	58

CHAP. I. 1065—1272.

Wye-lath. The lath of Wye comprehended the hundreds of Feverſham [*], Felborough, Calehill, Chart, Wye, and Longbridge, and probably a ſmall portion of Bolton and Blackburn. We ſhall travel through this diſtrict, from its northern ſide, Feverſham, to its ſouthern boundary by Liming-lath in a regular courſe.

Favreſhant. The hundred of [a] Feverſham contained twenty manours or hamlets, exactly the ſame number aſcribed by [b] Lambarde, in the reign of Elizabeth, though there is a trifling variation in their names. The town of Feverſham was one of the [c] four places in Kent, independant of cities and boroughs, that William retained in his own poſſeſſion. A [d] market was eſtabliſhed here at this early period, and the tolls produced four pounds to the deputy of the monarch. Odo was the only lay proprietor, in this diſtrict, holding in chief of the crown. The archbiſhop of Canterbury poſſeſſed Preſton and Leveland, the abbot of St. Auſtin's a village, by preſumption the modern Warden, in the Iſle of Sheppey, which conſtituted a part of this hundred. But though the lands of Edward and Godwin, with their tenants, were transferred to the biſhop of Baieux, yet in the [e] report of the aſſembled teſtimony of the four laths

[*] Favreſhant, Feliberg, Calehille, Cert, Wi, et Langabrige.

[a] FAVRESHANT.—Favreſhant, 2 a 2—Dodeham, 10 b 2—Wirentone, 12 a 2—Herſle, 10 a 2—Ore, 10 a 1 et 10 a 2—Ernoltun, 10 a 2—Bocheland 10 b 1 et 10 a 2—Nortone, 10 a 1—Oſpringes, 10 a 1—Preſtetone, 5 a 1—Perie, 10 a 2—Cildreſham, 10 a 1—Machehevet, 10 a 2—Nordeſling, 10 a 2—Trevelai, 10 a 2—Eſlinges, 10 b 2—Levelant, 4 a 2—Badeleſmere, 10 a 2—Staneſelle, 10 a 1.—Rongoſtone, 10 b 2.

[b] See Lambardes Perambulation, and the tenth and fifteenth of Kent, p. 45, 4to. 1596.

[c] Tarentefort—Elesford—Middletune—et Favreſhant. Domeſ. 2 b 2.

[d] Mercatum de 4 libris. 2 b 2.

[e] Has infra-ſcriptas leges reges concordant homines de quatuor leſtis, etc. De his terris ſcilicet Bocheland et alium Bocheland, Ernulfitone, Schildricheham, Piria, et alia Piria, et Oſpringes habet rex has foris-facturas Handſocam, Gribrige, Foriſtel. Domeſ. 1 b 1. See future general recapitulation of Eaſt-Kent.

of

of East-Kent, several hamlets in this quarter continued to pay their ordinary fines to the monarch, according to ancient custom. These lands had been held by Seward, the sheriff of the county, and were situated in the Isle of Hearty, Ore, Hurst, the two Bucklands, Hearne, Sheldwich, the two Peries, and Ospring. Basmere was occupied by Ansfrid, a knightly dependant of the earl, when the commissioners, attended by juries of hundreds, entered their circuitous report. At this period the abbey of St. Austin's entered their claim as the true proprietors, and supported their pretensions by the concurring testimony of the hundreds in their favour. But the [f] son of its late tenant, conscious that his own freedom and independance were strongly affected by the rank of his father, supported the right of Odo, as Earl, or Prince of Kent, and affirmed that his father was of liberal descent, could dispose of his property without the concurrence of this religious foundation, and owed it neither suit or service. This statement was controverted by the abbot and monks, and they appealed to a county court. In consequence, at the conclusion of the entries of their possessions in Domesday, it is particularly specified, that [g] Basmere appertained to the abbey by the testimony of the Shire, and that the occupier in the days of the Confessour was their vassal. By such verdict, repossession was obtained, the ratification of the Saxon-laws by William proved beyond controversy, and the slavery of our Saxon ancestors fully established.

[f] Hoc manerium reclamat abbas Sti. Augustini, quia habuit tempore regis Edvardi, et hundredi attestantur ei; sed filius hominis dicit patrem suum se posse vertere ubi voluerit, et hoc non annuunt monachi. Domes. 10 a 2.

[g] Scyra testificatur, quod Bedenesmere fuit Sti. Augustini tempore regis Edvardi, et de illo, qui eam tenebat, habebat abbas sacam et socam. Domes. 12 b 2.

CHAP. I. 1065—1272. Felbrough.

Felbrough [h] hundred consisted of nine manours or hamlets. Chartham and Godmersham appertained to the archbishop, and, like other ecclesiastical possessions, were better cultivated than the adjoining district. Their improvement had been so rapid, that their rental was more than doubled, in the short space of twenty years, for [i] all lands were frequently valued at this period, and let at rack rent. Each of these villages had a [k] church, but at Godmersham two ministers resided, at Chartham only one. The remainder of the hundred was almost solely possessed by Odo, who parcelled it to his military retainers. Of these Fulbert of Dover occupied the opulent manour of Chilham, which was well supplied with valuable mills, bacons, and fisheries, and to which thirteen houses in the city of Canterbury were annexed. We may form an estimate of the comparative insignificance of the other hamlets, when their mills were rated at half a mark, and the total of their value at twenty-two pounds. Of these, Deane, or Shottenden, occupied under the Confessour by four thanes, was seized by the sheriff of William, for defect of payment, probably, to the national land-tax; and Cumbe, or Winchcomb, furnished one military retainer to Odo, in addition to its assessed payments. There was a Grange, or mansion, to accommodate the abbot of St. Austin's in this hundred, denominated Charing-hall, let to a sub-tenant.

[h] FERLIBERG, Essamelesford, 10 a 2—Certeham, 5 a 1—Gomersham, 5 a 1—Hortone, 10 b 1—Cherinchelle, 12 b 1—Cilleham, 10 a 1—Dene, 10 b 2—Betmonteslune, 10 b 1—Cumbe, 10 b 1. Domesday.

[i] Quandò recepit, valuit 12l. modò 25l. et tamen reddit 30l. Cilleham et Gomersham similitèr. Domes. 5 a 1.

[k] In Gomersham æcclesia et 2 servi, et in Certeham æcclesia et 1 servi. Domes. 5 a 1. There can be little doubt that servi immediately following, æcclesia is synonimous with modern ministri.

CHAP. I. 1065—1272.

The hundred of Calehill comprehended seven [l] villages, or hamlets. Its most valuable district was occupied by the archbishops, and Lanfranc retained Charing, Welles, Pluckley, Little-Chart, and East Lenham, under his immediate jurisdiction. It is remarkable, that the Register of Domesday should not record one church to have been established at the productive [m] manours, either of Charing, or Welles, the occasional residence of the primate, and where numerous [n] ecclesiastics most probably attended him. Whilst at Pevington, a [o] feudal tenure, a [p] church with nine attendants is reported to have been founded, though its value was only estimated at six pounds. For other particulars, the tables may satisfactorily be consulted.

Calehill.

The peculiar hundred of Wye comprehended [q] seven distinct manours or places. But as there is an uncommon entry in Domesday, relative to the jurisdiction of this district, we cannot with propriety omit noticing it, though not certain whether our interpretation will be admitted. It is stated, that "of [r] the

Wye.

[l] CALEHELLE—Cheringes, 3 b 2—Lerham, 4 b 1—Rotinges, 12 a 2—Welle, 5 a 2—Litelcert, 5 a 1—Pluchelei, 3 b 2—Pevintone, 10 b 2. Domes. To these may be added a portion in Pistinges, held by Ralph Crookthorn, of which the particulars are not recorded. See Domes. 10 b 2.

[m] Value 100l. per annum.

[n] 19 servi.

[o] De feudo episcopi baiocensis. 10 b 2.

[p] Æcclesia et 9 servi. Ibid.

[q] WI—Wi, 11 b 2—Boltune, 14 a 1—Darenden, 12 a 1—Esmeresel, 12 a 2—Estwelle, 13 a 1—Manerium, 14 a 2—Manerium, 5 a 2.—These manours were probably Northburg et Gara, for Domesday, 1 a 2, de uno Jugo de Northburg 12d. aut unum Ineward. Et de Gara unum Ineward. Hæ terræ jacent in Wi.

[r] De 22 hundredis pertinentibus isti manerio, saca, et soca, et omnia forisfactura, [* quæ] justè pertinent regi. Domes. 11 b 2.

* Ignorance of the scribe.

twenty-

CHAP. I. 1065—1272. " twenty-two hundreds belonging to this manour, fac and foc, " and all fines juftly appertain to the monarch." [s] Lambarde reports, in his Perambulation, that the Chronicle of Battle-Abbey contains a fimilar Regifter. He endeavours to overcome the difficulty by a fuggeftion, that the lath of Sherwinhope contains an equal number of hundreds, and therefore Wye muft have included the whole of that divifion of Eaft Kent. This folution cannot be admitted, becaufe he includes Boughton, fituated in the Borough-lath, Blackburn, Rovenden, and Tenterden, in Liming-lath; Mylton, itfelf a lath at this æra; and enumerates Barkley, Branfield, and Cranebrooke, in his catalogue, names totally unknown at that period. Yet, with fuch inadmiffible additions, he only reckons nineteen hundreds in this lath, which by fuch well-authorized deductions are reduced to eleven. This extenfion alfo would totally deftroy [t] the oval form of Wye, from which probably it obtained the name. With fubmiffion then we fuggeft the following illuftration.

[u] Manour, in common acceptation, is a lefs general term than hundred, confequently in this paffage muft be ufed in an extraordinary fenfe. " Manour, in its original fignification, comprehended the refident inhabitants of a diftrict, fubjected to the controul of a particular court. But as there were courts of frank pledge, there were likewife baronial courts; as there were inferior manours of a knight, there were fuperior manours of an earl, vifcount, or baron, that controuled the fubordinate. From fuch, and other concurring difficulties, the ignorant fcribes of Domefday were reduced to a dilemma; for

[s] Page 284.

[t] Wi, an egg.

[u] From maneo, to refide upon.—Villani were fixtures at this æra, not capable of changing their abode. Domef. paffim.

if

if they had ſtated that in the lath of Wye there were twenty-two hundreds, the record would have been incorrect, and irrelevant, ſince ſpeaking of a juriſdiction, that extended not even to one-third of the number. If they had ſtated that one manour contained twenty-two manours, they muſt have explained their nature and difference. To avoid this difficulty, and yet render themſelves perfectly intelligible to a County jury, they report that the baronial manour of Wye, which the king transferred not to the abbey of Battle, but retained under the government of his viſcount, comprehended twenty-two [x] inferior juriſdictions, that occaſionally appealed to its court on litigated points, and that the fines ariſing from ſuch controverſies, yielded a revenue of twenty pounds to the proprietor. This entry was intended to diſcriminate between the petty manours that owed immediate ſuit and ſervice to the court of Wye, as the head of the barony, and the extenſive lordſhips, not only in Wye-lath, but in the appropriate hundred of Wye, occupied by peers of the crown, by [y] Odo and [z] Earl Euſtace, Hugh [a] Montfort, and [b] Haimo viſcount. This illuſtration is ſtrongly ſupported by other authorities, by proofs, that the feudal retainer [c] Montfort held diſtricts, that in Edward's time, ſupplied eels to the court of the lord. But as we are exceeding our preſcribed limits, we muſt refer to the tables.

[x] Manour and hundred ſynonimous, according to the Compilers of Domeſday. See Diſſert. on Laws, &c. p. 23.

[y] Montfort tenet unum jugum in Eſtwelle de *feodo* epiſcopi baiocenſis. Domeſ. 13 a 1.

[z] Tenet Boltune (in capite) pro 7 ſolinis. 14 a 1.

[a] Tria juga ſunt infra diviſionem Hugonis (in capite) 13 a 1.

[b] Haimo vicecomes tenet *de rege* unum manerium in Wit hundred. 14 a 2.

[c] De terrâ ſochmannorum. Hugo de Montfort habet duo juga reddentia 300 anguillas et duos ſolidos, et ſacam et ſocam, in T. R. E. reddebant (ipſe et Radulfus de Curbeſpinâ et Adelulfus. Domeſ. 11 b 2.

Longbridge

CHAP. I. 1065—1272. Longbridge. [d] Longbridge hundred probably contained only six hamlets, or manours, yet, as three of them were occupied by different tenants, are twice entered in Domesday, and designated by varying characters, we shall enumerate the nine names in our notes, and map, to avoid misrepresentation. Chenetone must be the Chelmington of [e] Pack, which he states to be the true western philosophical boundary of this county, and which this celebrated Autograph records to have been situated at that period in [f] Burmarsh, which at the present æra is denominated by the general name of Romney Marsh. There was a portion of this manour exempt from land-tax, and villains, consequently yeomen, or farmers, rented some share under the Confessour, from the abbey of St. Austin's, but the principal tenant's name is illegible.—Mersham was annexed to the archbishopric. These two villages were estimated at three times the value of the whole hundred, paid for eleven sowlings out of fourteen and a half, and contained seven-eights of the yeomen. The particulars of that [g] Mersham wrested from St. Martin's, Dover, by Alnod Cilt [h], or Prince, and afterwards occupied by Robert Romney, are not inserted in the Rolls.

Chart. [i] Chart hundred was of small extent, and solely occupied by ecclesiastics. It contained only two hamlets, the place from whence the name is assumed, and a small portion of Ripton. The Tables will furnish such information, as the Autograph of Domesday contains.

[d] LANGABRIGE—Merelesham, 2 a 2, vel Meresham, 3 b 2—Seivetone, 13 a 1, vel Suestone, 14 a 1—Estefort, 13 a 1, vel Essetesford, 13 a 1—Chenetone, 12 b 2—Essella, 13 a 1—Tevegate, 14 a 1.

[e] See Pack's Map of Kent.

[f] Chenetone, in Borchmers, 12 b 2—probably therefore another Chenetone, Kennington Common.

[g] Unum jugum quietum ab omni Scoto regio, 12 b 2.

[h] See History, p. 18.

[i] CERTH—Certh, 5 a 1—Rapentone, 12 a 2.

A SUMMARY

A SUMMARY TABLE OF THE HUNDREDS,

SITUATED IN

WYE LATH,

IN THE

REIGNS OF EDWARD THE CONFESSOUR, AND WILLIAM THE CONQUEROUR;

THEIR VALUE, POPULATION, &c. &c.

Hundreds.	Value under the Confessour. £. s. d.	Value under the Conquerour. £. s. d.	Sowlings.	Number of Villains.	Borderers.	Lords Ploughs.	Villains Ploughs.	Oxen.	Churches.	Ministers, or Retainers.	Fisheries.	Mills.	Salt-pans.	Acres of Meadow.	Hogs.	Thanes, or Knights, under the Confessour.	Knights, or Military Tenants, under the Conquerour.	No Manours.
Feversham	163 11 2	195 12 0	42½	236	118	25	72	238	10	72	7½	9	5	23	355	Siward, Turgis, Lewin, Alnod.	Fulbert, Port, Adam, Ansfrid, Osbern, Fitz-anschil, Fitz-fulbert, De-mare, Fitz-ivo.	20
Felbrough	81 10 0	164 0 0	22	204	46	14	38	160	3	8	2	14		194	197	Alred, Godric, Alnod, Wana, Alward, Leweron, Leweret.	Ansfrid, Fulbert, Athelwold, Montfort, Crookthorn, Wadard.	9
Calehill	75 6 4	146 13 4	22	165					1	50		7		108½	351	Sbern, and Ecclesiastics.	Crookthorn, Godfrey, and William Knight.	7
Wye	124 6 8	164 16 6	19½	215	56	17½	60½	212	4	42	1	8		222	550	Godwin, Frederic, and Ecclesiast.	Montfort, Adam, Crookthorn.	7
Longbridge	28 7 0	42 13 0	14½	79	32	7	31½	89	3	4		5	2	35	70	Brixi bold, 3 Freemen, a Socheman, Wirelm, God.	Maigno, and Ecclesiastics.	6
Chart	15 0 0	31 0 0	3½	38	23	3	22½	55		5		2½	1	38	110	Ecclesiastics.	Ansered.	2
Wye Lath	568 1 2	744 14 10	124	937	275	66½	224½	754	11	181	10½	45½	8	620½	1633	See future general Recapitulation.	See future general Recapitulation.	51

CHAP. I. 1065—1272. Liming-lath

The lath of [a] Liming comprehending ſixteen hundreds and Romney-marſh, completes the extent of Eaſt Kent, and we entertain little doubt relative to the accuracy of the preſumed correſponding ſituation of each hundred in our Map, if we except our modern Marden, to which we have appropriated the Domeſday SVMERDENE. Indeed we have ſtrong preſumptive evidence to fix on this ſcite, ſince in the numerous catalogue of the poſſeſſions of Earl Odo in this Autograph, there is not one place recorded in the four previous folios, or in the ſubſequent entries of his poſſeſſions, that lies not in Eaſt Kent. Since this lath is very irregular in its form, and the reader might otherwiſe find ſome difficulty in accompanying us in our progreſs, we ſhall commence our tour in its ſouth-weſtern quarter, and the mode, in which our Map is engraved, will remove the principal impediments, that might obſtruct his view.

Rovinden.

In viſiting the Wealds of Kent, we muſt not expect to find equal population, agriculture, rural implements of huſbandry, or accommodation for military chieftains. The hundreds in this diſtrict are inferior both in aſſeſſment to the land-tax, and value to their proprietor, to villages or hamlets in the vicinity of Canterbury or Dover; as is ſtrongly exemplified in [b] Rovinden, which conſiſted of a ſmall tract called Dean, or a dingle of wood, adjoining to Belice, a portion of Montfort's barony, and called elſewhere Benindene, or Belice Dene, our modern Beninden.

[a] LINWARTLEST vel LIMENOWART-LEST—Rovinden—S[a]. Mardene—Selebriſt—Blacheborne—Oxenai—Adelouteſbrige—Mareſc de Romenel—Hame—Neucerce—Lanport—Werde—Belicolt vel Briceode—Stret vel Eſtraites—Hen—Fulcheſtan—Stotinges vel Eſtothinges—Moniberge vel Nuniberg vel Honinberg.

[b] Rovinden—Benindene, 11 a 1—et Dena quæ remanſit extra diviſionem Hugonis de Montfort et jacet in Belice. 9 b 2.

Marden

[c] Marden hundred conſiſted of ſix paltry hamlets, without a mill, a church, a fiſhery, or an acre of meadow. The only circumſtance that can excite a comment, relates to a [d] transfer of ten villains, or yeomen, with their chattels, from Richard Fitz-gilbert to Robert Latin, by the Earl of Kent; where it is ſtated that the knight of Odo obtained them by royal authority, or ſanction of the name of the ſovereign, for the biſhop of Baieux probably, as juſticiary of the realm, had deſpoiled a peer of the crown, to gratify a military retainer. CHAP. I. 1065—1272. Marden.

The hundred of Selbrittenden extended not beyond the confines of Newedene, a [e] market town at this early æra, whoſe tolls yielded a conſiderable revenue to the archbiſhop of Canterbury, its proprietor. Biſhops and religious foundations were the general ſuperintendants of traffic and commerce at this period, and when the monarch retained a town under the juriſdiction of his military viſcount, an eccleſiaſtic was appointed to ſuperintend and regulate the ſale, purchaſe, or exchange of the articles expoſed, and ratify the bargain; hence denominated the clerk of the market, which title is ſtill retained to the preſent day. Selbritten-den.

The iſland of [f] Oxney is claſſed among the hundreds, though like many adjoining hamlets, ſo far from containing the number of ſureties or jurymen, the name originally imported, that only nine cottagers, ruſtics of the loweſt deſcription, reſided in the diſtrict; yet ſince a church was eſtabliſhed there, and an [g] exalted Oxney.

[c] Sm. MARDENE — Sm. Mardene—Ticheteſte—Waneſberge—Ece—Maſſeberge Eſmetone. Domeſ. 11 b 1.

[d] Robert Latin de novo dono epiſcopi habet in *manu regis* de Ricardo filio comitis Giſleberti 10 villanos cum tribus carucis et ſilvâ 50 porcorum.
Domeſ. 11 b 1.

[e] Newedene—Mercatum de 40s. 5d. minus. Domſ. 4. a 1.

[f] In Oxenai Hund. Paleſtrei. 10 b 2.

[g] Edwi preſbyter tenuit de rege Edvardo. Domeſ. 10 b 2.

CHAP. I. 1065—1272. prieſt was the occupier under Edward, it might properly perhaps have been denominated a tithing or petty manour, which the ſcribes of the commiſſioners have frequently confounded with hundred in the Record of Domeſday; eſpecially when ſeparated from the adjoining manour by a river or water-courſe. As only one manour is recorded to have exiſted in this hundred, and the national tax is eſtimated at three-fourths of a ſowling, or about 253 ſtatute acres, (not one-twentieth of the diſtrict,) we have great reaſon to preſume, that the cultivated, arable, or meadow land was ſolely or principally aſſeſſed to this contribution.

Aloes-bridge. Aloes-bridge is a hundred of a ſimilar deſcription. But as this and the hundreds of Lamport, Newchurch, and Worth are all included under the general title of Romney Marſh, and ſome places are recorded under that comprehenſive head; to form any tolerable apprehenſion of this diſtrict, the adjoining country muſt be included in our view. There is no hamlet ſpecified by name in this hundred, but the portions are denominated from their extent and proprietors, as Montfort's [h] yoke of land, or from their quality, as a [i] dingle annexed to Tenterden manour. In the former of theſe diviſions, twelve ſockmen continued to reſide, who muſt here be conſidered in the rank of yeomen, dependants of a manorial court; for it is impoſſible that ſo great a number could have received ſuit and ſervice from inferior vaſſals in a confine ſo limited.

Lamport. To the hundred of Lamport fifty [k] burgeſſes appertained in Romney. There were two [l] hamlets independant of the

[h] Ipſe Montfort tenet unum *jugum* in Adeloutesbrige hundred in ipſo Mareſch. Domeſ. 13 a 2.

[i] Dena de manerio Titentone. Ibid. 11 a 1.

[k] See Hiſtory, Romney.

[l] Aſettune, 10 b 2—Midelea, 11 b 1—Lanport, 12 b 2.

place

place whence it was ſo denominated, whoſe names are recorded, and ſome hundreds of acres in the Marſh. In theſe villages [m] ſockmen particularly abounded, and from this circumſtance we are led to infer, that theſe men, probably, ſuperintended the embankments, and acted as jurymen, in aſcertaining the proportionate payments of different proprietors, according to the wiſe regulations of the Saxon Alfred. It is certain that more perſons of this deſcription are found in this neighbourhood, than in the whole county.

Newchurch.

[n] Newchurch hundred was more extenſive, populous, and opulent, and conſiſted of five diſtinct villages or portions. Bliſſington, of which Alnod [o] Cilt, or Prince, was proprictor under the Confeſſour, had wonderfully encreaſed in value; and we muſt preſume that land was not let on long [p] leaſes at this period to the farmer, ſince four eſtimates had been taken in the ſpace of twenty years. This manour had indeed received an [q] addition, but this only conſiſted of three inconſiderable dingles. The occupancy of [r] Eton, a hamlet of Tenterden,

[m] Sex ſochemanni tenuerunt, 11 a 1. et duo ſochemanni, 11 a 1.

[n] NEUCERCE—Bilſuitone, 10 b 2—Etretone, 13 a 1—Rot (preſumed Rotinges) 13 b 2—Mareſc de Romenel, 13 b 2—Fane, 14 a 1.

[o] As this word, written *Child*, has puzzled many commentators on Shakeſpear,

"Child Rowland to the dark Tower came."

LEAR, Act 3d, Sc. 4th.

and many readers of Percy's Reliques of Ancient Poetry; by ſubſtituting Prince, or, at leaſt, the Son of a Noble, they will have a juſt conception of ſuch paſſages.

[p] Tempore regis Edvardi valebat 10 libr. et poſt 30 l. modò 50 l. et tamen reddit 70 l. *de firmâ*. Domeſ. 10 b 2.

[q] In hoc manerium miſit epiſcopus tres denas, quæ remanſerunt extra diviſionem comitis de Ow. Domeſ. 10 b 2.

[r] Etretone, terra appreciatur in Titentone, quia illuc arata eſt, cum dominicis carrucis. 13 a 1.

CHAP. I. 1065—1272. terden, in the days of the Conquerour, (becauſe its land was cultivated by Montfort's ploughs, the baron of the diſtrict,) had been [s] litigated betwixt this feudal lord, and the canons of St. Martin's. In this conteſt the eccleſiaſtics loſt their ſuit, by the verdict of the hundred, the burgeſſes of Dover, the knights of Saint Auguſtine's, and the lath of Eaſtrye. Its former poſſeſſour was proved to have held theſe premiſes by allodial tenure, (though recorded to have been a [t] ſockman) to have had five ſub-tenants, and a *mill* of twenty ſhillings per annum. To this land therefore the military retainer of William was juſtly entitled. But we are not hence to infer that all ſockmen were of this deſcription, for in the diviſion of Romney Marſh appertaining to this hundred, [u] twelve ſuch perſons occupied leſs than one hundred and forty modern acres equally under Edward, and when this Autograph was compiled.

Worth, and Romney Marſh. To the hundred of [x] Worth we ſhall annex thoſe remaining diſtricts in Romney Marſh, which are entered in Domeſday under that general title, though they might have been included in other diviſions. For [y] Hameſland moſt probably appertained to Warehorn, in Hame hundred, ſince the archbiſhop of Canterbury was proprietor of both. But [z] Burmarſh, or that

[s] Hoc teſtatur hundred, et burgenſes de Dovre, et homines abbatis Sancti Auguſtini, et Eſtrea leſt; quod terra Etretone, quam calumniantur canonici Sti. Martini de Dovre ſuper Hugonem de Montfort, quod Ulwile Wilde eam tenuit in Alodio, tempore regis, et defendebat ſe pro uno jugo, et hibi habebat unam carucam in dominio et quinque bordarios cum unâ carucâ, et unum molendinum de viginti ſolidis. 13 a 1.

[t] Tenuit unus ſochemannus. Ibid.

[u] Hugo tenet *dimidium* ſolinum in Mareſch de Romenel, &c. Duodecim ſochemanni *tenuerunt* et *tenent*. 13 a 2.

[x] WERDE, Eſtbrige, 13 a 1—Blachemenſtone, 13 a 1—Burwarmareſc, 12 b 2—Aſmeſlant, 5 a 2—Mareſc, 13 a 2.

[y] Aſmeſlant, 5 a 2.

[z] Burwar-mareſc as Borwar-leſt—Borough-marſh, and Borough-lath—for St. Auſtin's proprietors.

portion

portion of Romney Marſh that belonged to the borough of St. Auguſtine's, was certainly included in Worth diſtrict. [a] Eaſt-church, Blackmanſtone, and a nameleſs adjoining village, were poſſeſſions of the [b] principality, or earldom, of Godwin, under the Saxon dynaſty, and afterwards were included in Montfort's barony, part of which were held by him in demeſne, and others conferred on his military retainers.

Ham.

Ham hundred conſiſted of [c] three hamlets, and varied little from the adjoining diſtricts. While we tranſgreſs not the confines of the Marſh, ſockmen are found in conſiderable numbers under the Confeſſour's reign, for it was neceſſary to encourage this order of men, or the mounds would never have been ſupported againſt the attacks of the ſea and tide. But after quitting this neighbourhood, we ſhall in vain look for this deſcription of perſons, except on extraordinary occaſions.

Byrcholt.

[d] Byrcholt hundred comprehended [e] eight hamlets or inferior manours. But Aldinton was the [f] centre, from which many of the others emanated, and on which they depended.

[a] Eſtbrige, our modern Eaſtchurch, ſince two churches there; Blackmanſtone, from Blacheman, Edwards, tenant.

[b] Alſi tenuit de Comite Godwino. Domeſ. 13 a 1.

[c] Orlaveſtone, 13 b 2—Rochinges, 13 b 2—Werahorne, 5 a 2.

Orlaveſtune 11 ſochemanni tenuerunt. Domeſ. 13 a 2.

[d] BELICOLT, 4 a 1—BILESOLT, 2 a 2—BILISSOLD, 10 b 2—BRICEODE, 11 b 2—BERISOUT, 13 b 2—BERISCOLT, 14 a 1,—various entries of the hundred in Domeſday, by which readers, unacquainted with this Autograph, may form an inadequate idea of the difficulties to be overcome, in appropriating the particular ſcite of places.

[e] Staneſtede, 2 a 2—Aldintone, 4 a 1—St. Martin, 4 a 1—Limes, 4 a 1—Eſtothinges, 4 a 1—Haſtingelai, 11 b 2, & 14 a 1—Breburne, 13 b 2—Aldeloſe, 10 b 2.

[f] De eodem manerio tenet Comes de Ow Eſtothinges pro uno manerio—De ipſo manerio Aldinton jacet in Limes—Sanctus Martinus jacet in ipſo hundredo, 4 a 1.

Stowting,

CHAP. I. 1065—1272. Stowting, Limpne, and St. Martin's were branches from this ſtem, and numerous burgeſſes in Romney and Canterbury ſprung from its [g] root. This conſequently appertained to the barony of the archbiſhop, and in the language of that age was the head of the manour, the ſeat of wiſdom and power, that directed and controuled the other members.—The diſtrict of Haſtingligh, which Alnod ſolely poſſeſſed under the Confeſſour, was parcelled to the [h] feudal chieftains Odo and Montfort, tenants of the crown, who portioned it to their inferior military retainers. [i] Godric's Braborne was ſplit in a ſimilar manner by theſe powerful chieftains, and the village ſo denominated formed a portion of Eaſtwell, Hugh's barony, in Wye-lath and hundred, and the remainder was added to the earldom of the biſhop of Baieux.

Hen. The burgeſſes appertaining to the hundred of [k] Hen have already been enumerated in our deſcription of Hythe. Saltwood was an appropriate manour of the archbiſhop's, but as Montfort occupied the other moiety, the primate delegated to him the cuſtody of this diſtrict, ſo that the whole hundred was under government and ſuperintendance. For particulars we refer to our tables.

Stowting. In the hundred of [l] Stowting, which conſiſted of four hamlets, no circumſtance is recorded which merits particular ob-

[g] Quater viginti et quinque burgenſes in Romenel qui pertinent ad Aldintone, et 7 burgenſes in Canturaia, 4 a 1.

[h] De feudo epiſcopi—et Hugo de Montſort tenet aliam partem intra diviſionem ſuam, 11 b 2.

[i] Godric de Burnes tenuit de rege Edvardo Breburne et pro 7 ſolins ſe defendebat tunc, et modo pro 5½ ſolinis & dimidio jugo, quia alia pars eſt extra diviſionem Hugonis et eam tenet epiſcopus baiocenſis, 13 b 2—et eſt de feudo epiſcopi Aldeloſe, 10 b 2.

[k] HEN—Poſtinges, 13 a 2—Belice, 13 a 2—Saltcode, et Heda, 4 b 1.

[l] ESTOTHINGES—Bocheland, 9 b 2—Hortone, 13 b 1—Hortun, 13 b 1—Bodeſham, 12 b 2.

ſervation,

ſervation, which may not eaſily be known from an examination of the places arranged in alphabetical order, or the value of hundreds and therefore we ſhall not miſapply our time, through the formality of entering into detail on each diſtrict.

Stret.

The hundred of Stret was compoſed of nine [m] hamlets. Under the Norman government, Hugh Montfort was the lord paramount of the diſtrict, and engroſſed, in his diviſion, the various poſſeſſions of Siward, the viſcount of Edward, Alred the bold, Norman, and Alnod, with the poſſeſſions of their ſub-tenants, for two freeholders, of a ſuperior order, are found in this hundred. Excluſive of the two [n] eccleſiaſtical demeſnes of the canons of St. Auſtin's and the archbiſhop, every moiety appertained to this feudal baron, who parcelled it amongſt his military retainers, and Nigell his phyſician. No village is remarkably conſpicuous in this precinct, either for population, agriculture, or opulence, nor is there any circumſtance requiring particular obſervation.

Loningboro' Hundred.

The hundred of [o] Loningborough was compoſed of four manours, under the Confeſſour, but the two ſmalleſt had been conſolidated by the biſhop of Baieux, and preſented, as a portion of his barony, to a military retainer. Liming was populous and productive, was under the immediate juriſdiction of the primate, though three feudal knights poſſeſſed contiguous hamlets with inferior [p] courts; Alham was retained in the do-

[m] Stret vel Estraites—Stanetdeſte, 2 a 2—Berewice, 4 b 1—Sedlinges, 13 b 1—Siborne, 13 b 1—Suanetone, 13 b 2—Aia, 13 b 2—Bonintone, 13 b 2—Obtrepole, 14 a 1—Eſtraites, 13 b 1

[n] Sanetdeſte et Berewic.

[o] Moniberg, 4 a 1, Honinberg, 9 b 2, Nuniberg, 11 b 2—Leminges, 4 a 1—Alham, 9 b 2—Acres, 11 b 2.—The hundred is only thrice recorded, yet ſpelt three different ways.

[p] 2 Molini et 2 Æccleſiæ, 4 a 1.—We preſume infallible criterions.

main

CHAP. I. 1065—1272. main of the Earl of Kent; and [q] Acryſe, which two brothers had occupied, with ſeparate halls, was transferred, as a united manour, to Anſchitil of Roſs.

Folkſtone. The hundred of [r] Folkſtone conſiſted of many diſtinct villages, or hamlets, though their names are not recorded in Domeſday. Earl Godwin was the proprietor under the Saxon government, and yeomen or ruſtics [s] held extenſive diſtricts under his patronage or protection. The half-brother of William ſucceeded to the barony, and [t] governed the diſtrict by D'arcey, his deputy, though [u] ten military retainers occupied extenſive premiſes in various proportions, from three thouſand to one hundred and twenty acres, and had ſubordinate dependants to cultivate their grounds, erect their houſes, and ſupply neceſſaries to their halls or manſions. The [x] churches, in the demeſne of the lord paramount paid conſiderable tithes, or contributions, to the archbiſhop of Canterbury; though there is no proof of his cuſtomary right to demand and receive, in Kent, thoſe exceſſive exactions, which prevailed in the county of [y] Suſſex.

[q] Acres quod tenuerunt duo fratres, et quiſque habuit Haulam, modo eſt pro uno manerio. 11 b 2.

[r] Fulcheſtan.

[s] 9 ſolins de terrâ villanorum, 9 b 1.

[t] Quod habet in dominio valet 100 libras ibid.

[u] Hugo filius Willelmi, 9 ſolins—Walter de Appeile, 3 juga et 12 acras—Alured, 1 ſolin—Walterus filius Engelberti, ½ ſol. et 40 acras—Weſman, 1 ſol.—Alured Dapifer, ½ ſolin—Eado, ½ ſolin—Bernard de Sto. Audoeno, 4 ſol.—Baldric, ½ ſolin—Ricard, 58 acras terra. 9 b 1.

[x] Ibi 5 æccleſiæ, de quibus habet archiepiſcopus, 55s. Domeſ. 9 b 1.

[y] Every *ſeventh* pig of the ruſtics.—Archiepiſcopus de herbagio habet unum porcum de unoquoque villano, qui habet ſeptem porcos. Similiter per totum Sudſex. Domeſ. 16 b 1.

A SUMMARY TABLE OF THE HUNDREDS,

SITUATED IN

LIMING LATH,

IN THE

REIGNS OF EDWARD THE CONFESSOUR, AND WILLIAM THE CONQUEROUR;

THEIR VALUE, POPULATION, &c. &c.

Hundreds.	Value under the Confessour. £.	s.	d.	Value under the Conquerour. £.	s.	d.	Sowlings.	Number of Villains.	Borderers.	Lords Ploughs.	Villains Ploughs.	Oxen.	Churches.	Ministers, or Retainers.	Fisheries.	Mills.	Salt-pans.	Acres of Meadow.	Hogs.	Thanes, or Knights, under the Confessour.	Knights, or Military Tenants, under the Conquerour.	N° Manours.
Rovinden	2	10	0	3	0	0	½	6	9	1	2	8	1						5	Siward.	Adam Fitz-hubert, R. Romney.	2
Smarden	6	5	0	3	10	0	2	12	10	1	3½	11		2					50	Edric, Tochi, Siward, Godwin	Rob. Latin, Fitz-gilbert, Turstin, Osbern.	5
Selbrittenden	5	0	0	18	10	0	1	25	4		5	10								Archbishop.	Steward or Clerk of the Market.	1
Blackburn	21	10	0	30	2	6	42½	69	82	7	24½	77	1	10	9			40	46	Archbp. Norman, 11 Sockmen.	Montfort, Harold, 5 Sock. Canons.	5
Oxney	2	0	0	3	0	0	½		9	1	½	5	1	2	5			10	10	Edwi, Priest.	Osbern Paistforeire.	1
Aloesbridge	4	5	0	4	5	0	¼	13	11	½	2½	7			2					14 Sockmen	Montfort, Romney.	3
Lamport	26	19	0	33	0	0	6	78	30	6½	25½	77	1	2	1		7	20	12	Godric, Alsi, of Godwin, 8 Sockm.	Romney, Alured, St. Austin's.	5
Newchurch	34	17	0	96	17	0	6	59	78	15	21	102	1	1	2	1	10	10	50	Alnod Cilt, Ul. Wilde, 18 Sockm.	Montfort, Harold, Earl Bishop.	5
Worth & Marsh	39	8	0	61	8	0	6	69	54	10	23	90	3	1	9		9		3	Alsi, Athelelm, 17 Sockmen.	Hervey, Bertram, Roger, Robert, and Folet.	5
Ham	6	10	0	8	10	0	2½	33	12	3	5½	23	3		6			22	13	Leuret, 11 Sockmen.	William, Ralph, Fitz-Richard.	3
Byrcholt	117	19	10	159	9	10	33½	296	145	25	96	292	3	40	3	11		232	109	Alnod, Godric, Ecclesiastics	Ralph, Earl of Eu, Fitz-anschill, Osbert, &c.	9
Hen	29	0	0	47	1	4	11	52	43	5	17	54	3	2		12		81	120	Sbern, Alred, Turgis.	Montfort, Crookthorn.	4
Stowting	9	10	0	11	0	0	1⅛	19	13	4	8	32	1			2		44	18	Lewin, 5 Sockmen	Ansfrid, Fitz-richard, Alnod.	4
Stret	39	11	8	46	1	8	8⅛	60	83	12	19	86	6	17		2		113	39	Siward, Norman, Alred, Alnod.	Wm. of Edesham, Hervey, Nigell, Mandeville, Cock.	9
Loningborough	56	0	0	124	0	0	16	167	45	15½	79½	221	5	19	1	5		98	221	Ederic, 2 Thanes, Brothers.	Archbp. Earl Bp. Anschill of Ross	3
Falcheftan	110	0	0	145	10	0	58½	246	142	28½	65	244	8	3		11	1	128	42	Earl Godwin	D'arcey, Fitz-William, 9 Knights.	1
LIMING LATH	511	5	6	795	5	4	162	1204	770	135	309¼	1379	37	99	38	44	27	798	738	See future general Recapitulation.	See future general Recapitulation.	65

CHAP. I. 1065—1272.

For the cuſtoms and regulations that prevailed in Eaſt-Kent, we refer the reader to our future general recapitulation, where we ſhall comprehenſively review both diviſions of the county, with their tenants in capite, knights, and military retainers; their laws, ſines, for violation of the peace, infringement on the royal roads, or rivers, burglary, and other particular circumſtances. We now proceed with our ſurvey of Weſt-Kent, according to the principles adopted, and having previouſly deſcribed the ſtate of the city of Rocheſter, ſhall purſue our former plan, beginning with Greenwich hundred, in the lath of Sutton, and the north-weſternly diſtrict; and continue our route in a ſouth-eaſternly direction.

Rocheſter.

The city of Rocheſter, like Canterbury, and the boroughs of this county, contained a number of inhabitants, honoured with the title of burgeſſes, that had emigrated from the manours of their feudal lords, and continued under their power and patronage. This city was ſo [a] inconſiderable, of itſelf, in the days of the Confeſſour, that it was only eſtimated at the ſmall ſum of five pounds. It was principally occupied by eighty dependants of the biſhop, from the manour of Frindſbury, whoſe value was calculated with that diſtrict. But * ſubordinate

[a] Civitas Roveceſtre tempore regis Edvardi valebat 100 s. 2 a 1.

In Roveceſtre habuit epiſcopus et habet adhuc quater viginti manſuras terræ quæ pertinent ad Frandeſberie & Borcſtele propria ejus maneria. 5 b 2.

* Ad manerium Tarent pertinent 5 burgenſes in Roveceſtre, 3 a 1—Epiſcopus tenet in ſua manu—intra civitatem Roveceſtre quatuor domus ad hoc manerium (Ledeſdune) pertinentes, 7 b 1—In Oſeham una domus in civitate Roveceſtre, 7 b 1—habuit epiſcopus (Baiocenſis) tres Domos de 31 d. quas cepit de iſto manerio (Aigleſſa) in ſua manu, 7 a 2—Huic manerio Alnoitone adjacent tres manſiones terræ in Roveceſtre, 8 a 1—Huic Manerio (Hov) pertinebant 9 domus in Roveceſtre civitate, nunc ablatæ ſunt, 8 b 1—Huic manerio (Otringberge) adjacent 4 hagæ in civitate, 8 b 2—In manu ſuâ retinuit epiſcopus (Baiocenſis) in civitate Roveceſtre tres hagas de Celcâ manerio, 9 a 1—ad hoc manerium (Mildetone) hagæ in Roveceſtre pertinent, 14 b 1.

vaſſals,

CHAP. I 1065—1272.

vaſſals, or their ſons, had fixed their reſidence here, by the permiſſion of their lord from Darent, Oſham, Ludſdown, Aylesford, Norton, Hoo, Watringbury, Chalk, and Mylton. In the reign of the Conquerour its population and value were ſo much augmented, that, when the biſhop received it into his cuſtody, though the eſtimate was only ſtated at twenty pounds, his clerk of the market rendered him twice the ſum. Lanfranc became proprietor of the burgeſſes that appertained to the preceding archbiſhop; Odo, Earl of Kent, in transferring theſe hamlets to his feudal knights, principally retained the manſions annexed to the manours of Edward and Godwin in his own poſſeſſion; and Albert, the chancellor, ſucceeded to Eddiva's houſes, as parcel of her manour of Mylton. The number of resident burgeſſes reported, amount to one hundred and fourteen, and in delivering the rental of the city, we include not the valuable Roculf of the primate, which will be included in the hundred of Rocheſter.

Sutton Lath

The lath of [b] Sutton comprehended only five hundreds, Greenwich, Bromley, Litelai or Leſnes, Axtane, Helmſtrei or Rokeſley, Therham or Weſterham. We ſhall commence our deſcription with the modern Blackheath hundred.

Greenwich.

The hundred of [c] Greenwich comprehended ſeven diſtinct hamlets in the reign of Edward, under more numerous juriſdictions; for the place, whence the name was aſſumed, was divided into two [d] manours, analogous to our Eaſt and Weſt-

[b] SUDTONE-LEST—Grenviz—Bronlei—Litelai—Helmſtrei—Therham vel Oſtreham.

[c] GRENVIZ—Grenviz, 6 b 2—Lee, 6 b 2—Cerletone, 6 b 2—Alteham, 6 b 2—Witenemers, 6 b 2—Leveſham, 12 b 2—Hulviz, 14 a 2.

[d] Hi duo ſolini (in Grenviz) tempore regis Edvardi fuerunt duo maneria. Unum tenuit Heraldus Comes, et aliud Brixi, et modo ſunt in uno.

CHAP. I. 1065—1272. Greenwich, and [a] Charlton had two courts controuled by two brothers.

To Greenwich occupied by the bishop of Lisieux, as subtenant of the brother of the Conquerour, * two sowlings, adjoining to Deptford, then denominated Mereton, or the Town of the Marshes, in the hundred of Brixton, and included under its manorial jurisdiction, as part of the county of Surrey, in the days of the Confessour, and early part of William's reign, were annexed by the Earl to his principality of Kent. This fact was clearly proved by the testimony of the impannelled evidence of the jury of the district. When this military retainer was summoned to account for this infringement, or invasion, on the † royal demesne, he appealed to his feudal chieftain as his protector, who had guaranteed the possession to him. The commissioners then cited the bailiff of the bishop of Baieux to prove by what title, such lands were seized by him, and conveyed to his lord's vassal: but so great was the independant power and authority of Odo, and the general peers of the monarch, that his deputy refused to plead before this court, and considered himself superior to their controul. William probably overlooked this incroachment, and deemed such a trifling possession of too inconsiderable importance, for which to cite Odo before the high national council. Hence, probably the knight of this Norman noble continued to enjoy the district without farther molestation.

[a] Hanc terram tenuerunt de rege duo fratres pro duobus maneriis, Godwin & Alward, 6 b2.

* Episcopus Lisoiensis tenet in *Chent* [in *Meretone* in *Brixistan Hundred* in *Comitatu* de *Sudrie*] duos solinos qui huic manerio (Meretone) adjacuerunt tempore Regis Edvardi et *Regis Willelmi*, sicut testantur homines de hundred. Ipse reclamat advocatorem episcopum baiocensem, et præpositus suus *inde noluit placitare*. Domes. 30 a 2.

† *Ipse Rex tenuit.* 30 a 2.

To

To the whole of this hundred, except Lewisham and Woolwich, Odo, Earl of Kent, succeeded, as peer of the realm. He consolidated the divided manours, and presented five [f] of his Norman retainers to an equal number of villages. Lewisham [g] was possessed by the abbot of Ghent, in Flanders, not only under the government of William, but in the reign of the Confessour. This circumstance proves a considerable intercourse with the Continent under the Saxon monarchy, and the productive [h] customs of the port evince that the trade with the Netherlands was considerable, for abbots were the greatest merchants at this period, though the ships that navigated this river must have been of diminutive burthen. In this manour [i] eleven mills were erected, which, with some portions of land cultivated by rustics, and held by gavel-kind tenure, nearly [k] doubled the rental in twenty years. It is remarkable that not one church is entered in Domesday, as appertaining to this hundred, though a number of Servi are recorded, who certainly were either ministers of religion, or persons, superior to yeomen, that acted as squires to military chieftains, or held in petty serjeantry, on the condition of performing domestic offices to their lord. Woolwich, at this æra, was a poor village, where only the lowest class of [l] countrymen resided. Haimo the viscount succeeded to this portion of William's, the falconer, an officer of high honour and dignity with our Saxon ancestors. But such remarks infringe on our

[f] See Summary Table of Hundreds.

[g] Abbas de Gand tenet de rege Levesham, et de rege Edvardo *tenuit*. 12 b 2.

[h] De exitu Portus, 40 s. Ibid.

[i] 11 molini cum *gablo* rusticorum (50 villanorum et 9 bordarium) reddunt, 8l. 12s. 12 b 2.

[k] Tempore reg. Ed. 16l. et post 12l. modo 30l. Ibid.

[l] 11 bordarii reddentes 41 d.

intended

CHAP. I. 1065—1272. intended Dissertations, on Ranks and Services, Manners and Customs.

Litelai. The hundred of [m] Litelai, or Lesnes, was composed of the place so named, Erith, Hou, or Hall-Place, and the ecclesiastical and laical moieties of Plumstead. Odo, Earl of Kent, occupied the whole district, except the possessions of the archbishop and St. Augustine's; Latin and Ansgot were his subtenants; and the abbot was invested with another feudal portion, as an appendage to the manour of the abbey. It was not remarkable for extent, population, particular customs, or circumstances.

Bromley. [n] Bromley hundred was of still less dimensions, and inferior value. Beckenham, and the village whence it assumes the denomination, compleated its district. Anschil was the Saxon Thane, that controuled its jurisdiction, though his power extended [o] beyond its confines. The Tables will furnish the recorded information.

Rokesley. The hundred of [p] Helmstrei, our modern Rokesley, comprehended fourteen places, distinguished, either by name, or as a portion of different manours. Boxley and Orpington were annexed to the archbishopric, and were by far the most [q] populous districts, were best furnished with implements of hus-

[m] LITELAI—Loisnes, 6 b 1—Erhede, 3 a 2—Hou, 6 b 1—Plumestede, 6 b 1 et Plumstede, 12 a 1.

[n] BRONLEI—Bronlei, 5 b 1—Bacheham, 7 a 1.

[o] He held Witenemers, in Grenviz, 6 b 2.

[p] HELMSTREI—Bix, 3 a 1—Orpintun, 4 b 2—Rochelei, 6 b 1—Ciresfel, 6 b 1—Suderai, 6 b 1—Craie, 6 b 2—Craie alia, 6 b 2—Crai, 6 b 2—Wicheham, 6 b 1—Lafela, 6 b 2—Croctune, 7 a 1—Codeham, 7 a 1—Chestan, 7 a 1—Sentlinge, 7 a 1.

[q] 86 villains, 40 borderers, 37 ploughs, 82 oxen, 150 pigs, 6 mills, yielding 3l. 4s. 4d. three churches, &c.

bandry,

bandry, ſtored with proviſions for the eccleſiaſtics, and ſupplied by the moſt valuable mills. With the exception of theſe manours, a [r] moiety appertaining to the Lowy of Tunbridge, and a part [s] annexed probably by William to the royal foreſt, Odo poſſeſſed the entire hundred, and diſtributed the whole to his martial followers, not retaining even one manour under his immediate domain. Two Crays, that were of [t] ſeparate juriſdiction under the Saxon government, and held by different tenants from the Prince Alnod, and Edward, were conſolidated by the uterine brother of the Conquerour, and preſented, as one manour, to Anſchitill of Roſs, a knight inveſted with extenſive [u] poſſeſſions by him in the adjoining hundreds, and remarkable for [x] uniting his manours.

Axtane.

In the hundred of Axtane, ſuch numerous circumſtances occur, that merit the attention of the hiſtorian and antiquary, that we cannot but enter into conſiderable detail. It comprized, at leaſt, twenty-four places with different appellations, that were divided into more numerous diſtricts, and occupied, as [y] thirty-ſix diſtinct manours, or hamlets, by thanes or eccleſiaſtics,

[r] De Laſela Ricardus de Tonebridge tenet in ſua Leuga, quod appreciatur 6 l. Domeſ. 6 b 2.

[s] Quod rex tenet de hoc manerio (Laſela) valet 22 d.

[t] Hæ duæ terræ fuerunt duo maneria tempore regis Edvardi et modo ſunt in uno manerio. Alwin tenuit de Alnod Cilt, et Leuric tenuit de rege Edvardo. Domeſ. 6 b 2.

[u] Tarent, Hortune, Croctune, Elentun, Oſeham, Hou.

[x] He formed the four manours of Horton and Darent into one, as well as the the two of Acryſe. Vid. 6 b 2 et 10 b 2.

[y] ACHESTAN—Tarent, 3 a 1—Tarent, 6 a 2—Tarent alia, 6 a 2—Otcfort, 3 a 1—Sondreſſe, 3 a 1—Tarenteſort, 2 b 2—Hagelei, 2 b 2—Hagelei, 6 a 1—Forningeham, 4 a 2—Ferlingeham, 6 a 2—Ferningeham, 6 a 2—Ferningeham alia, 6 a 2—Elesford, 4 a 2—Orpinton, 4 a 2—Bricſted, 4 a 2—Olecumbe, 4 a 2—Sudfleta, 5 b 2—Eſtanes, 5 b 2—Facheſham, 5 b 2—Langaſel, 5 b 2.

ſiaſtics, under the government of Edward, by military retainers, dignified clergymen, or [z] favoured Saxons, in the reign of William. Dartford, though eſtimated remarkably low [a] to the national land-tax, was the moſt valuable poſſeſſion in the circuit. It was retained under the immediate juriſdiction of the crown equally by Edward, and William, who committed it to the cuſtody of their viſcounts, Siward and Haimo. Under the Saxon adminiſtration, the [b] Mayor of London had obtained conſiderable diſtricts from the deputy of the monarch, which were ſecured to Helto, his nephew and heir, by the Norman Conquerour, though the evidence of the hundred clearly eſtabliſhed this [c] apparently fraudulent tranſaction, and their connection with this manour, as a ſubordinate and dependant hamlet. Another [d] moiety had been alienated from the crown, by bribery, or a fine, to its officer. But, notwithſtanding ſuch diſmemberment, the rental increaſed, and the Norman ſub-tenant of the ſheriff rendered it more productive to its proprietor.—The examiners of the Autograph of Domeſday, who have accuſtomed themſelves to conſider

5 b 2—Suineſcamp, 6 a 1—Erclei, 6 a 1—Eddintone, 6 a 1—Mapledeſcam, 6 a 1—Malpleſcamp, 6 a 2—Redlege, 6 a 1—Eiſſe, 6 a 1—Didele, 6 a 1—Soninges, 6 a 1—Lolingeſtone, 6 a 1—Lolingeſtone, 6 a 2—Lolingeſtone alia, 6 a 2—Pinnendene, 6 a 2—Hortune, 6 a 1—Hortune alia, 6 a 1—Hortune tertia, 6 a 1.

[z] Helto, Uluret, et duo homines in Didele et Soninges, &c. Domeſ. 6 a 1.

[a] Tarentefort pro $1\frac{1}{2}$ ſol. Oteſort pro 8 ſol. Elesfort, Sudfleta et Eſtane pro 6 ſol. ſingul.

[b] Homines de hundredo teſtificantur, quod de iſto manerio regis ablatum eſt unum pratum, et unum Alnetum, et unum Molendinum et viginti acræ terræ, &c. dicunt autem quod Oſward tunc vicecomes præſtitite Aleſtan Præpoſito Lundoniæ, et modò tenet Helt Dapiſer et Nepos ejus. 2 b 1.

[c] See Hiſtory of Shammel hundred.

[d] Oſward vicecomes poſuit extra manerium per quoddam Vadimonium quadraginta ſolidorum. 2 b 1.

ſowlings,

fowlings, as an established and certain extent of land, will never be able to reconcile the diminutive [d] proportion of land, appertaining to the assessment of Dartford, with the immense number of [e] yeomen, rustics, and ploughs recorded to have existed in its confines. But this subject we shall fully discuss in our intended Dissertation on Agriculture. The [f] churches of this royal manour belonged to the bishop of Rochester, and yielded him a considerable revenue. This place was classed in the number of sea-ports at this æra, and had two havens, or harbours. CHAP. I. 1065—1272.

In this division of West-Kent, the archbishop of Canterbury possessed numerous and populous manours. Otford was in his immediate jurisdiction, yet three Saxon [g] thanes continued to hold extensive and [h] valuable premises in the district, with subordinate manorial rights, mills, yeomen, and rustics. Earl Fitz-gilbert's Lowy extended also to this barony of the primate's; but we shall reserve Tunbridge division, for a separate discussion, and distinct valuation. Sundrish and Darent were included likewise in the domain of the archbishop; Farningham, Aynesford, Orpington, Combe, and Brasted were occupied by his military retainers. Many manours in this hundred were dependant on the Earl of Kent, as peer of the realm, and subject to his baronial court. Swanscombe was held, on such conditions, by a nephew of [i] Alstan, the Mayor of London,

[d] 1½ fowlings.

[e] 142 villani, 10 bordarii, 52 carrucæ. Domesf. 2 b 2.

[f] Æcclesiam hujus manerii tenet episcopus de Rovecestre, et valet 60 s. extra hanc sunt adhuc ibi tres æcclesiolæ. 2 b 1.

[g] De hoc manerio tenent tres teigni 1½ folin, et ibi habent in *dominio* tres Carrucas, et 16 villanos cum 11 bordariis. 3 a 1.

[h] Appreciatur dominium Teighorum 12 l. Ibid.

[i] Osward viscecomes præstitit ea *Alestan* Præposito Lundoniæ, et modò tenet *Helto* Dapifer et Nepos ejus. Domesf. 2 b 1.

CHAP. I. 1065—1272. under the Saxon government, who continued to poſſeſs a [k] hall, or ſeat of juſtice, for the confines of his manour, had a [l] knight, ten attendants, and a port, or haven, within his diſtrict. Other Engliſhmen continued to enjoy the cuſtomary privileges of their order in this [m] neighbourhood. Ulred, though occupying a very ſmall territory in Halley, is clearly, and decidedly, ſtated to have been independant of every Norman knight or chieftain, and to be reſponſible to no other lord but the ſovereign of the realm. Adjoining to Aſhchurch, two other [n] freemen ſtill occupied their Saxon lands, were claſſed among the [o] *higher ranks*, though like many [p] Norman knights connected with the juriſdiction or court of a ſuperior vaſſal. South-fleet, Stone, Facombe, and Long-field were annexed to the biſhopric of Rocheſter, and yielded a revenue of ſixty pounds. There were conſiderable diſtricts in Lullingſton, Forningham, and Darent, which were preſented to [q] William, by the Earl of Kent, moſt probably for the enlargement of the royal foreſts.

Weſterham. Therham or Weſterham hundred completed the lath of Sutton, except the portions poſſeſſed by Richard of Tunbridge.

[k] Sexta Piſcaria quæ ſervit ad Hallam, 6 a 1—et de Sylvâ hujus manerii. Ib.

[l] Ibi unus miles et decem ſervi. 6 a 1.

[m] In hoc manerium tenet unus homo *viginti acras* terræ valentes per ann. 5s. Uluret vocatur, nec pertinet ad illud manerium, neque potuit habere *dominum* præter regem. 6 a 1.

[n] Præter hoc habet Hugo (de Port) duos homines tenentes dimidium ſolinum qui poterant, tempore regis Edvardi *ire quolibet ſine licentia*, 6 a 1. The criterion of freedom, for villains wandering beyond the limits of the manour, were *vagabonds*.

[o] Homines knights.

[p] In Eiſſe (the ſame manour) quidem miles habens 8 inter ſervos et Ancillas. Domeſ. 6 a 1.

[q] Rex habet de iſſo manerio (Tarent) pro *novo dono* epiſcopi—et Rex habet de ſilvâ hujus manerii (Ferningeham) quod valet 8s.—et Rex habet in manu ſuâ quod valet 10s. de Lolingeſtone, 6 a 1, et 6 a 2.

The

The [1] village of this name, and one other hamlet, are the only places whose value is recorded in this Autograph, or of which particulars are transmitted to us. In this portion of Kent, there was a wood appertaining to a manour in Surrey, which the monarch held under his immediate domain. This district was situated in the neighbourhood of Westerham, and may perhaps be termed the [2] Town in the Wealds, the Woldingham of the present day, which at that æra was a royal forest. The reader, in the progress of this work, will meet with frequent instances of hamlets, or inferior jurisdictions, that appertained to baronial manours, where the head of the barony was seated in a different county, of districts in [3] Hampshire connected with Sussex, in Hertfordshire with Essex.

CHAP. I. 1065—1272.

[1] OISTREHAM—Oistreham, 14 a 1—Scape, 4 b 1.

[2] Rex tenet in dominio Waletone [in *Waleton hundred* in *comitatu* de *Sudrie*] ibi Sylva, quæ est in *Chent*. Domesday, 30 a 2.

[3] Some of these districts were of considerable extent, as will be shewn in our future History of the respective Counties; which information it would be irregular and improper to anticipate in the county of Kent.

A SUMMARY

A SUMMARY TABLE OF THE HUNDREDS,

SITUATED IN

SUTTON LATH,

IN THE

REIGNS OF EDWARD THE CONFESSOUR, AND WILLIAM THE CONQUEROUR;

THEIR VALUE, POPULATION, &c. &c.

Hundreds.	Value under the Confessour.			Value under the Conquerour.			Sowlings.	Number of Villains.	Borderers.	Lords Ploughs.	Villains Ploughs.	Oxen.	Churches.	Ministers, or Retainers.	Fisheries.	Mills.	Salt-pans.	Acres of Meadow.	Hogs.	Thanes, or Knights, under the Confessour.	Knights, or Military Tenants, under the Conquerour.	N° Manours.
	£.	s.	d.	£.	s.	d.																
Greenwich	58	0	0	82	0	0	8½	151	41	11	39	122		21		15		131	140	Harold, Brixi, Alwin, Godwin, Anschil, Alwi the bald, Abbot of Ghent, William the Falconer.	Bishop of Lisieux, Walter of Douay, William Fitz-oger, Haimo Viscount, and Fitz-tyrald, of Rochester, Earl's Subtenants; Abbot of Ghent and Haimo, as Peers.	7
Lesnes	55	0	0	81	8	3	19½	126	14	6	44½	93	1	9	2	3		52	73	Archbishop, Azor, Anschil, Brixi Cilt.	Robert Latin, Ansgot of Rochester, Abbot of St. Austin's, of Odo.	4
Bromley	21	10	0	33	18	0	8	52	34	4	19½	55		4		2		14	160	Bishop of Rochester, Anschil.	Bishop of Rochester, Ansgot.	2
Rokesley	139	0	0	182	10	0	27½	249	90	24	80	256	7	58	1	13		78	319	Alward, Tochi, Toli, Godric, Brixi Cilt, Leuric, Godwin, Alwin, Sbern, of Edward—Alwin, of Alnod Cilt—Bonde, of Archbp.	Malger, Arnulph, of Hastings, Adam Fitz-hubert, Geoffrey, Anschitil of Ross, Fitz-oger, Gil. Maminot, H. Fitz-herbert.	14
Axtane	242	1	0	471	19	6	65½	589	195	58½	221	676	13	116	7	30½		476	671	Edward, Archbishop, Bishop of Rochester, Alnod, Brixi, Siward, Eustan, Alred, Ulstan, Ording, Godel, Helto, a Female.	Fitz-unspac, Hugh Port, Malger, Earl of Eu, Ansgot, Fitz-hubert, Osbern, Wadard, Arnulph, Anschitill, Helton.	36
Westerham	31	10	0	45	0	0	4½	42	9	3	30	72		14		1		16	100	Earl Godwin.	Earl Eustace, Godfrey Steward.	2
SUTTON LATH	547	1	0	896	15	9	133½	1209	383	106½	434	1274	21	232	11	64½		767	1463	See future general Recapitulation.	See future general Recapitulation.	65

The lath of Aylesford comprehended [a] twelve hundreds, and a considerable diftrict in Fitz-gilbert's Lowy of Tunbridge. We fhall continue our route through it, according to the eftablifhed order, commencing with the north-weftern divifion. CHAP. I. 1065—1272. Aylesford-Lath.

In the hundred of [b] Toltingtrow, Meopham and North-fleet were occupied by the archbifhop and his monks, and, like other ecclefiaftical poffeffions, were, comparatively [c] productive, populous, and well cultivated, abounding with cattle, and fupplied by a fifhery and mill. Thefe manours were more valuable than the four villages of Gravefend, Mylton, Ludfdown, and Nutftead, which Earl Lewin, and military tenants, occupied under the Saxon government, and were transferred to the Earl of Kent and his feudal dependants. [d] Gravefend was a port at this æra, but certainly independant of the city of London; it poffeffed three feparate jurifdictions in the reign of Edward, but thefe manours were confolidated under the Norman monarch, and its cuftody committed to Fitz-ivo, a knight of the bifhop of Baieux's. Toltingtrow

Shammel hundred comprehended [e] fourteen diftricts, either held as different hamlets or manours, or with various pro- Shammel.

[a] Elesford-lest.—Tollentreu—Effamele—Ceteham—Hov—Broteham—Laurochesfel—Roveceftre—Meddeftane—Haiborne—Litefel—Wachelftan—Tuiferde—et Leuga de Tonebrige.

[b] Tollentreu.—Norfluet, 3 a 2—Mepeham, 4 b 2—Melcftune, 7 b 1—Ledefdune, 7 b 1—Gravefham, 7 b 1—Noteftede, 7 b 1.

[c] Eftimated at 53 l. 10s.—16 fowlings—61 villains—71 borderers—41 ploughs 24 minifters or retainers, &c. For the whole hundred fee the Table.

[d] Ibi æcclefia et una *Heda*. Hoc manerium fuerunt [fuit] tria maneria tempore regis Evardi, Lewric et Ulwin et Godwin tenuerunt. Nunc eft in unum. Domef. 7 b 1.

[e] Essamele.—Clive, 4 b 2—Clive alia, 9 a 1—Cocteftane, 5 b 2—Danitone, 5 b 2—Hallinges, 5 b 2—Frandefberie—Celca, 8 b 2—Hecham, 9 a 1—Colinge, 9 a 1—Colinges alia, 9 a 1—Arclei, 9 a 1—Hanehcft, 9 a 1—Hadone, 9 a 1—Meleftune, 9 a 1.

prictors

CHAP. I. 1065—1272. prietors or fub-tenants, when Domefday was compiled. Frindbury, Halling, Cuckftone, and Denton were annexed to the bifhopric of Rochefter, Cliff to the metropolitan fee, and thefe five hamlets exceeded in [f] value, population, and agriculture the other villages in the hundred of which the Earl of Kent was the baronial poffeffor. If the extent of the ecclefiaftical property of this diocefe had not been much diminifhed, and its property feized for the accommodation of [g] Earl Fitzgilbert's Lowy, the difference would have been confiderably greater; for the affeffed eftimate of arable land was reduced from twenty fowlings of the Saxon computation to eleven in the reign of William. The burgeffes appertaining to the manour of Frindbury have already been noticed in our account of Rochefter [h].—The geographical reader that has previoufly perufed our introductory Explanation, infpected the Map, or examined the fummary Tables, muft have immediately noticed that the portion of land in Effex, generally delineated within the original boundaries of this county, is far removed from its accuftomed fcite. As fome perfons may attempt to controvert this point, it may be neceffary to enter more fully into the queftion, and attempt to produce fatisfactory evidence for fuch pofition.

The land afcribed to the county of Kent, fituated on the northern fide of the Thames, is decifively ftated, to have been in the tenancy of William Peverell, under the Norman monarchy. When we examine the Records of Domefday for the county of Effex, we find immenfe poffeffions occupied by this

[f] Rental 75 l. 5 s.—96 villains—64 borderers—40 ploughs—5 churches—130 acres, &c. For the hundred fee the table.

[g] See Lowy of Tunbridge. Quod Richardus tenet in fua Leuga valet 7 s. et 10 s. &c. 5 b 2.

[h] See Hiftory.

feudal

feudal chieftain, not only as peer, and joint lord, with Robert Greno, but as [i] ſub-tenant to the biſhop of London, in Barnſtaple hundred, on the concave ſhore to Chalk and Higham, but in Hame [k], a portion of Becontree hundred, oppoſite to Woolwich. Both theſe diſtricts were held by [l] Aleſtan, under the Saxon government. Hence, it is more reaſonable to preſume, that tradition, (attending only to general information, and tranſmitted reports, that a certain moiety in Eſſex appertained to ſuch noble, and lay in the county of Kent) might more probably err, as to its ſcite, than that [m] two Records, in this authentic Autograph, collected from the contemporary evidence of impannelled juries of hundreds, and ſanctioned by the authority of a ſhire-mote, could have been unwittingly admitted, or ungroundedly inſerted. That [n] Chalk and Higham have their proper deſignation and place, no reader of intelligence will be inclined to deny; and that perſon muſt be little

CHAP. I. 1065—1272.

[i] Hundred de Bardeſtapla. Terræ Ranulfi Piperelli. In Buratenet Serlo tenet de Ranulfo unam * Hidam quod tenuit *Aleſtan* liber homo. Little Domeſ. folio 71 b. fol. 34. tenet in capite.

De hoc manerio (Legenduna in Berdeſtapla) tenet Radulfus de epiſcopo. Ibid. 9 b 1.

[k] Hund. de Beventreu. Hame tenet Robertus in dominio, &c. De hoc manerio habet Ranulfus Piperellus † Medietatem, et in *dominio* Roberti *rectum*. Little Domeſday, 64 a—et Hame tenet Ranulfus in dominio quod tenuit *Aleſtan* liber homo tempore regis Edvardi, &c. De hoc manerio habet Robertus Greno Medietatem. Lit. Dom. 72 b.

[l] Vide ſupra.

[m] Two entries Chalk and Higham.

[n] Celca, et Hecham.

* This Hide is interlineated, having been omitted in the original Report; and an Ulſtan, here ſtated as its former poſſeſſor, occupied lands adjoining to Higham from Earl Lewin, whoſe tenant is not ſtated in the Survey of Kent, therefore probably the ſame perſon.

† They held in peerage, and could each proſecute their claim even in the *domain* of each other.

converſant

CHAP. I. 1065—1272. converſant with the topographical hiſtory of Saxon ages, when a military array was eſſentially neceſſary for the protection of property againſt lawleſs invaders, that can ſuppoſe a diſtrict, twenty miles diſtant from the caſtle of its feudal protector, and ſituated on a navigable river, could be an appendage to the manour of a minor thane. From ſuch, and other collateral conſiderations, we entertain little doubt that this [o] Aleſtan was the Mayor of London, deputy of the Biſhop, and the Superior of the cathedral of St. Paul's, for theſe, like other [p] dignified eccleſiaſtics, ſuperintended all commercial connections in the city, had the cuſtody of the courſe of the river Thames, and were [q] general proprietors of the land recovered from the encroachments of the ſea and tide. On this principle, we can eaſily account for that [r] diſtrict in Dartford manour, in the hundred of Axtane, which had been gained from the royal demeſne. Its ſituation was low, alders were there cultivated, and a mill erected in it. Siward the ſheriff had transferred it, according to the evidence of the hundred, to Aleſtan, the bailiff of London, and probably accordingly to the eſtabliſhed

[o] Aleſtan *Præpoſito* Lundoniæ. Domeſday, 1 b 2.

[p] Archbiſhop of Canterbury, Biſhop of Cheſter, &c. &c. See Hiſtory, and Domeſ. 262 b.

[q] Hoc * manerium dedit Willielmus rex Willielmo epiſcopo propterea quod *mare tranſivit*, quia in antiquo tempore fuit de *æccleſia Sancti Pauli*.

Little Domeſday, 10 b. a.

[r] Homines de hundred teſtificantur, quod de iſto manerio regis ablatum eſt unum *Pratum*, et unum *Alnetum*, et unum *Molendinum*, &c. Dicunt autem quod *Oſward* tunc vicecomes *præſtitit* ea *Aleſtan* Præpoſitio Lundoniæ, et modò tenet Helto *Dapifer* et Nepos ejus, Domeſ. 2 b 1.

* WARLEY, in the hundred of CHALFORD, in Eſſex, at this period overflowed by the ſea, and *therefore* committed to the cuſtody of William, *Biſhop* of London, *Conſerver* of the banks of the Thames, holding poſſeſſions in Barnſtaple, Chalford, and Becontree hundreds, in Eſſex, (of which Ralph Peverell was one of his ſub-tenants,) lord of the manours of Stepney and Fulham, in Middleſex. See Hiſt. of thoſe counties.

cuſtoms

cuſtoms of the age, ſince Helto, the nephew of Aleſtan, and ſteward [*] (moſt likely to the biſhop of London, and having ſuch tenancy continued to him becauſe an eccleſiaſtic) was ſtill permitted to hold it without moleſtation, when the Autograph of Domeſday was compiled. This may be that moiety aſcribed to Kent, on the northern ſhore of the Thames, at the preſent day, for the juriſdiction of Dartford was extenſive, and ſuperintended by the [s] viſcount. Having entered ſo largely in detail relative to this ſubject, we ſhall only briefly ſtate, that the diſtricts not previouſly deſcribed in this hundred appertained ſolely to the Earl of Kent. CHAP. I. 1065—1272.

In the hundred of [t] Chatham the archbiſhop of Canterbury, and Earl Godwin, were ſole proprietors under the Saxon government, to whoſe property Lanfranc and Odo ſucceeded in the reign of William. Gillingham, the diſtrict of the primate, was in his immediate domain, though a [u] Norman knight was inveſted with a moiety of the manour. Chatham was farmed by Robert Latin, a powerful military retainer of the biſhop of Baieux, and a [x] religious foundation, and numerous eccleſiaſtics eſtabliſhed there. The [y] value of theſe eſtates had been doubled Chatham.

[*] Helto *Dapifer.*

[s] Super hæc reddit præpoſitus vicecomiti 100s. Domeſday, 2 b 1.

[t] CETEHAM.—Gelingeham, 3 b 1—Gelingeham, 8 a 2—Ceteham, 8 b 2. Domeſday.

[u] De hoc manerio tenet quidam Francigena terram ad unam Carrucam et ibi habet duos bordarios. Quod tenet Francigena valet 40s. Domeſ. 3 b 1.

[x] Æccleſia et 15 ſervi. 8 b 1.

[y] Tempore regis Edvardi et poſt valuit (Ceteham) 12l. modo 15l. et tamen reddit 35l. Domeſ. 8 b 1. Ceteham in totis Valentiis, T. R. E. valuit hoc manerium 15l. quando recepit 12l. et modo 23l. et tamen reddit 26l.—12d. [*] minus. 3 b 1.

[*] Twelve pence leſs, or loſt, Leſan, a Saxon mode of computation, or payment, ſtill prevailing in the midland counties, where in *bargains* money is frequently agreed to be returned, and a certain proof that Saxons compiled the Survey, reckoning always Æn læſ twentig—Twa læſ twentig.

in

CHAP. I. 1065—1272. in a less space than twenty years, if we make our estimate from the raised rental, or actual payment.

Rochester. [a] Rochester hundred consisted of only four places distinguished by names, but comprizing six hamlets. The district of the archbishop comprehending the suburbs of Rochester, and the two villages of Norton, were [a] five times more valuable than the other part of the hundred, and were proportionally populous, well cultivated, and [b] civilized. The tables will supply the recorded information, that may be deemed worthy of attention, relative to [c] Bostle, annexed to the bishopric of Rochester, and the manours of Godric and Siward, transferred to the Earl Odo.

Hoo. In the hundred of [d] Hoo two places only were designated by distinctly appropriate titles, though containing several separate hamlets of powerful military vassals. To this district, Earl Godwin's baronial residence, particularly denominated the [e] hall, had most probably given such appellation. This Saxon noble occupied the whole hundred in the reign of Edward, but a subordinate [f] manour was claimed by the bishop of Rochester, from Odo Earl of Kent, that succeeded to such possessions in

[a] ROVECESTRE vel ROCULF.—Roculf, 3 b 1—Nortone, 3 b 1—Nortone Vitalis, 3 b 1—Delce, 8 b 1—Delce Ansgot, 8 b 1.

[a] Rental 108l. 7s. 8d. estimated at 24½ sowlings, with 182 yeomen, 94 cottagers, 96 ploughs.

[b] Three churches.

[c] Borchtelle.

[d] Hov—Estoches, 5 b 2—Stoches, 8 b 1—Hou, 8 b 1.

[e] Hou. Sometimes reported, Haia, Halla, Hame; hence our modern *the* Hough, Hawe, termination of a surname, Hall, Home.

[f] Hoc manerium fuit et est de episcopatu Rofensi, sed Godwinus Comes tempore regis Edvardi emit illud de duobus hominibus, qui eum [id] tenebant de episcopo, et eo ignorante facta est hæc Venditio—Postmodum verò regnante Willielmo rege diratiocinavit illud Lanfrancus archiepiscopus contra baiocensem episcopum, et inde est modo saisita Rofensis æcclesia. Domes. 5 b 2.

the

the reign of [g] William, as an appendage of the fee. These pretensions were grounded on the adduced evidence, that this land had been purchased by Earl Godwin, from two tenants of the bishopric, who had conveyed such premises to him, when they were vassals and dependants, not freemen or chief proprietors. In consequence of this testimony of the hundred or county jury, Lanfranc recovered this portion from the powerful Odo, restored it as an appendage to the diocesan chair, and annexed it to the cathedral of Rochester. Hoo was the [h] head of the barony, where subordinate retainers attended the court of their lord, and the litigations or controversies of inferior jurisdictions were determined. If the manour of the bishop of Rochester had not been subjected to the superior tribunal, though its immediate proprietor was a peer of the realm, it is impossible that such an error could have taken place, relative to the proper occupancy of the district of Stoake. To this feudal division nine houses in Rochester appertained, and three Norman chieftains held particular moieties of the district, and had [i] knights in their train of followers, the controulers of petty courts.

Wrotham.

The hundred of [k] Wrotham was confined to the precincts of the district of similar denomination. The archbishop was its proprietor, and four feudal chieftains occupied considerable

[g] Though agreeable to received usage William is frequently called the Conquerour in this history, we believe there is not a single authority throughout the whole Autograph of Domesday to countenance such a title, for it is uniformly stated post quam rex *venit* in Angliam, since the king arrived in England.

[h] TOTUM manerium tempore regis Edvardi valebat 60l. quando episcopus (Baiocensis) recepit similiter, et modo tantundem, et tamen qui eum [id] tenet reddit 113l.—Huic manerio pertinebant 9 domus in Roveceftre Civitate.

Domes. 8 b 1.

[i] Ibi habet unus *homo* ejus in *dominio*. 8 b 1.

[k] BROTEHAM, 3 a 2.

premises,

CHAP. I. 1065—1272. premiſes, within his manour, the value and population of which are included in the general value of the hundred, delivered in the table of this lath, except the moiety annexed to Tunbridge Lowy, which is reſerved for a ſeparate diſcuſſion.

Larkfield. The hundred of [l] Larkfield comprehended twenty diſtricts, poſſeſſed by different occupiers, and nearly as numerous denominations. But there was no [m] manour eminently conſpicuous for its opulence or population; and Aylesford, which William retained in his own cuſtody and controuled by his viſcount, was far leſs productive [n] to him, than his three other towns, or villages, of Mylton, Dartford, or Feverſham. Four, out of the eleven, baronial tenants of the crown occupied lands in this hundred; Lanfranc of Canterbury, the Biſhop of Rocheſter, the Earl of Kent, and Richard Fitz-gilbert of Tunbridge. The [o] manorial territory of Aylesford extended nearly to Rocheſter, and the biſhop of that ſee here occupied a moiety of land in exchange for that diſtrict where a caſtle had been erected.—[p] Woldham, Trotiſcliff, Snodeland, and one of the Mallings, were parts of the demeſne of the dioceſe. Each had its church and miniſters, and there were four mills under ſuch juriſdiction in the hundred, and ſome [q] houſes in Boreham,

[l] Laurochesfel.—Elesford, 2 b 1—Aigleſſa, 7 a 2—Metlinges, 3 a 2—Mellingetes, 5 b 2—Toteſclive, 5 b 1—Totintune, 7 a 2—Eſnoiland, 5 b 1—Oldeham, 5 b 1—Leleburne, 7 a 1—Elentun, 7 a 1—Dictune, 7 a 1—Siffletone, 7 a 1—Pelleſorde, 7 a 2—Rieſc, 7 a 2—Oſeham, 7 a 2—Oſeham, 7 b 1—Eſſedene, 7 a 2—Eddintune, 7 a 2—Berlinge, 7 b 1—Borham, 7 b 1.

[m] Malling of the archbiſhop moſt valuable, 15l. per ann. (Aylesford excepted.)

[n] Aylesford, 31 l.—Mylton, 200l.—Dartford, 80l. 11 s.—Feverſham, 80l.

[o] De hoc manerio tenet Anſgot *juxta* Roveceſtre tantum terræ, quod appreciatur 7l.—Epiſcopus etiam de Roveceſtre pro Excambio terræ in qua Caſtellum ſedet.

[p] Oldeham, Toteſclive, Eſnoiland, et Mellingetes ipſe epiſcopus tenet.

Domeſ. 5 b 1.

[q] Epiſcopus de Roveceſtre habet domos de hoc manerio et valent 7s.

Domeſ. 7 b 1.

a hamlet

a hamlet of Crookthorn's, a dependant of the Earl of Kent.—The royal foreſt of William had been enlarged in this neighbourhood, by conſiderable portions of [r] Leyborne, Ayles, and Peckham, which are ſtated as a new donation of his uterine brother. The remaining diſtricts appertained to Odo and Fitz-gilbert, whoſe knights may eaſily be aſcertained by a reference to the Tables. Crookthorn occupied Berling, which Sbern, the commiſſary of Edward, enjoyed, where was ſufficient paſture for [s] fifty animals, whether horſes or oxen, antiquaries may diſagree, probably the former, ſince occupied by the royal proveditor.

Maidſtone.

[t] The hundred of Maidſtone was formed of ſeven hamlets or manours. The place from whence it aſſumed the name was occupied in demeſne by the Primate; though three of his military retainers [u] occupied nearly one half of the diſtrict, and the accuſtomed ſuite of dependants, a mill, fiſhery, and ſalt-works. Salt, at this period, muſt have been an article of the firſt neceſſity, and importance, when ſuch eſtabliſhments for its preparation were formed on the banks of a river, at ſo great a diſtance from the ocean, and where the ſaline quality of the ſea muſt have been much reduced, by the union of freſh-water. The [x] monks of Canterbury had two clients in the manour,

[r] Rex tenet pro novo dono epiſcopi (in *Leleburne*) quod valet 24 s. Dom. 7 a 1—Rex 8 s. 5 d. pro novo dono epiſcopi in *Aigleſſa*, 7 a 2—Rex habet de manerio (*Pecheham* in Litefelle hundredo) tres *Denas*, 7 b 2.

[s] Paſtura 50 animalibus, 7 b 1.

[t] MEDDESTANE—Meddeſtane, 3 a 2—Pinnedene, 6 a 2—Bermelie, 8 b 2—Boſeleu, 8 b 2—Litelbrotcham, 8 b 2—Bichlei, 9 a 1—Bermelinge, 14 a 2.

[u] De hoc manerio tenent de archiepiſcopo tres milites quatuor ſolinos, et ibi habent 3½ carrucas in dominio, et 32 villanos cum 10 bordariis habentes 6 carrucas et 10 ſervos, &c. et 2 ſalinas. Domeſ. 3 a 2.

[x] Monachi Cantuarienſes habent omni anno de duobus hominibus hujus manerii 20 s. Domeſ. ibid.

who

CHAP. I. 1065—1272. who held by gavel-kind tenure. Farley also was a district of the metropolitan see, which the archbishop retained in his domain, though the produce was appropriated probably to the support of the monastic foundation of the Holy Trinity.— These villages, for Farley was then divided, are ranged amongst those places, which prior historians have attributed to the monks, as tenants in capite, but the Primate was doubtless their [y] lord, as the lord of his knights, and the *peer* of the realm, for no monk had a seat in the *high* national assembly. To corroborate this assertion, the twenty different places enumerated amongst their possessions, are [z] *all* held by Lanfranc, as *principal* tenant, and from him [a] Odo Earl of Kent, [b] Richard of Tunbridge, and [c] feudal [d] military retainers have inferior moieties. That he was the general patron of this foundation cannot but be admitted, and that he was the president of the baronial court, where appeals from their petty jurisdictions were terminated, will not, we believe, be denied.—But to resume our more immediate subject—[e] Farley was populous and well cultivated, abounded with mills, fisheries, and bacons, and was occupied by two [f] subordinate tenants, independant of Fitz-gilbert's district. Boxley was by far the most valuable

[y] Terra monachorum archiepiscopi, 4 b 2. Terra militum ejus, 4 b 1.

[z] See future recapitulation.

[a] Hunc solinum (in Horlingeborde) tenet episcopus biocensis de archiepiscopo ad gablum, 4 b 2.

[b] De eodem manerio (Pecheham) tenet Ricardus de Tonebrige—*recepit* archiepiscopus, 4 b 2.

[c] De terrâ hujus manerii (Ferlaga) tenet Godefrid in *feuo*, 4 b 2.

[d] De manerio (Edesham) tenent duo milites, 5 a 2.

[e] Great Farley, or the archbishop's Farley, had 91 rustics, 3 mills, 6 fisheries, 115 hogs, &c.

[f] Quod Abel modo tenet 6l.—quod Godefrid 9l.—quod Ricardus in sua leuga 4l. 4 b 2.

manour

manour that the Earl of Kent poſſeſſed in this hundred. CHAP. I. 1065—1272.
Robert Latin was the ſubordinate tenant, but what may appear extraordinary to ſome readers of our antient Hiſtory, [g] Helto, a *Saxon*, occupied an inferior portion, having a [h] *Norman* his domeſtic and dependant.

The hundred of Eyhorne was conſtituted of [i] twenty-two hamlets, or manours, though ſince many of them are contained in the eighth folio of Domeſday, where not one hundred is ſtated, we are leſs certain in our ſcite, than in any other diſtrict. [k] Hollingborne and Lenham, the property of Lanfranc, and the abbot of St. Auſtin's, were the moſt valuable villages, whether you conſider their population, rental, or agriculture. At [l] Leeds a church was founded, where eighteen eccleſiaſtics reſided, and a moiety of land was transferred to the abbey, for the portion of Lenham that Odo had encloſed in his park. Here vines were cultivated, and five mills were occupied by ruſtics, probably in gavel-kind tenure. The Tables will convey particular information. Eyhorne.

[g] Helto, Nepos Aleſtan Præpoſiti Lundoniæ. Vid. ſupra.

[h] De hoc manerio tenet Helto dimidium ſolinum et ibi habet unam carrucam cum uno bordario et unam *Francigenam*, &c. Domeſ. 8 b 2.

[i] HAIBORNE vel AIHORDE—Boltone, 4 a 2—Hoilingborde, 4 b 2—Harriardeſham, 7 b 2—Fereburne, 7 b 2—Fereburne alia, 8 a 1—Seleſburne, 7 b 2—Fredeneſtede, 7 b 2—Eſledes, 7 b 2—Audintone, 7 b 2—Stochingberge, 7 b 2—Alnoitone, 7 b 2—Sudtone, 8 a 1—Sudtone alia, 8 a 1—Certh, 8 a 1—Bogelei, 8 a 1—Merlea, 8 a 1—Languelei, 8 a 1—Otringdene, 8 a 1—Oteham, 8 a 1—Brunſelle, 8 a 1—Lertham, 12 a 1.

[k] Hoilingeborde, 61 villani, 16 bordarii, 25 carrucæ, duo molendini, et valet 30l. 4 b 2.—in Lertham, 40 villani et 7 bordarii, 18 carrucæ, 2 molendini et valet 28l. 12 a 1.

[l] Eſledes ibi æccleſia et 18 ſervi, ibi duo arpendi vineæ et 5 molini villanorum. Domeſ. 7 b 2.

Litcfield

CHAP. I. 1065—1272. Litefield.

[m] Litefield hundred consisted only of five hamlets. The Pechams were divided at this early æra, one appertained to the church of the Holy Trinity; the other belonged to a laical possessor. In the district of the archbishop, a freeholder resided, who was totally independant of the manour, except as connected with it in the payment of the national [n] land-tax. The royal forest extended to this district; and in the [o] Stockbury of this hundred, two freemen continued to reside in the subordinate district of Fitz-tyrald. The circumstantial Records may be found in the Tables.

Watliston, and Lowy of Tunbridge.

Since Watliston hundred consisted only of one recorded manour, Tudely, and this was occupied by Fitz-gilbert, we shall class its value with the Lowy of Tunbridge, in our summary Table of this lath. Richard occupied a moiety of twenty-four [p] manours, independant of [q] Birling and Yalding, which he held as peer of the realm. This land principally consisted of woods, or dingles, on the skirt of the district, and

[m] LITEFELLE—Pecheham, 4 b 2—Pecheham alia, 7 b 1—Haslow, 7 b 2—Estochingeberge, 7 b 2—Marourde, 14 a 2.

[n] De terra hujus manerii tenet unus homo archiepiscopi dimidium solinum, et cum his sex solins (de Pecheham) geldabat tempore regis Edvardi, quis [qui] non pertineret manerio nisi de * *Scoto*, quia libera terra erat. Domes. 4 b 2.

Rex habet de manerio tres denas [de Pecheham.] 7 b 1.

[o] In Estochinberge tempore regis Edvardi tenuerunt duo liberi homines et *modo similiter*. Ibid.

[p] WACHELESTAN et LEUGA de TONEBRIGE.—Tivedele, 7 b 2—Broteham, 3 a 2—Otefort, 4 a 1—Elesfort, 4 a 2—Norfluet, 3 a 2—Forningeham et Ferlingeham, 4 a 2—Pecheham, 4 b 2—Mepeham, 4 b 2—Ferlaga, 4 b 2—Hallinges, 5 b 2—Frandesberie, 5 b 2—Sudfleta, 5 b 1—Suinescamp, 6 a 1—Eisse, 6 a 1—Redlege, 6 a 1—Lasela, 6 b 2—Leleburne, 7 a 1—Aiglessa, 7 a 2—Meletune, 7 b 1—Ledesdune, 7 b 1—Ofeham, 7 b 1—Litelbroteham, 8 b 2 Colinge, 9 a 1.

[q] Bermelinge et Hallinges, 14 a 2. See alphabetical Table.

* Schot. Tribute.

the

the amazing extent of his chaſe may be tolerably aſcertained, by a reference to the places annexed, and examining their ſcite, in our Map. But as the whole of ſuch poſſeſſions are only eſtimated at two ſowlings and a quarter, it ſtrongly corroborates our opinion, that land in a ſtate of [r] agriculture was ſolely aſſeſſed to the national contribution. CHAP. I. 1065—1272.

The hundred of [s] Twyford, comprehending nine hamlets, completes the lath of Aylesford. There is little remarkable in this diſtrict but what may eaſily be known from the Tables. Two [t] hamlets indeed had houſes in Rocheſter, and the manour of [u] Yalding had been devaſtated, at leaſt deprived of its cattle, and its value conſiderably reduced, an extraordinary circumſtance in this county. Twyford.

[r] See Diſſertation on Agriculture.

[s] TUIFERDE, Pinpa, 8 b 1—[t] Neteſtede, 8 b 2—[t] Otringeberge, 8 b 2—Otrinberge alia, 8 b 2—Teſtan, 8 b 2—Haintone, 13 a 1—Hallinges, 14 a 2.

[u] Hallinges tempore regis Edvardi, et poſt valuit 30l. modo 20l. eo quod terra vaſtata eſt a * pecuniâ. Domeſday, 14 a 1.

* Value of all articles eſtimated from cattle.

A SUMMARY TABLE OF THE HUNDREDS,

SITUATED IN

AYLESFORD LATH,

IN THE REIGNS OF EDWARD THE CONFESSOUR, AND WILLIAM THE CONQUEROUR;

THEIR VALUE, POPULATION, &c. &c.

Hundreds.	Value under the Confessour.	Value under the Conquerour.	Sowlings.	Number of Villains.	Borderers.	Lords Ploughs.	Villains Ploughs.	Oxen.	Churches.	Ministers, or Retainers.	Fisheries.	Mills.	Salt-pans.	Acres of Meadow.	Hogs.	Thanes, or Knights, under the Confessour.	Knights, or Military Tenants, under the Conquerour.	N° Manours.
	£. s. d.	£. s. d.																
Toltingtrow	49 10 0	73 10 0	24½	103	89	11	43	130	6	52	1	2		39½	53	Archbp. Lewin, Leuric, Ulwin, Godwin, Ulstan.	Archbp. Fitz-tydald, H. Fitz-ivo, and Wadard, of Earl Bishop.	7
Sharnmel	61 0 0	122 15 0	37½	162	84	25	41½	183	7	51	1	4	Sheep 300	240	35	Godwin, Fitz-dudeman, Toli, Ulwin, Hennes, Alric, Odric, Siward, Goa, Wluard Wit.	R. Peverell, Fitz-tyrald, Ansgot of Rochester, A. Fitz-hubert, Arnulph of Hastings, Odo, Helto.	14
Chatham	29 0 0	55 19 0	12½	75	28	8	25½	83	2	19	9	2		56	20	Archbishop, Godwin.	Archbp. Earl Odo, Odo Knight, Robert Latin.	3
Rochester	52 5 0	128 17 8	28½	194	99	16	91½	247	3	110	1	3	12	177	71	Archbp. Bp. of Rochester, Godric, Siward.	Archbp. Bp. Rochester, Odo, Fitz-tahon, Ansgot, Archdea. Vital.	6
Hou	79 11 8	138 6 8	60½	116	92	9½	51	140	7	21	3	1		36	50	Earl Godwin.	Bp. Rochester, Earl Odo, [illegible]-gilb. Anschitile, Fitz-hubert, [illegible] Knt.	4
Wroteham	15 0 0	46 0 0	8	90	31	8	18½	69	1	20		3		9	500	Archbishop.	Archbp. Wm. Boteler, Geoffrey, Farman, Fitz-gilbert, Knights.	
Larkfield	90 0 0	167 6 4	48½	261	127	33	73	278	13	99	3	17½	Anim 50	329	355	Archbp. Bp. of Rochester, Lewin, Ulwin, Alnod, Godwin, Sbern, Alred, Ulric, Godric, Turgis.	Bp. Rochest. Odo, Haimo, [illegible]chitile, Vital, Fitz-tyrald, H. Port, Colville, Crookth. Latin, Ansgot.	20
Maidstone	63 1 0	144 5 6	31½	162	112	21	87½	259	2	58	10	17	2	77	372	Archbishop, Alnod, Godwin, Edwin, Lewin, Alred, Ulwin.	Archbp. Odo, Fitz-gilbert, Subtenants, Odo, Colville, Latin, Helto, Fitz-tyrald, Fitz-[illegible]. &c.	7
Eyhorne	161 5 0	199 10 0	45½	297	126	27	82½	273	16	124		15		94½	495	Archbishop, St. Austin's, Lewin, Godwin, Elveva, Alnod, Alwin, Siward, Sbern, Turgis, Lewenot.	Archbp. Abbot St. Austin's, Earl Odo, Earl of [illegible], Fitz-tyrald, Fitz-herbert, Ar[illegible]rold, Ansgot, Geoffrey, C[illegible]n, Port, &c.	22
Litefield	67 0 0	76 0 0	16½	105	52	8	34½	101	3	35	14	5		41	140	Arbp. Lewin, Eddeva, 2 Freemen.	Archbp. Fitz-[illegible]. Fitz-tydald, &c.	6
Watliston, and Lowy of Tonbr.		49 5 5	2½	7		14		56	1		1	1			122	Eddeva, Archbp. Bp. Rochester, Godric, Turgis, Alnod, Ulric.	Richard Fitz-gilbert of Tunbridge, Earl of Clare.	23
Twyford	58 6 0	56 10 0	12½	63	49	12½	20	90	5	51	6½	9		36	240	Godric, Leveva, Godil, Alnod. Norman, Edward, Aldret.	Fitz-gilbert, Haimo, Fitz-hubert, Colville, Montfort, Athelw. &c.	9
Aylesford Lath	725 18 8	1258 5 7	328½	1635	889	193	568½	1907	66	520	49½	49½	14	1135	2453	See future general Recapitulation.	See future general Recapitulation.	121

The lath of [a] Mylton extended only to the hundred fo denominated, though itfelf divided into two parts under the Saxon government, one moiety of which was under the immediate controul of the vifcount, as the officer of Edward, another, as the fuper-intendant of the Queen Eddiva. The diftrict occupied by the Confeffour devolved to William, and Haimo his fheriff had the cuftody of it. It was the moft [b] populous and valuable manour of the county, fupplied by numerous and productive [c] fifheries and falt-works. The fheriff had a [d] mayor or bailiff that acted as his deputy, collected the [e] tolls, received the [f] fines from the inhabitants of the Weald, when exempted from military or vaffal fervice, and rendered a handfome [g] prefent to his fuperior for the fituation. The [h] tithes and churches of this manour were annexed to the abbey of St. Auftin's, and if we may eftimate the produce of the hundred, from the payment of the royal domain, were immenfely [i] productive. We referve for our future Differtation on Weights and Mea-

[a] MIDDELTUNE LEST—in dimidio Left de Middletone in Mildetone hundredo—Tuneftelle, 9 a 1—Cerce, 9 a 1—Stepedone, 9 a 1—Middeltune, 2 b 1—et Newetone in dimidio Left de Mildetone, 14 b 1.

[b] In hoc manerio trecenti et novem villani et feptuaginta quatuor bordarii. Valebat 200l. ad *numerum*. Domef. 2 b 1.

[c] Salinæ et 32 Pifcariæ.

[d] Same denomination as the Mayor of London, Præpofitus Lundoniæ, Præpofitus Tarentefort, Præpofitus Middeltune dat Vice-comiti 12l. Domef. 2 b 1 et 2 b 2. Præpofitus Abbatis Sti. Ædmundi. Domef. 275—b 2—et quidam Præpofitus de Abbate nec potuit recedere. Domef. 58 b 2. Of the rank of villains, nor did the Mayor of London occupy one acre of ground in Middlefex, Surrey, Effex, or Hertfordfhire, under the Saxon government, as chief proprietor.

[e] De Theloneo 40s. 2 b 2.

[f] Homines de Walt reddunt 50s. pro Inenardis et Averis. 2 b 2.

[g] 12l.

[h] Æcclefias et decimas hujus manerii tenet Abbatia Sti. Auguftini, et 40s. de quatuor folinos regis exeunt ei. Domef. 2 b 2.

[i] 44l. per ann. 10s. per folin.

CHAP. I. ſures, the proportionate value between [k] money in tale, and
1065— ſilver weighed and refined, though we curſorily may remark,
1272. that William improved the coinage, at leaſt [k] one fifth, by diminiſhing the alloy, or augmenting the weight.—The other half lath of Mylton, which we preſume to have been ſituated in our modern Iſle of Sheppey, appertained to the [l] dower of Queen Eddiva, and was held by [m] Siward the viſcount of Edward, and immediate tenant of every diſtrict in the [n] hundred.

We are not ignorant that Queenborough was peculiarly inveſted with chartered immunities, as a borough, by Edward the third, perhaps in compliment to his queen Philippa, but as Eddiva was the [o] founder of the place, it might be ſo denominated from the conſort of the Confeſſour. In this diſtrict alone of the whole county [p] dairy-agriculture is reported to have flouriſhed. Twenty-eight weys of cheeſe appertained to Newton by eſtabliſhed cuſtom, from the royal manour of Mylton, and from nine ſowlings in that moiety of the hundred a ſtill [q] greater quantity with a gavel-kind rental of fifty-eight ſhillings. Here we could clearly prove that gavel-kind tenure

[k] Tempore regis Edvardi valebat 200 l. ad numerum, et tantundem quando Haimo Vicecomes recepit et *modo* ſimiliter—qui tenet reddit 140 l. ad ignem et ad penſam et inſuper 15 l. 6s. 2d. ad numerum.

[l] Sidgar tenuit de Regina Eddid. 14 b r.

[m] *Oſward* tenet Tuneſtelle, Stepedone, et Tangas, 9 a r, et Vicecomes Edvardi, 2 b r, but a different jury here reporting to the Commiſſioners it is entered—*Sidgar*—ſame leading Conſonants—S. R. D.

[n] Hundred and Lath here ſynonimous.

[o] Newetone—New-town.

[p] De manerio Mildentone redditur in Newetone una conſuetudo, id eſt 28 penſæ caſeorum; et de 28 ſolins de Mildentone pertinet in Newetone 10l. 10s. et de aliâ parte de novem ſolins de Middetone pertinet in Neutone [q] 28½ penſæ caſeorum,

tenure was subject to the late French[r] corvè, an occupancy, notwithstanding, far superior to that of villains, did we not hereby infringe on our arranged Dissertations. Albert the chancellor was tenant in chief of this district, in the reign of William, from whose manour, the archbishop, Geoffrey of Rochester, and Adam Fitz-hubert had considerable portions. CHAP. I. 1065—1272.

Having now surveyed every lath, city, and borough of the county, we shall present their state at one view, including the lath of Mylton not separately reported.

caseorum, et 58 s. de gablo ex his novem solins, et de *his* novem solinis reddebat * *Sigar apud Mildetone* [r] Averam. Domesf. 14 b 1.

* Consequently *Osward* the tenant and occupier of them.

A SUMMARY

A

SUMMARY TABLE

OF THE

LATHS, CITIES, AND *BOROUGHS,*

IN THE

COUNTY OF KENT,

THEIR VALUE, POPULATION, &c. &c.

LATHS, CITIES, and BOROUGHS.	Value under the Confessour.			Value under the Conquerour.			Sowlings.	Burgesses or Mariners.	Villains.	Borderers.	Lords Ploughs.	Villains Ploughs.	Oxen.	Churches.	Ministers or Retainers.	Fisheries.	Mills.	Salt-pans.	Acres of Meadow.	Hogs.	Ma[illegible], Hamlets, or Villages.	N° of Hund.
	£.	s.	d.	£.	s.	d.																
Borough-lath	524	18	0¼	776	15	3¼	161		926	618	76	328½	961	23	45	40½	23	56	479	750	[illegible]1	11
Eastrye-lath	480	2	4¼	627	9	2¼	136 6/8		592	436	94	223½	741	7	33	2	23½	4	85	33	[illegible]8	6
Wye-lath	568	1	2	744	14	10	124		937	275	66½	224½	754	21	181	10½	45½	8	620½	1633	[illegible]1	6
Liming-lath	551	5	6	795	5	4	162		1204	770	135	399½	1339	37	99	38	44	27	798	738	[illegible]5	16
Sutton-lath	547	1	0	896	15	9	133 3/8		1209	383	106½	434	1274	21	232	11	64½		767	1463	[illegible]5	6
Aylesford-lath	725	18	8	1258	5	7	328 1/8		1635	889	193	568½	1909	66	520	49½	49½	14	1145	2453	[illegible]21	12
Mylton-lath	261	10	0	266	13	4	99 1/8		334	141	9	154	344	4	17	33	8	28	30	266	[illegible]6	1
Canterbury	51	0	0	59	10	0		531														
Dover	18	0	0	54	0	0		420						3			10					
Sandwich	15	0	0	50	0	0		415														
Hythe	16	0	0	29	6	4		231														
Romney	14	0	0	21	0	0		156														
Sesaltre	1	5	0	1	5	0		45						1						10		
Forewic	5	0	0	11	0	0		79														
Rochester	5	0	0	40	0	0		114														
COUNTY of KENT	3784	1	8½	5632	0	7½	1144 7/8	1991	6837	3512	680	2332½	7522	183	1127	184½	268	137	3924½	7746	397	58

To those readers who have examined our statements, and are unacquainted with the barbarous Latin, in which these Records are transmitted, and consequently cannot be equally convinced, as the antiquary who will compare our references with the text and our deductions, we now take leave to observe, that there is *not one* villain, or [s] slave of villains, calculated in this general Table, that is not entered under such title in this celebrated Autograph. This state of society continued to exist throughout the [t] whole period which we have selected for our present discussion, and this system of slavery continued to be exercised over nine-tenths of the inhabitants of the realm. Numerous persons of this order of men were frequently transferred for a hawk, a hound, or a charger; their wives and their children were the *cattle*, or in modern language the chattels, of the lord, their daughters could not have their marriage [u] consummated in a state of virginity, and their sons emigrating were vagabonds. Since we are here infringing on our intended Dissertation on Manners and Customs, we must forbear farther observations on the subject.

Before we attempt to calculate the population of Kent, it may be necessary to view more distinctly those Norman knights or nobles, many of whom, though not immediately holding of the crown in this county, or members of such high national court, as that assembled when Lanfranc impleaded the cause of the bishop of Rochester against the powerful brother of William, were, notwithstanding, tenants in capite in other divisions of the realm, and here occupied valuable and extensive subordinate manours. It may be necessary perhaps to premise a few observations for illustrating our references, and ascertaining the feudal lords of these martial dependants, or the tenure of ecclesiastical dignitaries.

[s] Bordarii. [t] See Differ. on Laws. [u] Merchetum existed.

The

CHAP. I. 1065—1272.

The first folio of Domesday contains the general customs of the county; the second, denoted 1 b 1 and 2, the possessions of St. Martin's, of Dover, and the names found with such references designate the persons of its canons or prebendaries. The second sheet is occupied with a description of Canterbury, the continuation of the abbey's lands, and those towns which William retained in his own domain, and the lord-lieutenant controuled by his bailiff or deputies. The whole of the third and fourth sheets and first folio of the fifth, record the possessions of the archbishop of Canterbury, his knights, and ecclesiastics, consequently a reference to such pages and columns marks their true baronial lord. The second side of the 5th page, distinguished by b, transmits the bishop of Rochester's lands, who had only one sub-tenant, Anschitill, the archdeacon. The next six sheets are wholly filled with the extensive and numerous districts of Odo, except a moiety of the second column of the eleventh sheet, designated 11 b 2, appertaining to Battle-abbey, and therefore any dependant inserted from 6 a 1 to 11 b 2 proves him to be the military retainer or a favoured ecclesiastic of the earl of Kent. The twelfth sheet enregisters the lands of the mitred abbot of St. Augustine's, and his feudal vassals, or dignified [x] clerical tenants. The thirteenth sheet contains that appropriate division which Montfort superintended as [y] peer of the realm, and governed at his baronial court. The fourteenth sheet comprizes the whole lands occupied by Earl Eustace, Richard Fitz-gilbert, Haimo the Viscount, and Albert the Chancellor, as tenants of the crown, in this county, though the whole would not occupy

[x] Vital, abbot of Westminster.

[y] Tenet Hugo de Montfort rege, & habet caput manerii, has the jurisdiction over Ewell, a manor of *Odo*'s, occupied by *Ralph Crooktlorn.* Hugo de Montfort habet *caput* manerii, et ibi 5½ *molinos* de 6l. 11 a 2.

one

one page, if a portion of Montfort's was not added to them. By attending to theſe general diſtinctions, the reader may eaſily diſcover the peer or peers to whom the retainer owed ſuit or ſervice, and by printing the names of thoſe knights in italics, who held immediately from the monarch in other counties, we ſhall more accurately learn the number of perſons that may with propriety be claſſed as reſident inhabitants. The canons and prebendaries of St. Martin's are diſcriminated by an obeliſk affixed. The number of references to a name gives the number of manours or hamlets in the cuſtody or tenancy of ſuch perſon. We ſhall conſider the opulent proprietors of the realm at large in a future appropriate diſſertation.

The Names of the Nobles, Knights, Military Retainers, and Dignified Ecclesiastics, in the County of Kent, not holding immediately of the Crown, in this Diſtrict.

Abel, 4 b 2.
Alnod, 13 b 1.
†Alred, 1 b 1—2 a 2—11 b 1.
Alured, (Miles) 9 b 1—11 b 1.
Alured Dapifer (Miles) 9 b 1.
Altet quidam, 11 b 1.
†Alwi, 1 b 1.
†Anschill vel Anschitill, 5 b 1, 6 a 2, 2, 2—6 b 1, 1—6 b 2, 2—7 a 1, 1—1 b 2—7 b 1—8 b 1—11 b 2—12 a 2.
Anſgot, 6 a 1—6 b 1—7 a 1—7 a 2, 2—8 b 1, 1—9 a 1—2 b 1—4 a 2—7 b 2, 2.
Ansfrid, 12 b 1—10 a 1—10 a 2, 2, 2, 2, 2—10 b 1—9 b 2—11 a 1—11 a 2—12 b 2.
†Athelwold Camerarius, 7 b 2—9 b 2—8 b 2, 2—1 b 2—10 b 2.
Baldric, (Miles) 9 b B
Baldwin, 1 b 2.
Bernard de Sto. Audoeno, (Miles) 9 b 1.
Bertram, 13 a 1.
Blize, 5 a 2.
Braibowe, Hugh, 8 b 2.
† Bruman, Præpoſitus, 2 a 2.
Coc, Robertus, 13 b 1.
Columbellis de Ranulfus, 2 a 2—7 a 2—8 b 2—9 a 2—10 a 2—11 b 2, 2—1 a 1—12 b 1.
Curbespina de Ranulfus, 7 b 1, 1—8 a 2, 2—8 b 1—9 b 2—10 b 1—11 a 1, 1—11 a 2, 2—11 b 1, 1—11 b 2—2 a 2—10 b 2, 2—13 a 1.
De Arcis, William, (Miles) 3 b 2—9 b 1.
De Barbis, Robertus, 11 a 1.
De Maris, Ricardus, 10 a 1.
Dispensator, Wm. (Miles) 3 a 2.
Durand, 1 a 1.
Eddesham, Wm. de, 4 b 1, 1—5 a 2.
†Edwin, 1 b 2.
Eudo, Fitz-hubert, (Miles) 9 b 1.
Farman, (Miles) 3 a 2
Fitz-anschitill, Roger, 10 b 2—11 b 2.
Fitz-fulbert, Hugo, 10 b 2.
Fitz-jeoffrey, Wm. 1 b 2.
Fitz-grosse, Wm. 13 b 2.
Fitz-herbert, Hugh, 7 a 1—7 b 2, 2, 2, 2—8 a 2, 2, 2, 2—11 a 1.
Fitz-hubert, Adam, 6 a 1—6 b 1—7 a 1—8 a 1, 1, 1, 1, 1, 1—8 b 1—8 b 2, 2—9 a 1, 1, 1—9 b 2—10 a 1, 1—10 a 2—11 a 1—12 a 2—9 a 1, 1, 1—14 b 1.
Fitz-ivo (Taillgeſboſc) Herbert, 7 b 1 7 b 2, 2, 2—8 a 2, 2, 2, 2—10 a 1 10 a 2, 2—11 a 1—2 a 2—9 b 2—13 b 1.
Fitz-letard, Osbern, 6 a 2—9 b 2, 2 10 a 2, 2—10 b 2—11 b 1—11 b 2 4 b 1—11 a 2, 2—12 b 1.
†Fitz-oger, Wm. 1 a 1—1 b 1—6 b 2, 2.
Fitz-richard, Ralph, 13 b 1.
Fitz-robert, 1 a 1—8 a 1—11 a 1.
Fitz-tahun, Wm. 10 b 1—8 b 1.
†Fitz-tydald, Wm. 1 b 2—1 a 1.
Fitz-tyrald, Ralph, 4 a 2—6 a 1, 1 6 b 2—7 a 2, 2—7 b 1, 1—8 b 2—9 a 1.

Fitz-

CHAP. I. 1065—1272.

In addition then to the [a] *eleven Peers of Kent*, there were twenty-three tenants in chief, holding lands immediately from the crown, in other diſtricts, that occupied inferior moieties within this county, by ſubordinate tenure. There were ſeventy-ſeven, diſtinguiſhed by different titles, of an inferior rank. Of theſe hundred proprietors, fifteen are particularly ſtiled [b] knights, and twenty-one were [c] canons, prebendaries, or dignified eccleſiaſtics. To theſe muſt be added twenty-one [d] knights, not diſtinguiſhed by name, ninety-four [e] eſquires, thirteen [f] thanes, two [g] Normans, thirteen [h] bailiffs, eight [i] prieſts, and forty-four [k] freeholders.

[a] Archiepiſcopus Cantuarienſis—Epiſcopus Roſeceſtrenſis—Epiſcopus Baiocenſis—Abbas de Batailge—Abbas Sti. Auguſtini—Abbas de Gand—Hugo de Montfort—Comes Euſtachius—Ricardus de Tonebrige—Haimo Vicecomes—Albertus Capellanus. Domeſ. 2 a 2.

[b] Milites.

[c] Three canons of St. Martin's, Sired, Godric, and Sewen—12 prebendaries. Domeſ. 2 a 2, & 1 b 1, et 2.

[d] *Milites* 3 in Tanet, 12 a 2—1 in Sondreſſe, 3 a 1—4 Francigenæ, 12 a 2 in Ciſtelet—1 in Suineſcamp, 6 a 1—1 in Eiſſe, 6 a 1—1 in Berham, 9 b 2—1 in Cildreſham, 10 a 1—1 in Ewelle, 11 a 1—3 in Meddeſtane, 3 a 2—2 in Edeſham, 3 a 2—1 Heltonis—Servitium 1 Militis in Cumbe, 10 b 1.

[e] *Homines* 6 in communi terra Sti. Martini, 2 a 2—2 in Medeſtane, 3 a 2—5 in Eſturſete, 3 b 1—5 in Wingeham, 3 b 2—3 in Leminges, 4 a 1—1 in Pecheham, 4 b 2—1 in Haſtingelei, 14 a 1—2 Hugonis Port, 6 a 1, in Eiſſe—8 ſub illis molinis Sti. Martini—6 cum 1½ carrucis, 2 a 2—Homo Adam, 8 a 1—Homo Adam, 8 b 1—Homo Archiepiſcopi in Gecham, 5 a 1—Uluret Homo—Hugo quidam, 11 a 2—Homines de Walt, 50s. *pro Inewardis*, 2 b 2. Therefore 50 eſquires for 1 s. for a body-guard, 1 a 2.

[f] Teigni tres in Oteſort, 3 a 1—Teigni 10 in Bedeſham, 11 a 2.

[g] Francigena in Gelingeham, 3 b 1—Francigena in Boſeleu, 8 b 1.

[h] Canterbury, Dover, Sandwich, Hythe, Romney, Seſaltre, Forewic, Rochester, Feverſham, Mylton, Aylesford, Dartford, Newinden. See their references.

[i] *Preſbyteri* 7 in Romney, 4 a 1—1 in Monocſtune, 12 a 2.

[k] *Sochemanni* 14, 13 a 2—12, 13 a 2—5, 13 a 2—12, 13 a 2—Fæmina Sochemanni, 13 b 2.

The

The monks of St. Auguſtine's and Chriſt Church, in Canterbury, were certainly more numerous than the prebendaries of St. Martin's, and it cannot be ſuppoſed that Dover could furniſh four hundred and twenty mariners, if not containing a much greater number of inhabitants. But as we are reporting facts, not opinions, we now ſtate that the population of Kent, according to the Record of Domeſday, amounted to thirteen [1] thouſand ſeven hundred and ſeventy-three mature males. If we eſtimate five to a family, the population, from this report, will amount to nearly ſeventy thouſand ſouls. But ſince we are certain that many foreigners and troops of William reſided in this county, who are not recorded in this Survey, we might, with great propriety, augment this calculation, if not incompatible with the ſyſtem that regulates our hiſtory.

With reſpect to the Saxon Nobles and Thanes, we muſt refer our readers to a future diſſertation on the opulent proprietors under Edward and William. The cuſtoms of this county varied little from the general received uſages of the kingdom,

[1] 11 Tenants in Chief.
100 Subordinate Tenants.
21 Knights.
94 Eſquires.
13 Thanes.
2 Normans.
13 Bailiffs.
8 Prieſts.
44 Freeholders.
1991 Burgeſſes.
1127 Miniſters, or Retainers.
6837 Villains.
3512 Borderers.

13,773

CHAP. I. 1065—1272. kingdom, and will be delivered with greater precision and clearness when we examine that subject distinctly. Gavelkind tenure was certainly not confined to this district, nor was the honour of forming the [m] van of an army in attack, or the rear in a retreat, limited to the men of this county, but wisely extended to other places, whose inhabitants were best acquainted with the seat of war. The cathedrals, castles, or palaces within this district will more properly be considered in our Dissertation on Arts and Sciences, and the State of Society, and Commerce, in our Essays on Agriculture, Trade, and Ranks and Services. If we convert the sowlings into square miles, we shall find them amounting to little more than [n] one-third of the county, probably the proportion of cultivated land in the district.

Should Providence permit us, and the patronage of the public encourage us, to continue our researches, we shall shew the progressive advancement of this county at a future period. For the present we shall summarily conclude this portion of our History with a few observations, and extracted authorities. The grand mass of the people received few immunities or advantages during this æra selected for discussion. The cities, boroughs, towns, or villages that were not annexed to the monarchy, appertained to archbishops, earls, bishops, or barons, who ruled them with an iron sceptre. The immunities purchased from one sovereign were frequently disregarded by him, at a subsequent æra of his reign, and always by his successor.

[m] The words to which Kelham applies the note, "the Kentish men, *accordingly*, "at the battle of Hastings, were in front of the English army, as their antient "privilege," p. 158.—Refer to part of Wales, in Herefordshire. Cum exercitus in hostem pergit, ipsi (homines de Arcenefeld) per consuetudinem faciunt avantwarde, et in reversione redrewarde. Domes. 179 a 9. Nor is there any such custom relative to Kent transmitted in this period.

[n] 589 square miles.

When

When [o] lands and charters had been conferred on the abbot of Feverſham, by Stephen, Maud, and ſeveral opulent nobles, ſuch poſſeſſions or privileges could not be enjoyed, till the third Henry was bribed to ratify them. The [p] city of Canterbury purchaſed its liberties three times from this Henry, and again redeemed them from his ſucceſſor. [q] Poll-taxes, [r] quinzimes, [s] ſcutages, and other arbitrary aſſeſſments were univerſal, burthenſome, and oppreſſive, and [t] fines and aids were levied by the viſcount, his bailiff and deputies.

Since the origin of the Cinque Ports has been much controverted, we ſhall conclude this chapter by endeavouring nearly to aſcertain the time when they received ſuch denomination. In the year 1229, when the [u] archbiſhopric of Canterbury

[o] Abbas de Faverſham reddit Compotum de 25 Marcis pro 5 palefredis, pro habenda confirmatione regis Johannis de [h]iis quæ habent de dono regis Stephani & Mattillidis quondam reginæ Angliæ & Ricardi de Lucy et quinque aliorum, &c. Mag. Rot. 12 a. Kent. Anno 1212.

[p] Adam de Vallibus, et Thomas de Beuveys Cives Cantuariæ, &c. et pro ſe et tota Communitate Civitatis prædictæ finem fecerunt cum rege 100 marcarum, pro confirmatione hujus regis habendâ de *tribus Cartis* ipſis civibus factis tempore regis Henrici, ſuper diverſis libertatibus eis conceſſis tempore ipſius regis Henrici, &c. Mich. Fines. 26 et 27 Edv. 1ſt.

[q] Taillagium Roffe (Rocheſter) aſſiſum per capita. Rot. 1 a Kanciæ. Anno 1237.

[r] Quinzime Doura et Sandwice. Anno 1205.

[s] De ſcutagio de Kery (Chriſt-Church, Canterbury) 89l. 15s. 4d. de 67 $\frac{1}{2}$ $\frac{1}{8}$ feodis. Mag. Rot. 13 H. 3.

[t] Jacobus Salvagius debet 3 paleſridos, ut omnes tenentes eccleſiæ ſuæ de Ocham [in Kent] et Capellarum ad eandem eccleſiam pertinentium liberi ſint et quieti in perpetuum de ſectis ſcirarum, et hundredorum, ed de auxiliis vicecomitis, et omnium baillivorum et miniſtrorum ſuorum, et de omnibus aliis quæ ad vicecomitem vel baillivos, vel miniſtros ſuos pertinent. Mad. vol. 1. p. 408.

[u] Compotus archiepiſcopatus Cantuariæ a 18° die Julii anno 12 regis uſque ad ultimum diem Marcii anno ejuſdem 13°, &c. et de 10l. 13s. 11½d. de Exitibus Portus de Romenel et de Hee, &c. Summa 1927l. 15s. 5½d. Mag. Rot. 13 H. 3. in Rot. compot. m 2 b.

CHAP. I. 1065—1272. terbury was vacant, and its emoluments received by commissioners for the crown, the port fees of Romney and Hythe are included in the one thousand nine hundred and twenty-seven pounds, fifteen shillings and five-pence farthing, the produce of the see for little more than nine months. Consequently the burgesses of these towns were under the patronage of the see at this period, though the [x] five ports had been distinguished even in the reign of John. In the reign of Edward the first however they were totally exempted from all [y] customary payment to the primate, their barons are distinguished by name, and had a seat in the national representation. But as we are infringing on our intended continuation, we must defer our authorities for the present.

[x] Americamenta hominum de quinque Portubus pro Bladis missis inimicis regis in Flandria. Mag. Rot. 1 Joh. Rot. 56. Kent.

[y] Consuetudo here and in Domesday signifies customs transmitted from time immemorial, the foundation of the English common law.

END OF THE TOPOGRAPHICAL DISSERTATION.

THE

HISTORY OF SOUTH BRITAIN;

FROM

Authentic Documents.

CHAP. I.

On the Nature of the Laws, their Variety, and Execution, from Edward the Confeſſor, to Edward the Firſt, ſurnamed the Engliſh Juſtinian, a Period of 207 *Years.*

UNDER every [a] feudal government, the military leader CHAP. I.
preſided in the ſupreme court of judicature; and, though 1065—
he might aſſociate with himſelf other chieftains, to exerciſe the 1272.
legiſlative power, and aſſiſt his judgment, by their united wiſdom and counſel, arrogated to himſelf the ſole right of deciſion, on all controverted points [b]. His will was the law.

[a] Dr. Tucker, dean of Glouceſter, and Dr. Adam Smith, author of the Wealth of Nations, are the only moderns, that have entertained juſt ideas relative to the Saxon government.

[b] Cum hoc ipſum lex ſit, quod principi placet, legis habet vigorem. *Fleta* in Commentarii Jur. Anglic. Procemio.

 From

CHAP. I. 1065—1272. From his decree there was no appeal[c]: an enrolled record of his perſonal verdict, or his judicial ſentence, muſt implicitly be obeyed.

In the earlieſt periods of this æra, the high national court was not confined to a particular place, nor was there a regular appropriate term for its ſeſſion. A Saxon, or Norman, prince had numerous palaces, extenſive domains, and a ſplendid ſuite of noble attendants; the moſt opulent and powerful barons of the realm were honoured with the domeſtic offices of his houſhold, and marſhalled in his train of followers. He traverſed the kingdom with a pompous cavalcade of retainers; and the royal preſence was ever attended by the moſt [d] able and intelligent clerks, the braveſt warriors, and moſt diſtinguiſhed nobles. In whatever diſtrict he ſojourned, a council could ſpeedily be aſſembled, a conference of the moſt learned and experienced eaſily be obtained. Hence the monarchs of England frequently decided the controverſies of their vaſſals while they made the [e] circuit of their ſeigneury, whilſt they ſucceſ-

[c] Regis curia, in quâ ipſe in propria perſonâ ſuâ, jura decernit, quod nec recordationi, nec ſententiæ in ea latæ, licet alicui contradicere—* Lib. niger Scaccarii tempore Hen. II. Lib. I. c. 4.—c Nemo quidem de factis regis præſumat diſputare—*Bracton*, Lib. I. c. 7. De legibus & Conſuetudinibus Angliæ †.—c De chartis verò regiis & factis regum, non debent nec poſſunt juſtitiarii, nec privatæ perſonæ diſputare. Ibid. Lib. II. c. 16.

[d] De melioribus & antiquis hominibus totius comitatus—Domeſday, 44 b.

[e] Qui non veniebat ad ſciremote, ſummonitus, totam terram ſuam erga regem foris faciebat—Berkſhire Domeſ. 56 b.—Qui non veniebat ter in anno ſine ammonitione (in Kent) qui non veniebat ad ſtabilitionem ſylvæ emendabat regi 50 ſolidos. Domeſ. 56 b. Similar inſtances in almoſt every county, with various fines.

* This book, generally aſcribed to Gervaſe of Tilbury, is inconteſtibly proved, by the correct Madox, to have been compoſed by Richard Nigell, biſhop of London.
Madox—Exchequer, Vol. II. p. 345.

† This work was completed by the illuſtrious Bracton, about the concluſion of the reign of Henry the Third.

ſively

ſively ſported in their widely-ranging foreſts, or viſited their ſtately palaces: but, at ſtated feſtivals, and on particular occaſions, [f] the community of the realm [g], the barons and knights, aſſembled in general council, where the monarch preſided on his throne, adminiſtered juſtice to his ſubjects, and tranſacted ſuch important affairs as demanded greater ſolemnity, or required peculiar notoriety. Theſe courts were held at the royal palaces of [h] Weſtminſter, Winton, Oxford, or Windſor; occaſionally at Northampton, Glouceſter, Saliſbury, or Woodſtock; and ſometimes at St. Albans, Dunſtable, Marlborough, &c. Here he received the homage of his vaſſals, on the grand feſtivals of Chriſtmas, Eaſter, or Whitſuntide; here an immenſe concourſe of nobility, prelates, and knights, was collected in the common hall of their feudal lord, feaſted at his round [i] table, deliberated on the national intereſts, arranged and received the eſtabliſhed ordonnances of the realm. None but immediate tenants of the crown were admitted to the preſence of their ſeigneur, allowed to participate of the ſovereign controul as peers and con-vaſſals, or conſidered as true

CHAP. I. 1065—1272.

[f] Communitas pertotam Berchefciram, confined ſolely to the Thanes, or royal knights. Vid. Doomſday, 56 b.

[g] The realm conſiſted of earldoms and baronies—Caput comitatus propter *jus gladii dividi* non poteſt, vel caput baroniæ, caſtrum, vel aliud ædificium, & hoc ideo, ne ſic caput per plures particulas dividatur, & plura jura comitatuum & baroniarum, deveniant ad nihilum, per quod deficiat regnum, quod ex comitatibus & baroniis dicitur eſſe conſtitutum. Bracton, 2—34.

[h] Ventilata eſt hæc cauſa prius ad uuentanam civitatem & poſtea in villâ regia quæ vocatur uuindiſor. Madox Exchequer, Vol. I. p. 7, 4to ed. In natali tenuiſſet curiam Willielmus apud Glouceſtre, ad Paſcha apud Winceſtre, et ad Pentecoſten apud Londoniam. Mad. ibid. quod vide.

[i] Qui conventuri ſint ad rotundam tabulam colloquium habituri cum Lewelino. Rym. Fœd. Vol. I. p. 324.

CHAP. I. 1065—1272. [k] liege-men of their chief lord. The other inhabitants of the kingdom had but a * ſecondary intereſt in the tranſactions of the royal conſultation, and were preſumed to acquieſce in the perſons of their lords; they were amenable alſo to the awards and controul of inferior courts of judicature, which however were, in ſome degree, regulated by the proceedings of the ſupreme council, at ſubſequent periods. Theſe national aſſemblies were not only neceſſary for ſupporting the dignity of the monarch, ſecuring the fidelity of his ſubjects, preſerving the unity of the nation, and eſtabliſhing general regulations for the government of the realm, but for the effectual promulgation of their irregular ſtatutes, through every diviſion of ſuch an empire, where few could read, and the [l] prince, probably, not write.

It is by no means extraordinary, therefore, that the laws of England ſhould not be enrolled in a regular code, but ſhould depend on traditionary evidence, and tranſmitted deciſions. Theſe varied in every diſtrict. Long ſubſequent to the conqueſt, the realm of England experienced diſtinctions, that originated in its heptarchical government. In the edicts of the

[k] Law-worthy. Pacem regis habentes.

* In the ever-memorable Magna Charta, John had the penetration to inſert a clauſe of the higheſt importance to the commonalty, whoſe obſervation would elevate the people, and controul his imperious barons. Its ſpirit is this; that whatever liberties or favours he conferred on them as his vaſſals, theſe lords ſhould beſtow on their villains. Omnes autem iſtas conſuetudines prædictas, et libertates, quas nos conceſſimus in regno noſtro tenendas, quantum ad nos pertinet, erga noſtros omnes de regno noſtro, tam clerici quam laici obſervent, quantum ad ſe pertinet erga ſuos. Mag. Chart. § 60.—This is the ſole clauſe that affects the body of the people.

[l] Vid. Madox Exchequer, Vol. I. 7. where the marks of William and his queen Mathilda are affixed to an Autograph, in the archives of Canterbury. This record was engroſſed in the year 1072, in the vigour of the conqueror's life. And again: Neuſtria pia, p. 16.+Signum Willelmi Regis Anglorum. Mad. Vol. I. 49.

Confeſſor,

Confeſſor, ratified by William, theſe diſcriminations are reduced to three appropriate diviſions, [m] the Daniſh, Mercian, and Saxonic laws. In the [n] eaſtern and northern diſtricts of the kingdom, the Daniſh laws prevailed, in the midland the Mercian, and in the weſtern and ſouthern counties the Saxon preponderated. The fines annexed to the violation of the royal peace, or eſtabliſhed ordonnances of the nation, were proportioned to the preſumed civilization of the [o] country, the refinement of its inhabitants, received uſages, or prevailing cuſtoms, that had immemorially obtained in that quarter. Oral teſtimony, and eſtabliſhed opinions, ſuperſeded the law of nations, and the natural principles of juſtice and equity. Law was little defined, and leſs underſtood. Tradition ſupplied ſuch precedents as precluded the neceſſity of dry [p] reaſon-

[m] Foris-factura regis quæ pertinent ad vice comitem, quadraginta ſolidi in *Merchenelega* & L ſol in *Weſtſenelega*, & de libero homine qui habet ſac & ſoc, &c. 40 Oræ in *Danelega*, & de alio homine qui ejuſmodi libertatem non habet Oræ XXXII. Wilkins leges & conſuetudines Willielmi, p. 219, § 3. In *Merchenelega*, ſi quis appellatus fuerit de latrocinio, ſeu de furto, & plegiatus fuerit venire ad juſtitiam, & fugerit interim, plegius ejus habebit 4 menſes & unum diem ad eum querendum, & ſi poſſit eum invenire, juret ſe duodecimâ manu, quod tempore, quo eum plegiavit, latro non fuerat, neque per eum eſſet quod fugerit, nec eum prehendere poſſit. Tunc reddat Catallum & XX ſolidos pro Capite & IV Denarios ei, qui ceperit ipſum & unum Obolum pro Inquiſitione & XL Sol. Regi. *In Weſt ſaxenelega* C ſol. ad Clamorem pro Capite & IX Libras Regi, et in Danelega Foris-factura eſt VIII Libræ (XX *Solidi* pro Capite) & VII Libræ Regi, § 4.

[n] Vid. Lambardes Perambulation of Kent, pag. 4, 5, 6. 4to. London, 1596.

[o] In ſummam grandem argenti centuriata fiſco condemnaretur, quædam ſcilicet in XXXVI, quædam in XLIV ſecundum locorum diverſitatem & interſectionis frequentiam. Dial. de Scac. 2 Mad. p. 391.

[p] Non enim in ratiociniis, ſed in multiplicibus judiciis excellens ſcaccarii ſcientia conſiſtit. [Dial. de Scac. per Ric. Epiſ. Lond. 1178. Mad. 2. 360.]

ing,

CHAP. I. ing, elaborate illuſtrations, ingenious argument, or defined
1065— ſtatutes, in the realm of [q] England peculiarly, ſo late as the
1272. conclusion of the reign of Henry the Third, the period limiting our preſent obſervations.

The dictatorial Conqueror augmented the glorious uncertainty of the law, and encreaſed the probable abſurdity of the deciſion of its judges, by ſeparating the civil and eccleſiaſtical courts. Accuracy in inveſtigation, ſound judgment, or wiſe verdicts, are little to be expected from that aſſembly; the majority of whoſe conſtituents are incapable of reading or writing, and whoſe knowledge is confined to the narrow ſphere of ſcience, acquired ſolely by their own experience, unaſſiſted by the wiſdom of ages. But though [r] William wiſely, perhaps, ſuppreſſed clerical appeals to eccleſiaſtical courts in lay cauſes, his judgment was certainly defective, if, at this dark æra, he excluded clergymen from deciding civil points of controverſy. On intereſted principles, or affectionate attachment to his Norman followers, ſuch conduct, indeed, may be juſtifiable and laudable; for the clergy alone, dared to retain any poſſeſſions or property from his martial bravoes, or vindicate the ſecondary rights of *non-reſiſting* Engliſhmen to their hereditary eſtates, (even when ſubmitted to the controul and patronage of the church) againſt lordly plunderers, whoſe ſword guaranteed their tenure. In this view alone can we account for ſuch conduct. For at this period, ſuch an indiſtinctive twilight pervaded the Britiſh horizon, that the few

[q] Sola Anglia uſa eſt in ſuis finibus jure non ſcripto & conſuetudine. [Henricus de Bracton de Legibus & Conſuetudinibus Angliæ. Lond. 1569. 4to. p. 1.]

[r] Mando et regiâ authoritate præcipio, ut nullus epiſcopus, vel archi-diaconus, de legibus epiſcopalibus amplius in hundred placita teneant. [Leges Will. Wilkins. 292. an. 1085.]

luminaries, capable of projecting ſplendour, thus loſt their effect, for want of a proper medium to tranſmit their rays; and the dim ſtars, whoſe feeble beams might have aſſiſted the viſual faculty, were thus clouded from the ſight.

But notwithſtanding ſuch pernicious diviſion of the canon and civil law, we find eccleſiaſtics appointed juſticiaries of the kingdom, judges of the circuit, or [s] barons of the exchequer, in every ſucceſſive reign. The royal exchequer was the king's peculiar court, where controverſies of every deſcription were terminated. Its aſſeſſors not only examined the accounts of the ſheriffs, regulated the revenue, or tried the ſuits of the crown, but occaſionally ſummoned every tenant in chief to attend its bar, as jurors or defaulters, to determine litigated queſtions, or common pleas, to anſwer for neglect of ſervice, or non payment of fines, aids or ſcutages. This high national [t] council aſſembled principally at Wincheſter, ſometimes at Weſtminſter, in the twelfth century; and, as the celebrated [u] roll of Winton tranſmitted the real poſſeſſors of landed property in its day, ſucceeding ages deemed no [w] transfer equally good, no ſecurity or compact equally valid, as that atteſted before this tribunal, and regiſtered in its records. Hence an

[s] Vid. Madox Exchequer, Vol. II. p. 312, &c. where we find, in the forty-ſecond and forty-fifth years of Henry III. the abbots of Weſtminſter, Perſhore, and Peterborough, in the tranſmitted rolls, and a regular uninterrupted ſucceſſion, from the biſhops of Baieux, Conſtance, and Durham, to thoſe of Lincoln, Ely, and Wincheſter, the archdeacons of Poictou and Salop, the dean of Waltham, and maſters Belet, Giffard, and Thomas de Wymundeham.

[t] Majores quique de regno, qui familiariùs regiis ſecretis aſſiſtunt. Dial. de Scaccario, Lib. I. c. 4.

[u] Domeſday Book.

[w] Gilebertus de Gillin debet dimidiam marcam, ut ſcribatur in magno Rotulo, &c. Prior de Ledes, Henricus Biſſet, Abbas de Stanelega debent ſinguli dimidiam Marcam, multique alii. Mad. 1. 217.

immenſity

CHAP. I. 1065—1272. immenſity of fines, paſſed for ſuch purpoſes, are found in the great rolls. In the reign of every prince, who pretended to adminiſter juſtice, [x] pleas at common law were not only removed from the [y] immediate judgment of the monarch, but transferred from the Exchequer to the [z] courts of Common Pleas and King's Bench. There is an expreſs [a] ſtipulation on this ſubject in Magna Charta. Previous to this æra, however, regular circuits had been preſcribed to the juſticiaries, and their route extended through every diſtrict of the kingdom. In the early part of his reign, Henry the Second, with the [b] approbation of his peers, ſeparated England into four grand diviſions, and appointed five judges to hold the aſſizes in each county. In his twenty-ſecond year, a different arrangement was adopted: the number [c] of circuits was augmented to ſix, and of aſſeſſors reduced to three. As, on ſubjects of this nature, Hoveden's and Spelman's authority are indiſputable; as

[x] Judicio baronum regis, qui placitum tenuerunt. Vid. Domeſday 2 a 1.

[y] Domini regia curia, in quâ ipſe in propria perſona jura decernit. Dial. de Scaccario, Lib. I. c. 4.

[z] The court of King's Bench, inſtituted for the trial of criminal cauſes only, took cognizance of civil ſuits; the plaintiff pretending that the defendant, in not doing him juſtice, had been guilty of ſome treſpaſs or miſdemeanour. The court of Exchequer, inſtituted for the levying of the king's revenue, and for the enforcing the payment of ſuch debts only as were due to the king, took cognizance of all other contract debts, the plaintiff alleging that he could not pay the king, becauſe the defendant would not pay him. Dr. Smith's Wealth of Nations, Vol. III. p. 88.

[a] Communia placita non ſequantur curiam noſtram.

[b] Conſilio archiepiſcoporum, epiſcoporum, comitum & baronum. Hoveden, p. 590.—c Alnod cilt et ſimilum ejus. Domeſ. p. 1.

[c] Anno 1157. Cives eboraci reddunt compotum de XL Marcis argenti, pro reſpectu ne placitarent extra comitatum ſuum donec *rex veniret*. Mag. Rot. 3. H. 2. Mad. 1. p. 397. et anno 1180. Homines de Briſtou red. comp. de 50l. pro habendo reſpectu, et ne placitent extra muros villæ ſuæ, donec rex veniat in Angliam. Mad. 1. p. 398.

we

we find their ſtatement corroborated by Gervaſe of Canterbury, and ſtill more authoritatively aſcertained by the Rolls of the Exchequer, edited by Madox, we ſhall preſent the antient and modern circuits to the reader, in one view.

It is foreign to our purpoſe to enter into the controverſies of lawyers, relative to the priority, or dignity, of the different courts. It is equally foreign to pretend to decide when theſe juſticiers were firſt inſtituted to diſtribute juſtice in the ſeveral circuits, or diviſions allotted them; for facts, not conjectures, are the objects of our enquiry. We know that [e] pleas were held in the reign of the Conqueror; and there were, doubtleſs, [f] pleas of the foreſt, and pleas of the crown, equally with [g] common pleas, circuits for the receipts of the royal exchequer, and the trials of criminal offenders, in the reign of every ſubſequent monarch. As little variation has taken place in this excellent ſyſtem, even to the preſent day, we ſhall preſent the ameliorated arrangement of Henry the Second, as delivered by Spelman, Hoveden, and Gervaſe of Canterbury, with the corrections of Madox, and our modern circuits, in one view, to the reader.

This plan was arranged at Nottingham, in a general aſſembly of the royal barons.

[e] Vid. ſupra Domeſday. Placita autem dicimus pœnas pecuniarias in quas incidunt delinquentes.

Dial. de Scac. Mad. Vol. II. p. 210.

[f] De placitis, de novis placitis, de aſſiſis & novis conventionibus.

Mad. Vol. I. p. 123.

[g] Communia placita. Magna Charta.

CHAP. I.
1065—
1272.

MODERN CIRCUITS.

NORFOLK.

Buckingham, Bedford, Huntingdon, Cambridge, Norfolk, Suffolk.

MIDLAND CIRCUIT.

Northampton, Rutland, Lincoln, Nottingham, Derby, Leicefter, Warwick.

HOME CIRCUIT.

Hertford, Effex, Kent, Suffex, Surrey.

OXFORD.

Berkfhire, Oxford, Worcefter, Gloucefter, Monmouth, Hereford, Shropfhire, Staffordfhire.

WESTERN.

Hampfhire, Wiltfhire, Dorfet, Devonfhire, Cornwall, Somerfetfhire, and Briftol.

NORTHERN.

Yorkfhire, Durham, Northumberland, Cumberland, Weftmoreland, and Lancafhire.

Hen. II. 22 & 23. 1176. magnum Nottinghamiæ concilium CHAP. I.
adhibens regnum totum in 6 divifit partes earumque fingulis tres 1065—
conftituit juftitiarios: fuas (at nondum) portiones itineraturos. 1272.
Nomina fubfequuntur.

Retinemus antiquam fcripturam.

	Justitiarii	Comitatus
1	Hugo de Creiffi Walterus fil. Roberti [h] Robertus Mantell	* Norfolc, Suffolc, *Cantebrigefire*, *Huntedunes*, *Bedefordfire*, *Bukinhamfire*, *Eftfexe*, *Hertefordefire*
2	Hugo de Gundevilla Willielm. fil. Radulfi [h] Willielmus Baffet	*Lincolnefire*, *Notinghamfire*, *Derebifire*, Staffordefire, *Warwikefire*, *Northamptfire*, *Leiceftrefire* (Roteland Madox)
3	Robertus fil. Bernardi Richardus Giffard Rogerus fil. Reinfrai	*Kent*, Surrie, *Suthantefire*, *Suthfexa*, *Berkefire*, *Oxenifordfire*
4	Willielm. fil. Stephani Bertram de Verdun Turftinus fil. Simonis	*Herefortfire*, *Glouceflerfire*, *Worecefterfire*, Salopefire
5	[h] Radulfus fil. Stephani Willielmus Ruffus Gilebertus Pipard	*Wiltefire*, *Dorfete*, Sumerfete, *Devonia*, *Cornubia*
6	Robertus de Vallibus [h] Radulfus de Glanvile Robertus Pikenot	*Everwikefire*, *Richemundfire*, Loncaftre, Coplande, Weftmerilande, *Northumberlande*, Cumberlande

Spelmann *Iter*. Hoveden,
Part II. p. 548.

* Correfponding with Madox, without deviation.

[h] Barones Scaccarii, vid. Mad. 2. 312.

 We

CHAP. I. 1065—1272. We are not to imagine, however, that justice was administered with that integrity, judgment, equity, or [i] equality, so pre-eminently conspicuous in our courts of judicature, in the eighteenth century, the pride, and security, of Englishmen. The chancellor's situation was venal, and purchased for an enormous sum, three thousand and six pounds, thirteen shillings and four-pence, [k] in the reign of Stephen. John granted the chancellorship for life to [l] Walter de Grey, on receiving a fine of five thousand marks; and [m] Richard Fitz-alured, the king's *butler*, was assessed in fifteen marks, for the privilege, and perquisites, of holding the pleas of Buckinghamshire jointly with Ralph Basset.

When the appointment of a judge is conferred on the highest bidder, we may readily presume that bribes and fees, well applied, will supersede the [n] verdict of justice. This inference, indeed, is fully justified by incontrovertible evidence. Not only were the dispensers of right and equity corrupt, but the fountain was impure. Before a [o] suit could be instituted, a donum must be deposited in the royal exchequer: before a debt could be recovered, a [p] compromise must be entered into with

[i] English, not French equality; equitable decision, without respect of persons.

[k] Idem Cancellarius (Galfridus) debet 3006l. 13s. 4d. *pro* Sigillo.

M. Rot. 5 Steph. Rot. 14. Mad. 1. p. 62. an. 1140.

[l] An. 1206. 7 John. Vid. Spelman Gloss. in Voce-Cancellarius.

[m] Ricardus filius Alured, Pincerna, debet 15 marcas argeniti, ut sederet cum Radulfo Basset ad placita regis.

Mag. Rot. 5. Steph. Rot. 11. a Buckinghamcira. Mad. 1. 63.

[n] Verèdictum.

[o] Simon filius Eustachii debet 2 uncias auri, pro habendo recto de vadio suo versus Willelmum Coterell.

An. 1189. M. R. 1. R. 1. Mad. 1. 427.

[p] Theophania de Westland debet medietatem de 212 marcis pro justiciando Jacobum. 6 H. 3. Kantia. Alexander debet tertiam partem 13 marcarum pro habendo

with his majesty's barons, what portion should be appropriated to his service; and we find an half, a third, a fourth, but seldom less than a fifth part of the whole amount agreed upon. Sometimes a determinate [q] sum was paid, and a farther stipulation made, if the cause should be favourably terminated. Brian Fitz-ralph acknowledged himself indebted to the king in 100 marks, for permission to prosecute his claim to the barony of Petworth, against Henry Percy, and promised an additional 200 if successful in his action: for there was much uncertainty and dilatoriness in the law proceedings of this æra, and the longest purse generally prevailed in the contest. It was frequently necessary to [r] hasten its decision by a second tender of money, the present of a beautiful palfrey, charger, or well trained and rapid hawk or falcon. A rich defendant could easily nonsuit a plaintiff, by applying to the intercsted feelings of the monarch, who, on such an application, dispensed with his defence, and dismissed the suit. Such exceptions against

CHAP. I. 1065—1272.

habendo recto de illis 13 marcis. 4 Joh. Wilts. Robertus de Mara et uxor ejus debent quartam partem de 20 marcis pro justiciando Robertum Bloy.

M. R. 5. H. 3. Cant. & Hunt. Mad. 1. p. 452, &c.

[q] Brianus filius Radulfi debet C marcas, pro habendo recto de baronia de Petewarda, et de xv militibus feffatis pertinentibus ad prædictam baroniam, versus Henricum de Perci. et si prædictam baroniam dirationaverit, dabit 200 marcas.

Mag. Rot. 7. Ric. 1. Rot. 18 b. Sudsex. Mad. 1. 427.

Reddit compotum de 10 marcis, Walterus de Burton, ut filius ejus habeat liberam legem ut placitet, ut habeat judicium, ut habeat rectum.

Mad. 1. 429. passim, more than 100 instances.

[r] Robertus Malherbe debet C libras pro festinando recto. Fulco filius Warini deb. C libr. et dextrarium, pulchrum, et talem, quod non sit eo melior in Wallia pro festinando judicio. Falkesius debet unum osturum pro festinando judicio.

18 H. 2. 12 Joh. & 7 H. 3. Mad. 1. 448.

appear-

CHAP. I. 1065—1272. appearance, and pleading, are to be found in the records of every prince, from the fifth year of[1] Stephen to the twenty-ninth of Henry the Third, in considerable numbers. To give every[2] instance that occurs, would be tedious; but we shall select a conspicuous name to convey a striking illustration.

Ellen of Pepworth, and her son, had agreed to pay 20 marks into the exchequer, and deliver a horse to king John, for permission to enquire, whether the lands of Pepworth, which Robert Russel had forcibly possessed, were her right and inheritance, by descent, from her ancestors, or whether she held it in frank-almoigne; (i. e. on the terms of supporting two poor persons from the produce or revenue, thence arising). In the mean time, Russel had sent to the king four palfreys, (probably of fine form and good action, otherwise their value would not have much exceeded the fine of Ellen). Influenced by such a present, John instantly guaranteed his possession of Pepworth by a royal charter; and the national rolls, recording this infamous transaction, and iniquitous alienation of property,

[1] Rogerus de Hachouse 6l. 19s. 6d. de fine, ne procederetur ad inquisitionem. Mag. Rot. 28. Hen. 3. Rotla. Notlin & Dereb. Mad. 1. 451.

[2] Robertus Russel reddit compotum de quatuor palefridis pro habenda carta regis de * 10 virgatis terræ cum pertinentiis in Pappewurð, quas Helena de Pappewurð tenuit per servicium pascendi in perpetuum singulis diebus duos pauperes, pro anima regis & antecessorum suorum.

Elena de Pappewurð & Walterus filius ejus debent xx marcas & unum palefridum pro habenda inquisitione, si terra de Pappewurð unde Robertus Russel eos dissaisivit, sit Jus & Hæreditas ipsius Helenæ de Anceseria, an ipsa eam tenuerit in Elemosina pascendi duos pauperes pro rege: sed non debent summoneri, quia non potuit [erunt] habere inquisitionem, propter finem, quem Robertus Russel fecit.

Mag. Rot. 10 J. Rot. 9. a Cant. & Hunt. tit. Nova Oblata. Mad. 1. 517.

* Equal to 400 Cheshire acres, equal to 847.27 statute acres.
Vide Dissertation on Weights and Measures.

unequi-

unequivocally state, at the same time, that Ellen had a right to these lands, by such charitable title, but that justice was withheld, from such interested inducement. CHAP. I. 1065—1272.

Under the [u] Saxon or Norman princes it recked little by what claim or title an estate was held by an inferior tenant. Land, which had been inherited by a regular succession from the conquest, by the [x] Levelands, in Westminster, was given to Osbert Longchamp, by the first Richard, because five hundred marks, the fine of Osbert, greatly outweighed their sixty-five. Charters or liberties were little regarded by these monarchs, when their interest was concerned; and their justices were actuated by a similar spirit, and regulated their proceedings from the prospect of advantage presented to them. The circuits appear to have been principally framed to collect the royal revenue, and enrich the treasury and themselves. The barons of the exchequer frequently received fines from both parties interested, but the greatest sum generally preponderated in their scale of justice. The men of [y] Whitby had obtained a grant of liberties from the abbot and convent, which had been ratified by a royal charter, and for which, doubtless, they had paid an ample consideration: a succeeding

[u] Alnold Cilt per Violentiam Heraldi abstulit Sto. Martino Mereclesham and Havochesten, pro quibus dedit canonicis iniquam commutationem.

Domesday, Kent, p. 2. a. 2 presumedly the best regulated county.

[x] Vide Mad. 1, 514.

[y] Abbas de Whiteby debet C. Marcas, ut Burgenses de Whitebi non possent *uti* libertatibus sibi concessis ab abbate & conventu de Whitebi, et *Carta Domini Regis* confirmatis, donec judicatum sit in Curia Regis, &c. Willelmus Clericus, &c. & debent 80 Marcas pro habenda confirmatione de libertatibus, &c.

Mag. Rot. 1 Joh. Rot. 4. Everwichscira.

Sciatis, &c. & quod Carta, quam Burgenses de Whiteby habent, et quæ est contra Dignitatem Ecclesiæ non confirmabitur a nobis.

Chart. 2. J. m. 16. Mad. 1. p. 515.

abbot

CHAP. I. 1065—1272. abbot appealed to the itinerant judges, and tendered one hundred marks (twenty more than his opponents) that the inhabitants of the town might not enjoy those privileges, but judgment be respited, till an appeal was made to the king in person, or his superior court. The abbot prevailed, and the charter was annulled, because derogatory to the *dignity* of his church.

But ecclesiastics, however opulent, did not always prevail; their tenants sometimes outbribed them, and purchased their liberties. The prior of [z] Spalding had a controversy with his dependants relative to the services they owed him, and wished to decide it by the verdict of a jury. Apprehensive of the event, his men presented three palfreys, that the sitting justiciaries might not permit him to convict them of slavish services by such trial, which is contrary to the established usage and custom

[z] Homines Prioris de Spaulling, de Pincebec & de Muleton debent tres palefridos, ut Justiciarii de Banco non permittant Priorem de Spaulling convincere eos, de Servilibus Consuetudinibus, per Juratam, quia hoc est contra Assisam & Consuetudinem Angliæ. Mag. Rot. 3. H. 3. Rot. 10 b. Lincolnescia. Mad. 1. 508.

Madox has translated this curious passage "to convict them, by a jury, of "servile customs, the same being contrary to the assize and law of England;" but even the inaccurate grammarians of that day would not make *hoc* refer to an antecedent in the plural number, *Consuetudinibus*, which might be presumed from his arrangement of the words.—The true meaning of the passage we presume to be this,—The tenants were assured that the jury would convict them, or find against them, for the jurymen were * Milites and Normans probably, and to have such a jury was contrary to the † usage of England, for these men should have been tried by their peers, *rusticos*, or at least half of the jury rustics.

* Hundreds were frequently fined for summoning rustics on juries, by the sheriffs; as Spelethorn hundred, London and Middlesex, &c. Vide Madox 1, 546.

† Of the tenements which are holden in gavelkinde, there shall no battail be joined nor grand assize taken by 12 knights, &c. but by 12 men being tenants in gavelkind. Usages of Kent, confirmed 21 of Edward 1st. Lambardes Kent. ed. 1596. p. 584.

custom of England. Probably they obtained their point, and emancipated themselves from slavery. CHAP. I. 1065—1272.

When wealth possessed such omnipotent power, could change right into wrong, and make the worse appear the better cause, it became of little consequence what was the nature of the laws, since their just execution was so shamefully obstructed. We are assured then, from better authority than Matthew Paris's, the original record, that judges, or lawyers, could receive fees from both parties, and act the part of a Janus bifrons; that justice was venal; that by money every violation of right or property could be canceled; by money a plunderer could not only defer, or escape, but prevent responsibility for his oppressions, in direct contradiction to [a] Magna Charta, and long subsequent to the period when that presumed palladium of liberty and property was extorted from John. Towards the conclusion, however, of the reign of Henry the third, the immense fines for recovery of debts were no longer paid into the exchequer; the denial of right was not openly avowed, or justice publicly prostituted.

That the itinerant justices originally and principally traversed the circuits for the emolument of the prince, cannot be easily doubted, when we examine their instructions, as delivered by Bracton, a contemporary author. The rights even of the privileged orders, the administration of the laws, or the good of the community, appear only incidentally considered. These are the [b] outlines of their directions in modern language. To enquire,

[a] Nulli vendemus, negabimus, deferemus Rectum aut Justitiam.

[b] De valectis & puellis, qui sunt & esse debent in custodia domini regis, qui sunt, et qui illos habent, et per quem, et quantum terræ eorum valent. De dominabus, quæ sunt et esse debent de donatione domini regis, sive sunt maritatæ sive non, et si sint maritatæ, quibus & per quem, et quantum terræ illarum valent

CHAP. I. 1065—1272. enquire,—What wards appertain to the royal guardianſhip,—their quality, their occupiers, and value of their poſſeſſions;—What ladies are at the diſpoſal of the crown—the widows that have married again—their huſbands—the perſons who gave them away—and the rental of their eſtates;—What churches are in the preſentation of the king,—their ſituation—incumbents—and annual value;—What honours—baronies—biſhoprics—or monaſteries had lapſed to their ſovereign lord, or infringements been made on the crown, the royal foreſts, or demeſnes.—They are then to examine whether the ſtatute weights and meaſures have been obſerved, or if any of his majeſty's ſervants have authorized their peculiar favourites to purchaſe by

valent per annum. De eccleſiis quæ ſunt de advocatione domini regis, quæ eccleſiæ illæ ſunt, et qui illas habent et per quem, et quantum valent per annum. De eſchaetis domini regis, quæ ſunt, et quis illas tenet, et per quod ſervitium, tam de terris *Normannorum* quam de aliis, & ſi quæ teneantur ſine warranto, capiantur in M. D. R. De ſerjantiis. D. R. quæ ſunt, et qui illas tenent, et per quem, & cujuſmodi ſerjantiæ illæ ſunt, et quantum valent, et quæ ſervitia reddant. De purpreſturis factis ſuper D. R. ſive in terra, ſive in mari, ſive in aqua dulci, ſive infra libertatem, ſive extra, ſive alibi ubicunque. De menſuris factis & juratis per regnum, ſi ſervatæ ſint ſicut proviſum fuit, et ſi cuſtodes menſurarum mercedes ceperint ab aliquo, quod poſſint per alias emere, et per alias vendere, quod quidem intelligatur de omnibus menſuris, tam ulnis, quam ponderibus, & ſi aſſiza de latitudine pannorum ſervata ſit, ſicut fuit proviſum, et ſi quis denarios ceperit pro pannis contra aſſiſam venditis. De vinis venditis in civitate, burgis, et aliis villis mercatoriis, ubi vina vendita ſunt, contra aſſiſam, et quis ea vendiderit, et quot dolia per annum, et per quot annos. De vicecomite & aliis ballivis capientibus miſericordias pro defaltis, vel pro uthesio non levato vel non ſecuto. De uſurariis Chriſtianis mortuis et quis eorum catalla habuerit. De catallis Judæorum *occiſorum* et vadiis & debitis & chartis. De falſonariis denariorum & retonſoribus. De moneta & chambio, burglatoribus, fugitivis utlagatis, mercatis remotis ab uno die in alium ſine licentia D. R. (niſi de die dominica) de novis conſuetudinibus, de mercede capta pro blado & aliis Catallis dimittendis, ne caperentur ad caſtella.

Bracton de Legibus Angliæ. Lib. 3. tr. 2. c. 1°.

one,

one [c], and fell by another; whether the ftandard meafure of cloth and wine has been violated, by the connivance or permiffion of officers, and to what extent.—They are then to inveftigate the conduct of the fheriffs and bailiffs, what fines they have levied, what offenders, houfe-breakers, or outlaws, profecuted, or overlooked. But ftill the intereft of the king was the grand object of their miffion; and there is not one article fpecified for their attention or enquiry, that was not immediately connected with the revenue. The ufury, mortgages, or debts of Jewifh money-lenders *flain*, or Chriftian money-lenders *dead*, were productive of great emolument to the royal coffers, confequently merited particular obfervation from the judges. The regulation of the mint, coiners and clippers, the change of market-days without a charter, (unlefs from Sundays,) innovation of eftablifhed cuftoms, and bribes received by the wardens of caftles, or their fervants, for difpenfing with the regular fupply of corn and provifions by the tenants, all tended to the income, or infringed upon the prerogative, of the prince, and were therefore fubjects for their inveftigation.

But the liberty or property of the fubject appear very little attended to in thefe directions or inftructions; and we learn from the fame refpectable writer, that [d] civil fuits principally appertained to other courts. For at thefe periods every manor had its hall or feat of judicature, where the petty feffions of the diftrict were held, and at which the lord prefided. To

[c] Merchant, 15 ounces to the pound;—Statute, 12;—Englifh hundred, 120, &c. &c. Diff. on Weights and Meafures.

[d] Actiones quæ funt in rem, ficut rei vendicationes, per breve de recto, terminari debent in curia baronum vel aliorum, de quibus ipfe petens clamaverit tenere. Bracton. Lib. 3. cap. 7.

 this

CHAP. I. 1065—1272. this court-leet or baron, every tenant muſt ſue for right in all civil actions, and if juſtice was denied him, he had little proſpect of redreſs from application to other courts. For though in equity he might appeal to the hundred or county court, and in the time of Henry the ſecond, probably, this privilege had been [e] occaſionally granted to ſubordinate tenants; yet, in the thirteenth century, the nobles and barons had obtained ſuch exorbitant power, that they allowed no action to be transferred to a ſuperior tribunal, but at their will, or unleſs, through inability to redreſs the party aggrieved, or ignorance to decide ſatisfactorily, they voluntarily remitted the cauſe to the king in council.

Here it is neceſſary to diſtinguiſh betwixt the court of a knight or military tenant of the crown in chief, and the ſuperior court of a baron, the [f] head of the barony, to whoſe common hall [g] ſubordinate chieftains reſorted, and whoſe lord was their general patron, leader, and judge. In the time of the Confeſſor, we are fully aſſured that this conſtitution prevailed generally throughout the kingdom, which, in the language of our ancient lawyers, conſiſted of [h] baronies. Indeed we entertain little doubt that Saxon tythings were ſyno-

[e] Sed transferri non debet contra voluntatem dominorum, ſicut olim fieri ſolet per principem. Bracton. Lib. 3. cap. 7.

[f] Caput baroniæ tenet Hugo de Montfort. Kent. Domeſday. Quod vide. Alnod Cilt & Brixi Cilt of Weſt & Eaſt Kent, &c. under the Saxon government.

[g] Communem Aulam. Gr. Domeſ. 322. b.

[h] De feodo militari meſuagia capitalia inter cohæredes dividuntur, niſi capitale meſuagium illud ſit caput comitatus propter jus gladii, quod dividi non poteſt, vel caput baroniæ, caſtrum, vel aliud ædificium, et hoc ideò, ne ſic caput per plures particulas dividatur, & plura jura comitatuum et baroniarum deveniant ad nihilum, per quod deficiat regnum, quod ex comitatibus & baroniis dicitur eſſe conſtitutum. Bracton. Lib. 2. c. 34.

nymous

nymous to manors, [i] hundreds to baronies, and counties to earldoms.

Though the language of the celebrated Autograph of Domesday is not the most correct or precise, (for the Norman commissioners were unacquainted with the customs of the country, had to learn them from the natives, and transmit English terms in *their* Latin jargon,) yet we can easily collect the necessary information from a particular scrutiny of the vocabulary adopted by the different persons, that entered the record. Thus the same reporters consider [k] hundred and manor, manor and hamlet, as synonymous, but an intelligent observer will easily form a necessary discrimination by a reference to the context.

In conformity to our opinion, and as a strong proof of its justness, we find more frequent disputes in this authentic document, between a baron, or powerful noble, and his free dependants, thanes, or military tenants, whether suit and service are due to him as their lord, or as their patron, than on any other point whatsoever. The evidence of the hundred is generally, if not universally, repugnant to the insolent presumptions of the Norman tyrants, whom William at this period had endeavoured to restrain, by confirming the laws of the Confessor; but their bravoes were admitted to determine the controversy by appealing to the decision by [l] combat, and

[i] Manerio de Wi. 22. Hundred pertinent. Vide Kent.

[k] Ad hoc manerium vel hundret (Salford) pertinebat 21. Berewich, tenebant totidem taini pro totidem maneriis. Gr. Domesday. Fol. 270.

[l] Homo Hermeri offert judicium quod suus antecessor habuit omnem consuetudinem tempore regis Edvardi præter Soccam Sanctæ Adelredæ, et quod poterat terram suam vendere—testatur hundred quod suus antecessor nullam consuetudinem habuit præter commendationem—ex hoc dederunt vades.

Norfolk. Little Domesd. Fol. 208.—et passim.

The possessions of this Hermer were immense, and occupy four folio pages.—Judicial combat was probably introduced by the Normans.

doubtless

CHAP. I. 1065—1272. doubtless oftentimes prevailed. By such means, the laws and customs of Edward were violated, annulled or changed.

In these days of universal rapine, there were other causes also, which subjected these inferior possessors, even of extensive districts, with their vassals and colonists, to the immediate controul and government of their feudal chieftain. If the manorial house or mansion was deemed an insufficient security for the protection of their [m] flocks or herds, but they folded them in the castle of the baron, and by such conduct acknowledged his [n] protection, thenceforward, they and their dependants became amenable to the judicature of the court of their lord, who received all forfeitures attached to the violation of the laws or customs. By such innovations and changes the establishment was altered, but we presume that we can adduce more than probable evidence, in support of our assertion.

The privileges and emoluments resulting from an independent court were considered so important and great at this early æra, that it is recorded in Domesday, as a remarkable circumstance, that [o] two brothers, who had each distinct mansions, and the liberty of changing their residence, should continue to reside in the same jurisdiction. Thanes or minor barons necessarily occupied [p] five hydes of land, must possess a church

[m] Erant consuetudinarii ad faldam antecessoris sui, alii erant liberi præter commendationem. Little Domesday. 273.

Super omnes istos qui faldam comitis requirebant, habebat comes socam & saccam. Little Domesd. 129.

[n] Quidam liber homo hanc terram tenens, et quo vellet abire valens, submisit se in Manu Walterii pro defensione sui. Great Domesday. 36.

[o] Scaldefor duo fratres tenuerunt, tempore regis Edvardi. Unusquisque habuit domum suam & *tamen* manserunt in una curia, et quo voluerunt, ire potuerunt. Great Domesd. Fol. 35.

[p] Habens quinque hidas terræ, ecclesiam & culinam, turrim sacram et atrii sedem. Wilkins Leg. Anglosax. p. 70.

and

and a tower, a kitchen, and feat of juftice, and were the prefidents [q] of the free-borough, or tything, fuperintended the men of their divifions, were refponfible for their conduct, and had at leaft ten yeomen dependant upon them. Their courts (where the fuits of the diftrict were determined) were the general [r] receptacle for the cattle of the village, or hamlet, and confifted of an extenfive inclofure, round the manfion-houfe of the lord, formed of a fpecies of [s] wicker-work, or paling of fhingles. Such was the court-leet, or view of frank-pledge, which each tenant regularly attended every third week [t]. That fuch inferior manors exifted, numerous proofs are to be adduced from Domefday, and doubtlefs they had their own huftings, courts-leet, or houfes of decifion, though its lord was the [u] client of a more powerful noble. Thus in the hundred of [x] Salford (in Lancafhire) twenty-one hamlets were occupied by as many thanes, and poffeffed manorial privileges; and in Yorkfhire, [y] Wallef had a common-hall, to which thirteen fubordinate chieftains reforted. Thus were the petty

[q] Ipfe capitalis Frithborgi. Hoveden, p. 605. Ad rectitudinem novem haberent decimum. Ibid.

[r] Faldam. Domefday paffim.

[s] Silva ad claufuram. Domefday paffim.

Materiem invenit ad unam domum 60 pedum & virgas ad curiam circa domum. Great Domefday. Fol. 205.

[t] Querge le fein per agard de fa court de tres femeynes en tres femeynes. Charter of the Ufages of Kent. Lambard, p. 581. 4to.

[u] Alvict liber homo *commendatus* Alfio Nepoti Comitis Radulfi 30 acras tenuit pro manerio T. R. E. 322 a.

[x] Ad hoc manerium vel hundret pertinebant 21 Berewich. Tenebant totidem taini pro totidem maneriis. G. D. 270.

[y] In hallun habebat Wallef communem aulam, funt 16 Berewitæ pertinentes manerio. 322. b.

CHAP. I. 1065—1272. tyrants of the realm [z] subdivided, they ruled the [a] district of their villa with an iron power, and were masters of all persons and property within the precincts of their domain. That manours had their hall or court of justice can be little doubted, since it is recorded as a peculiar circumstance, that many manors had no hall; and if all manors had their peculiar jurisdiction, we must allow that not only military tenants, thanes [b], or radmans, but even free-men, free-holders, or, in modern language, gentlemen, had their subordinate courts, at least in the county of Lancaster, though these *great* men built the royal palaces, and performed villains services in the days of the Confessor. But we shall discuss the gradation of ranks more fully in another place.

When villages, hamlets, or their proprietors had a controversy, the suit was then referred to a higher court, from a petty jury of rustics to a grand jury of knights or esquires, assembled in the hall of the chief baron. We have not much hesitation in ascribing the origin of hundred courts to these baronial courts, since [c] Bracton assures us that the kingdom is composed of earldoms and baronies, (counties and hundreds,) since in the thirteenth century a suit between the men

[z] Sub-commendatus Antecessori Malet. 322 a Domesday.

[a] Si autem ex nativo unius et ex nativa alterius, tunc refert in cujus villenagio. Bracton. Lib. 1. c. 6.

[b] Manerium in ternuce sine haula. 308. Great Domesday. Vide Kent.

Tres taini tenebant alretune pro tribus maneriis et quatuor radmans tenebant cildewelle pro quatuor maneriis. In Lailand 12 Carucatæ Terræ quas tenebant 12 Homines liberi pro totidem maneriis. G. D. 270.

Taini de Derbei (hundret) faciebant domos regis sicut villani. G. D. 269. b.

[c] Vide supra.

of

of [d] Litton and Bilſdon is referred to an hallmote: even at the present day the county of Weſtmoreland is divided into two baronies, and Kent has two grand juries. CHAP. I 1065—1272.

Under the Saxon monarchs [e], earls certainly poſſeſſed a ſpecies of ſubordinate principality, and received part of the emoluments of the revenue of the county, independant of that hundred over which they peculiarly preſided. This uſage ſtill continued, ſubſequent to the conqueſt, in thoſe ſhires which were committed to favourite commanders, with unlimited powers, who held it by the right of the ſword [f], and were inveſted with the liberties of their predeceſſors. Thus the earl of Moreton's agents [g] received thirty pence from each village of the county of Devon, independent of the cuſtoms of his appropriate hundred. But at this turbulent and diſorganizing period, the eſtabliſhed ſyſtem was relinquiſhed or aboliſhed. The miniſters of the monarch controuled the privilege and juriſdiction of the military officer, and viſcounts, or ſheriffs, the repreſentatives of the prince, and receivers of his revenue, were the general magiſtrates of the county, and preſidents of its court. Theſe were immediately appointed by the king, were wardens of the royal demeſnes, aſſeſſed the value of the towns, villages, and manors, collected the fines of hundreds, and ſuperintended all criminal offences and puniſhments. But it appears highly probable that commiſſioners were appointed by

[d] Homines de Lechton x Marcas pro habendâ inquiſitione per proxima hallimotta & per legales milites & alios homines de viſneto, quas conſuetudines ipſi fecerint tempore Henrici Regis Patris. M. R. 4 John. Rot. 2. b. Mad. 1. 437. et de finibus de halimot in maneriis. Mad. 1. 720.

De 22 hundredis manerio Wi pertinentibus, & Kent Hiſtory paſſim.

[e] Eorl or Scyrman. Lambard. 502.

[f] Jure Gladii. Bracton ſupra.

[g] Homines comitis Moreton habent 30 denarios de unaquâq; villa comitatus & conſuetudinem hundret. Great Domeſday, 100. b.

CHAP. I. 1065—1272. the royal mandate, at a very early period ſubſequent to the conqueſt, to regulate all civil controverſies, and all claims relative to landed property. When the book of Domeſday was compiled, the nobles that formed the ſurvey, were certainly inveſted with ſuch powers, decided on many appeals, and were attended [h] by juries both of the county and hundred. National courts had certainly been held in various diſtricts previous to this æra; for we find Ulſtan aſſerting his right to an eſtate by the deciſion of queen Matilda, four viſcounts, and the teſtimony of the county of Warwick. But a century elapſed before we can deciſively pronounce, that a juriſdiction exiſted independent of the controul of the viſcounts or ſheriffs, except when the monarch, or his conſort, perſonally viſited the county. In the twentieth year of the ſecond Henry, however, we find juſtices in Eyre, where ſheriffs are not inſerted, and a diſtinction eſtabliſhed relative to their offices. When the ſheriff and conſtable were included under the ſame commiſſion with the judges, they form an *aſſize*; [i] but wherever Ralph Glanville, or Hugh de Creſſi, hold their courts, new *pleas* are inſtituted. Whether this diſcrimination was univerſally made, we will not preſume to determine; but that it generally prevailed, can

[h] De melioribus & antiquis hominibus totius comitatus & hundred.
Domeſday, 44 b.

Ulſtan epiſcopus dicit ſe hanc terram deplacitaſſe coram regina Mathilde in præſentia quatuor vicecomitatuum & inde habet breve regis Willelmi & teſtimonium comitatus Warwicenſis. Domeſday, 238 b.

[i] Ralph Fitz-ſtephen, Alured de Lincoln, Richard de Wilton, William Fitz-ralph, Robert Mantell, Alard Banaſtre, William Guy a foreigner, William Braioſe, and Hugh Gundeville, are ſheriffs of different counties, and form, with other commiſſioners, an aſſize: in the ſame manner the conſtable of Oxford, and Reginald Warren the ſubſtitute of the conſtable; but Ralph Glanville and Hugh de Creſſi tenent nova placita & novas conſuetudines *paſſim*.
Mad. I. 123, 4, &c.

be

be little doubted, when we find it observed in more than twenty records near this period. The forest laws were enforced and maintained by a separate officer; and, at this period, [k] Alan de Neville presided over its pleas. The civil courts also still continued separated from the ecclesiastical; and we find not only laics, but dignified [k] clergymen, rendering payments into the exchequer for suits relative to feudal tenure, being tried before the courts of christianity.

It appears highly reasonable to imagine, that commissioners continued regularly to traverse the kingdom, and enquire into the conduct of the sheriffs, bailiffs, and foresters of the realm, not only in the reign of the Conqueror, but his sons William and Henry. The laws of Edward were sanctioned by his successor; for Chernet appeals to a jury, [l] and rejects the Norman corsnet or ordeal; consequently, the ancient customs and usages must have been then renewed, (if ever they had been discontinued,) though commissioners might preside in the court of a quondam earl. In conformity to this opinion, the oldest records of the crown now extant (those of the fifth [m] of Stephen) transmit the names of justices, or inquisitors, that visited the several counties, and assessed their pleas, fines, aids, and farms. But the power of these men extended not to the barons, or privileged orders, who were solely responsible to their peers, or claimed an exclusive right of being judged by the king in council, or chief justiciary of the crown.

[k] Mad 1. 133.

[k] Prior de Wirecestria reddit compotum de 10 marcis quia tenuit placitum de laico feodo in curia *christianitatis*.

Mag. Rot. 31 H. 2. Rot. 3. and many others. Mad. 1. 561.

[l] Picot contraduxit suum testimonium de villanis & vili plebe & de præpositis qui volunt defendere per sacramentum aut per Dei judicium, &c. testes Willelmi de Chernet nolunt accipere legem nisi regis Edvardi. Domesday, 44 b.

[m] Mad. 1. 148.

 Whatever

CHAP. I. 1065—1272. Whatever perſon had fraudently obtained poſſeſſion of property, eaſily ſecured his right and title, by obtaining a charter from the crown, not to plead his cauſe, only in the royal preſence. Theſe grants are neither few, nor in a particular reign; and when the king received plunderers under his protection, there was no appeal. Such briefs were not limited to the reſidence of the monarch, or its immediate neighbourhood, but prevailed in [n] Cornwall and Yorkſhire, the counties of Glouceſter and Lincoln, Lancaſter and Norfolk. Theſe immunities were not to be obtained without conſiderable preſents, termed oblata, and may be conſidered as the peace-offerings of iniquity. For when ſuch privileges had been granted, a redreſs of grievances depended not on right, or juſtice, but on the [o] fine tendered at the exchequer. Hence the poſſeſſions of the ſubject were held by a precarious tenure, and greatly depended on the dictatorial will of the lord, his avarice, his prodigality, or his favour. Sometimes, indeed, theſe deſpotic princes held a formal court of judicature, with the ſplendour of a ſovereign, and affected to adminiſter juſtice; and ſometimes decided litigated points on their journey [p]; for it was impoſſible that a ſuit could ariſe, or be terminated, without emolument to themſelves. Fines [q] were paid for inſtituting a

[n] Ailwardus filius Serici reddit compotum de 20 marcis, pro brevi regis habendo, ne placitet niſi coram eo. M. R, 22. H. 2. Cornubia. Robertus pro confirmatione de perquiſitionibus ſuis, & ne ponatur in placitum niſi coram rege. Everwich, &c. Vid. Mad. I. 118. & ſequent.

[o] Pleas continually ſtaid propter finem ſubſcriptum. Mad. paſſim.

[p] In curia & itinere.

[q] Fines & amerciamenta de itinere regis. Ricardus de Clendon reddit compotum pro licentia concordandi de XIIII marcis, Willelmus de Clendon pro eodem VI de marcis.

M. Rot. 10 Joh. 12 b. Norhamteſcire. Mad. I. 151. & paſſim.

plea,

plea, fines were paid for the liberty of amicably adjuſting it, even in the royal preſence.

Subſequent to the reign of Henry the Second, the juriſprudence of the kingdom was entirely neglected, and the executive authority much enfeebled. When Richard had completed his armament for the cruſade, he compiled, indeed, a code of laws, calculated for a horde of barbarians, rather than the inhabitants of a civilized ſtate. The puniſhment was ſummary; the trial, probably, by martial law. This digeſt, or proclamation, was iſſued by the king in council, and with the approbation and advice of his moſt experienced miniſters. As ſuch a precious fragment ſhould not be entirely diſregarded, we ſhall epitomize its articles.[1]

The murderer of a man, by ſea, ſhall be tied to the corpſe, and immerſed in the ocean; on ſhore, be bound to the body, and buried alive. Whoever is convicted of drawing his dagger, and ſpilling blood, ſhall loſe his hand; of ſtriking, without bloodſhed, ſhall be thrice plunged in the ſea. To revile an aſſociate

[1] 1189. Charta Ricardi I. Omnibus hominibus ſuis hieroſolymam per mare ituris ſalutem. Sciatis nos de *communi* proborum virorum conſilio, feciſſe has juſtitias ſubſcriptas. Qui hominem in navi interfecerit, ligatus cum mortuo projiciatur in mare. Si autem eum ad terram interfecerit, cum mortuo ligatus in terram inſodiatur. Si quis atem per legitimos teſtes convictus fuerit quod cultellum ad alium percutiendum extraxerit, aut quod alium ad ſanguinem percuſſerit, pugnum perdat. Si autem de palma percuſſerit ſine effuſione ſanguinis, tribus vicibus mergatur in mari. Si quis autem ſocio opprobrium aut convitia aut odium Dei injecerit: quot vicibus ei conviciatus fuerit, tot *uncias** argenti ei det. Latro autem de furto convictus tondeatur ad modum campionis & pix bulliens ſuper caput ejus effundatur, & pluma pulvinaris ſuper caput ejus excutiatur ad cognoſcendum eum & in prima terra, qua naves applicuerint, projiciatur. Rym. Fœd. 1. p. 65.

* Theſe laws were framed for the leaders or barons, for none under the degree of a knight could pay ounces of ſilver for a fine.

in

CHAP. I. 1065—1272. in the expedition, or charge him with irreligion, shall subject the offender to a penalty of an ounce of silver for each aspersion. A robber shall be tarred and feathered, and sent on shore at the first port.

The laws of [s] Oleron, published by the same monarch, are of a different description, and certainly form a good maritime code for that æra; but as they principally relate to commerce, we shall descant on them under another head.

The celebrated Magna Charta, which, in the language of Blackstone, [t] "*protected every individual of the nation, in the free enjoyment of his life, his liberty and property,*" would certainly merit our attentive consideration, if we entertained similar sentiments of it. Doubtless we have deliberately examined this boasted bill of liberty, but cannot find any clause that affects the body of the nation, the commonalty, or even yeomen, except the cited stipulation, that inferior feudal chiefs should model their behaviour towards their respective vassals, according to those regulations and restrictions that their seigneur had adopted. The descendants of [t] Englishmen were slaves; and, except of the clerical profession, had no rights. How could their life be secure, when their murder subjected not the assassin, or his hundred, to a fine? How could they enjoy liberty, when they were a chattel and fixture of their tyrant? How could their property be protected, when the extravagance of their patron subjected their house and utensils to instant confiscation? Such circumstances might have taken place, without an infringement of the charter. But we may

[s] A small island in the Bay of Biscay, which Richard inherited in right of his mother.

[t] Commentaries, Book 4. ch. 33. p. 424.

[t] Englescheria, a distinguishing criterion betwixt Englishmen and Normans, still in force. Vid. Dissertation on Customs, &c.

judge

judge how frequently these compulsively extracted privileges were violated, when even [w] Coke allows, that these ordonnances were more than thirty times ratified. Indeed, if we had no other authority for the Anglo-saxonic slavery and feudal subordination, we might reasonably presume, that the ancestors of Englishmen, or Normans, had never enjoyed great independence or liberty, since their posterity were perfectly satisfied with such inconsiderable concessions.

To justify our statement, we shall adduce authorities from Bracton, the great law luminary of the kingdom, in the latter part of the reign of Henry the Third, and other incontrovertible documents; and if lord [x] Bacon's excellent definition of a *good* law, " that its language and object should be clear, its principle just, its execution easy, its spirit congenial to the government, its effect virtuous," must be admitted, not one good law was extant in England at this period.

Slavery, at this æra, so generally prevailed, that every member of the community was subjected to its oppression. The monarch was insulted and harassed by the collective bodies; whilst each individual baron, when separated, necessarily submitted to the tyranny of his superior. The children even of the most potent earls were not less exempt from the dictatorial controul of their feudal lord, than the inferior vassal from the power of his chieftain. Whatever ancient or modern [y] lawyers may assert to the contrary, it is an indisputable truth, that

[w] 32. 2 Institut. proœmium.

[x] Lex bona censeri possit, quæ sit intimatione certa, præcepto justa, executione commoda, cum forma politiæ congrua, et generans virtutem in subditis.
Bacon de Augmentat. Scient. L. 8. c.

[y] The clause in Mag. Char. hæredes maritentur absque disparagatione, meant certainly by Hæredes, heirs female, as there are no traces before this to found of the lords claiming the marriage of *heirs male*; and as Glanville expressly confines it to heirs female. Blackstone, B. 2. ch.

he

CHAP. I. 1065—1272. heirs male, equally with females, were married to what persons the sovereign willed, both prior and subsequent to Magna Charta. In every reign, from [z] Stephen to Edward the First, fines are recorded to have been paid by men for permission to marry according to their inclination. In the reign of Henry the Second, both [a] parties fine for such privilege, when their parents were living, and desirous of the connection. [b] Henry the Third stipulates with the prince of Savoy for his daughter's marriage, either to the earl of Warren or Lincoln, who are minors under his protection, and whose hands are at his disposal.

The inequality of the law to persons of different conditions, might here lead us to an enquiry relative to ranks and services; but this subject we reserve for a select discussion. It is sufficient for our present purpose to state, that every inferior tenant of the crown was subject to similar restrictions and impositions, as every vassal owed such services to his proper lord. But the lower classes, and slaves, experienced more cruel treatment. The Scotish [c] Merchetum prevailed also in England. This

[z] Walterus de Canceio reddit compotum de 15 libras ut ducat uxorem ad velle suum. Mag. Rot. Steph. Rot. 3. a Mad. 1. 464. Ricardus de Luci pro se maritando ubi voluerit. 1. 465.

[a] Adam filius Norman. r. c. de 18l. 16s. 8d. pro maritanda filia sua filio Willelmi de Leclai. Willelmus filius Hugonis de Leelay r. c. de 22l. 8s. pro maritanda filia prædicti adæ filio suo.

Mag. Rot. 31 Hen. 2. Rot. 5 a. Mad. 1. 512.

[b] 1246. Rex maritari faciet filiam comitis Sabaudiæ vel Johanni de Warenna, qui si vixerit, comes erit, Warennæ, vel Edmundo de Lacy, qui si vixerit, comes erit, Lincolniæ. Qui quidem pueri sunt in custodia regis & maritagium eorum ad regem pertinet. Rymer Fœdera, Vol. I. 441.

[c] Merchetum verò pro filia dare non competit libero homini, inter alia propter liberi sanguinis privilegium, et unde in dominicis Domini regis distinguendum

This [d] fine was the characterizing diſtinction betwixt a free-man, (whoſe daughter was exempted from ſuch infamous proſtitution by the purity of her deſcent) and a Soccage villain, in the royal demeſnes. The [d] free yeomen of the royal manors had been lately inveſted with ſome peculiar privileges, becauſe the monarch was contending with his turbulent barons, and wiſhed to attach them to his cauſe. But the copy-holders and their ſervants, the majority of the nation, were the [d] chattels of their lord, the animals attached to his ſoil, whoſe implements of huſbandry, and poſſeſſions, he could ſeize at pleaſure for his own uſe. The natural energy in the human character, that impels us to ſeek our own good, and ſtimulates to ſuch exertions of activity and labour, as neither the goad or the whip can produce in beaſts of burthen, is ſpeedily ſuppreſſed or extinguiſhed in the breaſt of that man, who is conſcious that he is toiling for another, and that the acquiſitions of his induſtry, real or perſonal, are the property of his maſter. Thus a vegetating ſtream, that, flowing in proper channels, might have fertilized the country, ſtagnated and inert, yields the nauſeous and pernicious weeds of the green-mantling pool.

CHAP. I. 1065—1272.

guendum erit inter liberos et villanos Sockmannos, qui in dominico Domini regis nati ſunt, et ab antiquo tenuerunt in villenagio.

Bracton, Lib. 2. c. 8.

[d] Poteſtas dominorum in ſervos nunc coarctata eſt per jus civile, &c. Hoc autem verum eſt de illis ſervis, qui tenent de antiquo Dominico Coronæ, ſed de aliis ſecus eſt; quia quandocunque placuerit Domino, auferre poterit a villano ſuo Waynagium ſuum & omnia bona ſua. Bracton, Lib. 1. c. 9.

[d] Fine paid to the lord for not claiming his right of firſt ſleeping with a bride.

" I cannot learn that ever this cuſtom prevailed in England."

Blackſton, book 2. ch. 6.

[d] Quandocunque placuerit domino auferre poterit a villano ſuo Waynagium ſuum & omnia bona ſua—quicquid per ſervum juſtè acquiritur, id domino acquiritur. Bracton, Lib. 1. c. 9.

CHAP. I. 1065—1272.

These miserable beings were not only ſlaves themſelves, but the cauſe of ſlavery to all connected with them. If they married a free woman, their offspring were [*] villains. If their daughters were married to a gentleman, ſtill the children were ſlaves, if born within the juriſdiction of their deſpot, though married with his concurrence, and he had received the Merchatum fine. Theſe topics will be more fully diſcuſſed in our diſſertations on cuſtoms and manners, ranks and ſervices. But ſurely no unprejudiced writer, who will candidly inveſtigate the annals of the reign of Henry the Third; peruſe the Commentaries of Bracton, Fleta or Britton; examine the Fædera of Rymer; conſult the records of Madox; or impartially read the evidence adduced in this chapter; can hereafter proclaim, that Magna Charta, paſſed fifty years previous to many of our authorities, protected every individual of the nation, in the free enjoyment of his life, his liberty and property, either in theory or practice.

But though national franchiſes received ſo little augmentation, extenſive charters of rights were conferred on corporate bodies, boroughs, abbey-villages, and individuals. Particular cities and diſtricts had continued to regulate the police of their diviſion, according to the received uſages and cuſtoms that had prevailed in the time of the Confeſſor; for William had ratified the laws of the country, prior to the formation of Domeſday, and various abſtracts of them are there recorded. As our ſtatements, on this ſubject, will vary much from thoſe of preceding hiſtorians, we take leave to premiſe a few obſer-

[*] Si villanus ingrediatur ad liberam in liberum tenementum, partus proveniens erit ſervus. Item dicitur ſervus nacione de libero genitus, qui ſe copularit villanæ in villenagium, ſive copula maritalis intervenerit ſive non, &c. &c.
Bracton, Lib. I. c. 6.

vations.

vations. That, however we may be ſtigmatized as a [f] "ſlaviſh, or narrow-minded writer;" however abuſed by the friends of that (fictitious) conſtitution, which our Anglo-ſaxon anceſtors poſſeſſed, and which their poſterity have glorioufly [g] "redeemed, after a conteſt of ſix centuries"; we ſtill ſhall obey the dictates, that ariſe from the conviction of rational evidence candidly examined, and declare, without heſitation, thoſe ſentiments, which truth commands a faithful hiſtorian to detail. Miſrepreſentation is never juſtifiable, though the goodneſs produced, may, in particular caſes, ſomewhat palliate the deception that has been practiſed. But at the preſent æra, deceit is unneceſſary. Rational liberty is founded on a firmer foundation, than aboriginal preſcription, or viſionary perfection, and is beſt known by its fruits, and experimental excellence. Though the ſtrong advocate of manly freedom, we can ſtill admit the ſlavery of our forefathers; yea, view, with ſatisfactory exultation, our enfranchiſement from their thraldom.

The authorities we produce to prove the truth of our ſtatement, will be extracted from Domeſday, and from thoſe diſtricts where the three different laws, then exiſting, prevailed; from the [h] Saxon laws in Somerſetſhire, the Mercian laws in Buckinghamſhire, and the Daniſh laws in Norfolk. In the reign of the Confeſſor, Stigand, archbiſhop of Canterbury, was the proprietor of the borough of Taunton. He was the general patron, on whom all were dependant, not only the villains, cottagers, ſervants or ſwineherds, but even merchants, an aſſociated guild of freemen, appertained to him, were his property, and he could levy contributions on them

[f] Blackſton. [g] Ibid.

[h] Taunton—Tempore regis Edwardi Stigandus habebat ibi 80 villanos, 91 bordarios, 70 ſervos, 16 *colibertos*, 17 porcarios.

Great Domeſday, 87 b.

at

CHAP. I. 1065—1272. at pleaſure. In the town of [i] Buckingham we have a very diſtinct account of different burgeſſes, their owners in the time of Edward, to whom they are transferred by the Conqueror; their value to their reſpective lords, and payments to the king. In [k] Norwich, the third city of the kingdom, the burgeſſes had no peculiar corporate rights, which all equally poſſeſſed, for they belonged to different proprietors, and were, conſequently, ſubject to different regulations; the majority of them paid their cuſtoms and rent to the king, and their earl, or alderman; ſome to the archbiſhop, and others to Harold. The only places that appear to have enjoyed ſuperior privileges, are the cities of London, York, Wincheſter, and [l] Exeter. Theſe were not taxed, except when the whole realm was taxed; and the kingdom, or the lands of the nobility, could not probably be taxed, without the concurrence of a national council, or general aſſembly of earls and barons, the peers of the monarch.

[i] Buckingham Great Domeſday, 143.

Epiſcopus conſtantienſis habet 3 burgenſes.				Reddens Domino. Den.	Reddens Regi. Den.
Hugo Comes habet	1.	Burgenſem qui fuit Homo	Burnardi	26	5
Robertus de O'gi	— 1	———	Azor	16	5
Rogerus de Juri	— 4	———	Azor	76	13
Hugo de Bolebec	— 4	———	Alrici	28	12
Haſcoius Muſart	— 1	———	Azor	16	2
Manno Brito	— 4		fæminæ Syred Eddevæ	28	nil
Ernulf de Heſding—	1	———	Wilaf	2	3
Leuuin de Neuucham	5			4	12
Willelmus de Caſtellon	2			16	nihil

[k] In Norvico veteri rex et comes habebant ſacam, ſocam & conſuetudinem de 1238 burgenſes. Stigandus de 50. Heroldus de 22.

Little Domeſday, 118.

[l] Exeter. Hæc civitas tempore regis Edvardi, non geldabat niſi quando Anglia, Londonia, Eboracum, Wintonia geldabant.

Great Domeſday, 100.

The

The variety of classes, that inhabited the towns and cities, is so great and uncertain, that we cannot treat of burgesses in general with any tolerable precision, at this period. This, however, may be asserted, that their houses belonged either to the king, the earl, some powerful baron, dignified ecclesiastic, or pious foundation. Many of the burgesses were attached to particular manors; even in the most privileged cities, in [m] London, [m] Winchester, and [n] Chester. Their annual assessments varied in proportion to their circumstances, under the government and laws of the Confessor; and however boroughs may have asserted their right and claim to a certain stipulated payment, a fixed tribute and farm, or the ancient privilege of lot and scot; we are assured that the burgesses of [o] Nottingham paid an additional sum on account of their opulence. There are evident proofs, that all the towns were frequently surveyed, a new estimate formed, and their rental augmented. [p] Wallingford, previous to the conquest, was valued at thirty pounds, afterwards at forty, when Domesday was compiled, at sixty, and yet produced eighty pounds per annum. This great increase in the price of houses, occurred in a period of twenty years; and the annual estimates of the burgesses, by the different sheriffs or wardens, were still more various. The average value of a house in Wallingford was more than six

[m] Inter Francigenas & quosdam *Burgenses* Lundoniæ 23 Hidæ de terra *Villanorum*. Domesday, 127 b.

[m] 7 Burgenses pertinent manerio Sarisberie. Great Domesday, 76.

[n] 10 Burgenses pertinent de manerio de Roelau.

Anhlote & Anschote, Consuetudinem Anglorum quod ipsi dicunt. Leg. Willelmi anno 4to regni (i. e.) unum tributum & una solutio Æn unus hloð tributum et Schoð solutio. Lye Saxon Diction.

[o] Tempore regis Edvardi de censu & opibus 10l. Great Domesday.

[p] Wallingford. 250 hagæ diversorum hominum tempore regis Edvardi valebant 30l. post 40l. modo 60l. tamen reddunt de firma 80l. in numero. Great Domesday, 56.

shillings,

CHAP. I. 1065—1272. shillings, in Colchester six-pence; the rich inhabitants of Nottingham paid three shillings and six-pence each, the poor burgesses of Ipswich one penny. All the boroughs and cities of the realm were doubtless dependant on some patron, prior to the conquest, though invested with different privileges and liberties, by the favour or mercy of their lord. If William had no intention of continuing the franchises they enjoyed, why did he command that they should be particularly specified, and recorded, in his survey? If he intended to violate their rights and established customs, why would he transmit a memorial of them to posterity? But we have more than presumptive authority. The English [q] burgesses resident in Hereford are expressly stated to possess all their former customs, we cannot say enjoy their privileges, for immunities like theirs, rather constitute slavery, than establish liberty. But on this subject we shall enlarge hereafter.

As prodigality, and avarice, are alternately conspicuous in the conduct of the Norman princes, as their intestine commotions, with their turbulent barons, emptied their exchequer, and compelled them to adopt extraordinary means of supplying their necessities, (when the aids and rents of their towns gave them little assistance, when even the talliages or poll-tax of them were insufficient for their wants,) they appealed to the interest of their subjects, and proposed to confer privileges and franchises for stipulated advances of money. By such means were liberties obtained, and mild laws procured. There is not a city or borough in the realm, that has not frequently bought its charter, that has not paid for the establishment of its corporation, the renewal of its market, the formation of its guild, or the exemption of its inhabitants from the judicial combat

[q] Anglici burgenses ibi manentes habent suas priores consuetudines.

Great Domesday. 179.

of

of the ordeal; for Norman princes esteemed themselves little bound by the acts of their predecessors. When a new monarch ascended the throne, a [r] renovation of charters must take place, if the burgesses wished to enjoy their franchises; and their own grants were considered of so little consequence, that there was frequently a necessity of purchasing their ratification. We may judge how insecure the property of burgesses must be, when so late as the year 1258, (the year that Simon Montfort established the Oxford aristocracy,) Henry authorized his brother, earl of Cornwall, and king of the Romans, to [s] talliage all his boroughs and manors, which once belonged to the crown, and to collect a subsidy from all his free tenants in the kingdom. It little signified that the word reasonable poll-tax was inserted in this proclamation, for we must recollect that there was no appeal, at this æra, from the court or will of the lord, and that his wants or avarice established the proportion, and fixed the competency. Boroughs doubtless possessed privileges and customs both by charter and prescription, which villages enjoyed not, and which, if inviolably observed, constituted, at least, great immunities from slavery, and some portion of freedom. Burgesses could marry their children without obtaining the consent of their lord, had a peculiar

CHAP. I. 1065—1272.

[r] Omnes chartæ & confirmationes, quæ prioris sigilli impressione roboratæ fuerint, irritæ forent, nisi posteriori sagillo roborentur. Rot. Ric. 1. ex Radulfo Cogshill.

Qui suis libertatibus volebant gaudere, ut innovarent Chartas suas. M. R. 10. Henri 3tii.

[s] 1258. De tallia pro rege Romanorum. Concessimus ei, quod burgos & maneria sua, quæ fuerunt Dominica nostra, rationabilièr talliare possit hac vice, licet Dominica nostra per Angliam ad præsens non fecerimus talliam—et omnibus liberè tenentibus de illustri rege Romanorum in Anglia. Universitatem vestram rogamus attentè quatenus, &c. eidem hac necessitate sua jam competens subsidium impendere studeatis. Rymer. Fædera. tom. 1. p. 669.

court

court and jurisdiction, were to be tried by a jury, and other important rights, which will be particularly exhibited in another chapter.

In the reigns of John and Henry, London became conscious of its importance, and occasionally derived advantages from the conflicts of the king and barons. But the principal privileges obtained were granted from pecuniary considerations, and she purchased the election of her sheriffs or receivers of her ferm, the formation of her merchant-guilds, and choice of her mayor. Her internal police doubtless was much improved, the recovery of debts facilitated subsequent to 1240, but her aldermen were only empowered to act for their own ward, for magistrates or justices of the peace were not appointed till the succeeding reign, the grand age of reform in English jurisprudence. London indeed, equally with every other borough, that had not a peculiar proprietor, (some powerful noble or ecclesiastic,) was still considered as the royal property, was talliageable, at the mercy of the king, and assessed twenty thousand marks, in 1271, the year previous to the period limiting our present observations. This we pledge ourselves fully to prove in a particular dissertation.

In the turbulent reign of Henry the third, no good laws were framed, but many customs gradually introduced, that ameliorated the situation of rustics and burgesses, and heightened their importance. In the year 1264, boroughs had obtained so great consequence, and their co-operation, in the civil wars, was of so great assistance to the party, whose cause they espoused, that when Montfort had Henry his prisoner, and the prince of Wales was in arms against him, (to derive the greatest possible advantage from the name and possession of the royal captive) he compelled the monarch, to issue summonses for assembling not only four knights from each county, but two

citizens

citizens and burgeſſes from each royal borough. This we heſitate not to declare the firſt ſummons for a [t] parliament of commons, and the true origin of our excellent conſtitution and laws. This aſſertion we ſhall maintain beyond controverſy in a ſeparate [u] chapter, and for the preſent ſhall decline farther obſervations on the nature of the laws and their execution: which ſubject, when reſumed by the author, will be repreſented like [x] a dawning twilight to an obſerver emerging from the gloom of a cavern, till in gradual progreſs from the darkened ſhade of the fourteenth and fifteenth centuries, he arrives to the blaze, ſplendour, and clearneſs of meridian light illuminating our Britiſh horizon.

[t] We find not the word parleamentum uſed in any official record previous to 1260. Rymer's Fœdera. Vol. I. p. 705.

[u] Vid. Diſſert. on national aſſemblies.

[x] Quale eſt quod ex obſcuro ſpecu enitentibus, &c. Grot. de Veritate Rel. Chriſtianæ. Lib. 5.

citizens and burgeſſes from each roya
heſitate not to declare the firſt ſummon
commons, and the true origin of our
and laws. This aſſertion we ſhall maint
in a ſeparate chapter, and for the par
obſervations on the nature of the laws
like a dawning twilight to an obſcure
gloom of a cavern, till in gradual progr

www.ingramcontent.com/pod-product-compliance
Lightning Source LLC
Chambersburg PA
CBHW020254170426
43202CB00008B/373

* 9 7 8 3 3 3 7 2 0 3 8 7 0 *